Frommer's® 98

PORTABLE

Las Vegas

D0772184

by Mary Herczog

Macmillan • USA

ABOUT THE AUTHOR

Mary Herczog lives in Los Angeles and works in the film industry. As a freelance writer, her work has appeared in several major publications (the *Los Angeles Times* and *Rolling Stone,* among others) and essay collections, as well as *Frommer's Los Angeles.* She still isn't sure when to hold and when to hit in blackjack.

MACMILLAN TRAVEL

A Simon & Schuster Macmillan Company
1633 Broadway
New York, NY 10019

Find us online at **www.frommers.com** or
on America Online at Keyword: **Frommers**.

ISBN 0-02-862225-1
ISSN 1090-5472

Editor: Douglas Stallings
Production Editor: Robyn Burnett
Design by Michele Laseau
Digital Cartography by John Decamillis & Ortelius Design

SPECIAL SALES

Bulk purchases (10+ copies) of Frommer's and selected Macmillan travel guides are available to corporations, organizations, mail-order catalogs, institutions, and charities at special discounts, and can be customized to suit individual needs. For more information write to: Special Sales, Macmillan General Reference, 1633 Broadway, New York, NY 10019.

Manufactured in the United States of America

Contents

List of Maps

ACKNOWLEDGEMENTS

Thanks to Doug Stallings, Becka Hemingway, Cheryl Ladd-Campbell, Jan Laverty, James Randi, Paula Tevis, Wayne Newton, Cary Hern, "Uncle" Lou, Kelly Benway, Bob Bell, Barbara Ciartantini, Tom Hawley, Brittany and Kitty, Chuck Taggert, Jesse Garon, and *Scope* magazine.

AN INVITATION TO THE READER

In researching this book, we discovered many wonderful places—hotels, restaurants, shops, and more. We're sure you'll find others. Please tell us about them, so we can share the information with your fellow travelers in upcoming editions. If you were disappointed with a recommendation, we'd love to know that, too. Please write to:

Frommer's Portable Las Vegas '98
Macmillan Travel
1633 Broadway
New York, NY 10019

AN ADDITIONAL NOTE

Please be advised that travel information is subject to change at any time—this is especially true of prices. We therefore suggest that you write or call ahead for confirmation when making your travel plans. The authors, editors, and publisher cannot be held responsible for the experiences of readers while traveling. Your safety is important to us, however, so we encourage you to stay alert and be aware of your surroundings. Keep a close eye on cameras, purses, and wallets, all favorite targets of thieves and pickpockets.

WHAT THE SYMBOLS MEAN
✪ Frommer's Favorites

Hotels, restaurants, attractions, and entertainment you should not miss.

The following abbreviations are used for credit cards:

AE	American Express	JCB	Japan Credit Bank
CB	Carte Blanche	MC	MasterCard
DC	Diners Club	V	Visa
DISC	Discover		

FIND FROMMER'S ONLINE

Arthur Frommer's Outspoken Encyclopedia of Travel (www.frommers.com) offers more than 6,000 pages of up-to-the-minute travel information, including the latest bargains and candid, personal articles updated daily by Arthur Frommer himself. No other Web site offers such comprehensive and timely coverage of the world of travel.

Introducing Las Vegas

As often as you might have seen it on TV or in a movie, there is nothing that prepares you for that first actual sight of Las Vegas. The skyline is hyperreality, a mélange of the Statue of Liberty, a giant lion, a pyramid and a Sphinx, and preternaturally glittering buildings. At night, it's so bright, you can actually get disoriented—and also get a sensory overload that can reduce you to hapless tears or fits of giggles. And that's without setting foot inside a casino, where the shouts from the craps tables, the crash of coins from the slots, and general roar combine into either the greatest adrenaline rush of your life or the eleventh pit of hell.

Las Vegas is a true original; there is nothing like it in America and arguably the world. In other cities, hotels are built near the major attractions. Here, the hotels *are* the major attractions. Las Vegas can be whatever the visitor wants, and for a few days, the visitor can be whatever he or she want. Just be prepared to leave all touchstones with reality behind. Just for this time, you will rise at noon and gorge on endless amounts of rich food at 3am. You will watch your money grow or (more probably) shrink. You will watch a volcano explode and pirates fight the British. And after awhile, it will all seem pretty normal. This is not a cultural vacation, okay? Save the thoughts of museums and historical sights for the real New York, Egypt, and Rome. Vegas is about fun. Go have some. Go have too much. It won't be hard.

The result of all this is that once you go to Vegas, you will want to come back again, if only to make sure you didn't dream it all. Love it, loathe it, or both, no one has ambivalent feelings about Vegas.

1 Frommer's Favorite Las Vegas Experiences

- **A Stroll on the Strip After Dark.** You haven't really seen Las Vegas until you've seen it at night. This neon wonderland is the world's greatest sound and light show. Begin at Luxor and work your way down past the incredible new New York New York. If your strength holds out, you will end at Circus Circus, where live

Favorite Vegas Movies from the Mayor of Las Vegas

—Jan Laverty is the mayor of Las Vegas.

- *Oceans 11*
- *Viva Las Vegas*

10 Other Vegas Movies the Mayor Didn't Pick & Possible Reasons Why

- *Leaving Las Vegas.* Alcoholics and hookers not good role models.
- *One from the Heart.* Shot on sound stage rather than in real Las Vegas.
- *Vegas Vacation.* Griswald family *not* typical Vegas tourists.
- *Casino.* Puts squeeze on heads rather than on wallets.
- *They Came to Rob Las Vegas.* The title says it all.
- *The Electric Horseman.* Robert Redford successfully steals valuable horse from casino.
- *Indecent Proposal.* Robert Redford successfully wins million dollars from casino.
- *Con Air.* In real Vegas, planes land at airport, not on the Strip.
- *Showgirls.* Need we say more?
- *Honeymoon in Vegas.* Beats us. Who doesn't love Flying Elvises?

acrobat acts take place over head while you gamble. Make plenty of stops en route to take in the ship battle at Treasure Island, see the Mirage volcano erupt, and enjoy the light, sound, and water show at Bally's.

- **Casino-Hopping on the Strip:** The interior of each lavish new hotel-casino is more outrageous and giggle-inducing than the last. Just when you think they can't possibly top themselves, they do. From Rome to ancient Egypt, to a rain forest to a pirate's lair, to King Arthur's castle to New York City, it is still all totally, completely, and uniquely Las Vegas.
- **The Penny Slots at the Gold Spike:** Where even the most budget-conscious traveler can gamble for hours.
- **A Dinner Show at Caesars Magical Empire:** A solid dinner plus hours of entertainment, including your own personal magic show, make this one of the best values in Vegas—and a heck of a good time.

- **Buffets:** They may no longer be the very best of bargains, as the cheaper ones do not provide as good food as the more pricey ones, but there is something about the endless mounds of food that just screams "Vegas" to us.

- **Cirque du Soleil:** You haven't really seen Cirque du Soleil until you've seen it at Treasure Island. The showroom is equipped with state-of-the-art sound and lighting systems and a seemingly infinite budget for sets, costumes, and high-tech special effects. It's an enchantment.

- **An Evening in Glitter Gulch:** Set aside an evening to tour downtown hotels—unlike the lengthy and exhausting Strip, you can hit 17 casinos in about five minutes—and take in the overhead light show of the Fremont Street Experience.

- **The Liberace Museum:** It's not the Smithsonian, but then again, the Smithsonian doesn't have rhinestones like these. Nowhere else but here.

- **The Shopping Forum at Caesars Palace:** This is an only-in-Vegas shopping experience—an arcade replicating an ancient Roman streetscape, with classical piazzas and opulent fountains. Don't miss the scary animatronic statues as they come to glorious, cheesy life.

2

Planning a Trip to Las Vegas

*B*efore any trip, you need to do a bit of advance planning. When should I go? Should I take a package deal or make my own hotel and airline reservations? Will there be a major convention in town during my visit? We'll answer these and other questions for you in this chapter, but you might want to read through chapter 6 if you tire of gambling.

1 Visitor Information

For advance information call or write the **Las Vegas Convention and Visitors Authority,** 3150 Paradise Rd., Las Vegas, NV 89109 (☎ 800/332-5333). They can send you a comprehensive packet of brochures, a map, a show guide, an events calendar, and an attractions list; help you find a hotel that meets your specifications (and even make reservations); and tell you if a major convention is scheduled during the time you would like to visit Las Vegas. Or stop by when you're in town. They're open Monday to Friday 8am to 6pm and Saturday and Sunday 8am to 5pm.

Another excellent information source is the **Las Vegas Chamber of Commerce,** 711 E. Desert Inn Rd., Las Vegas, NV 89109 (☎ 702/735-1616). Ask them to send you their *Visitor's Guide,* which contains extensive information about accommodations, attractions, excursions, children's activities, and more. They can answer all your Las Vegas–related questions, including those about weddings and divorces. They're open Monday to Friday 8am to 5pm.

And for information on all of Nevada, including Las Vegas, contact the **Nevada Commission on Tourism** (☎ 800/638-2328). They send out a comprehensive information packet on Nevada.

2 When to Go

Since most of a Las Vegas vacation is usually spent indoors, you can have a good time here year-round. The most pleasant seasons, as you'll see from the chart below, are spring and fall, especially if you want to experience the great outdoors. Weekdays are slightly less crowded than weekends. Holidays are always a mob scene and come accompanied by high hotel prices. Hotel prices also skyrocket when big conventions and special events are taking place. The slowest times of year are June and July, the week before Christmas, and the week after New Year's. If a major convention is to be held during your trip, you might want to change your date.

One thing you'll hear again and again is that even though Las Vegas gets very hot, the dry desert heat is not unbearable. This is true. The humidity averages a low 22%, and even on very hot days there's apt to be a breeze. Also, except on the hottest summer days, there's relief at night when temperatures often drop as much as 20°. But it also gets cold—really cold (for us from Southern California, at least), especially in the winter when at night it can drop to 30° and lower. The breeze can also become a cold, biting wind. If you aren't traveling in the height of summer, bring a wrap. Also, remember your sunscreen and hat—even if it's not all that hot, you can burn very easily and fast.

LAS VEGAS CALENDAR OF EVENTS

You may be surprised that Las Vegas does not offer as many annual events as most tourist cities. The reason is Las Vegas's very raison d'être: the gaming industry. This town wants its visitors spending their money in the casinos, not off at Renaissance fairs and parades. When in town, check the local paper and call the **Las Vegas Convention and Visitors Authority** (☎ 702/892-0711), **Las Vegas Events** (☎ 702/731-2115), or the **Chamber of Commerce** (☎ 702/735-1616) to find out about other events scheduled during your visit.

January
- **The PBA Classic.** The Showboat Hotel, 2800 Fremont St. (☎ 702/385-9150), hosts this major bowling tournament every January.

March
- **The PBA Invitational.** Another major annual bowling tournament, also at the Showboat Hotel.

April
- **The World Series of Poker.** This famed 21-day event takes place at Binion's Horseshoe Casino, 128 Fremont St. (☎ 702/382-1600), in late April and early May, with high-stakes gamblers

and show-biz personalities competing for six-figure purses. There are daily events with entry stakes ranging from $125 to $5,000. To enter the World Championship Event (purse $1 million), players must put up $10,000. It costs nothing to go watch the action.

- **TruGreen-ChemLawn Las Vegas Senior Classic.** This 4-day event in mid- to late April or early May takes place at the Tournament Players Club (TPC), The Canyons, 9851 Canyon Run Dr., in nearby Summerlin. For details and driving information, call ☎ **702/382-6616.**

June

- **Helldorado.** This Elks-sponsored Western heritage celebration takes place over a several day period in mid-June. It includes bull riders, a trail ride, a barbecue, and four major Professional Rodeo Cowboys Association (PRCA) rodeos at the Thomas and Mack Center at the University of Nevada, Las Vegas (UNLV). For information call the Elks Lodge (☎ **702/870-1221**) or check the local papers. The ticket office number is ☎ 702/895-3900.

September

- **Oktoberfest.** This boisterous autumn holiday is celebrated from mid-September through the end of October at the Mount Charleston Resort (☎ **800/955-1314** or 702/872-5408) with music, folk dancers, sing-alongs around a roaring fire, special decorations, and Bavarian cookouts.

October

- **PGA Tour Las Vegas Invitational.** This 5-day championship event, played on three local courses, is televised by ESPN. For details call ☎ **702/382-6616.**

December

- **National Finals Rodeo.** This is the Super Bowl of rodeos, attended by close to 170,000 people each year. The top 15 male rodeo stars compete in six different events: calf roping, steer wrestling, bull riding, team roping, saddle bronco riding, and bareback riding. And the top 15 women compete in barrel racing. An all-around "Cowboy of the Year" is chosen. In connection with this event, hotels book country stars in their showrooms, and there's a cowboy shopping spree—the NFR Cowboy Christmas Gift Show, a trade show for Western gear—at Cashman Field.

  Where: At the 17,000-seat Thomas and Mack Center of University of Nevada, Las Vegas (UNLV). When: For 10 days during the first 2 weeks of the month. How: Order tickets as far in advance as possible (☎ **702/895-3900**).

- **Las Vegas Bowl Week.** A championship football event in mid-December pits the winners of the Mid-American Conference against the winners of the Big West Conference. The action takes place at the 32,000-seat Sam Boyd Stadium. Call ☎ **702/895-3900** for ticket information.

- **Western Athletic Conference (WAC) Football Championship.** This collegiate championship event takes place the first week in December. Call ☎ **792/731-5595** for ticket information. Tickets prices range from $15 to $100.

- **New Year's Eve.** This is a biggie (reserve your hotel room early). Downtown, Fremont Street is closed to traffic between Third and Main streets, and there's a big block party with two dramatic countdowns to midnight (the first is at 9pm, midnight on the East Coast). Of course, there are fireworks.

3 Tips for Travelers with Special Needs

FOR PEOPLE WITH DISABILITIES   Write or call **The Independent Living Program,** Nevada Association for the Handicapped, 6200 W. Oakey Blvd., Las Vegas, NV 89102 (☎ **702/870-7050**). They can recommend hotels and restaurants that meet your needs, help you find a personal attendant, advise about transportation, and answer all questions.

In addition, the **Nevada Commission on Tourism** (☎ **800/638-2328**), offers a free accommodations guide to Las Vegas hotels that includes access information.

FOR SENIORS   Always carry some form of photo ID that includes your birth date so you can take advantage of discounts wherever they're offered. And it never hurts to ask.

If you haven't already done so, consider joining the **American Association of Retired Persons (AARP)** (☎ **800/424-3410** or 202/434-2277). Annual membership costs $8 per person or couple. You must be at least 50 to join. Membership entitles you to many discounts. Write to Purchase Privilege Program, AARP Fulfillment, 601 E St. NW, Washington, DC 20049, to receive their *Purchase Privilege* brochure, a free list of hotels, motels, and car-rental firms nationwide that offer discounts to AARP members.

FOR FAMILIES   Las Vegas in the '90s is discussed in the "Especially for Kids" suggestions in chapter 6 and in the "Best Bets" in chapter 4. Here are also a few general suggestions to make traveling with kids easier.

Children under 12, and in many cases even older, stay free in their parents' rooms in most hotels. Look for establishments that have pools and other recreational facilities (see "Family-Friendly Hotels" in chapter 4).

FOR GAYS & LESBIANS   The *Las Vegas Bugle,* a monthly magazine serving the gay community, provides information about bars, workshops, local politics, support groups, shops, events and more. A subscription costs $20 for 12 issues. For details call ☎ **702/ 369-6260.** See also listings for gay bars in chapter 8.

4   Getting There

BY AIR
THE MAJOR AIRLINES
The following airlines have regularly scheduled flights into Las Vegas (some of these are regional carriers, so they may not all fly from your point of origin): **Air Canada** (☎ 800/776-3000), **Alaska Airlines** (☎ 800/426-0333), **America West** (☎ 800/235-9292), **American/American Eagle** (☎ 800/433-7300), **American Trans Air** (☎ 800/543-3708), **Canadian International** (☎ 800/426-7000), **Condor** (☎ 800/524-6975), **Continental** (☎ 800/525-0280), **Delta/Skywest** (☎ 800/221-1212), **Frontier** (☎800/432-1359), **Hawaiian** (☎ 800/367-5320), **Kiwi** (☎ 800/538-5494), **Midway** (☎ 888/226-4392), **Midwest Express** (☎ 800/452-2022), **Northwest** (☎ 800/225-2525), **Reno Air** (☎ 800/736-6247), **Southwest** (☎ 800/435-9792), **Sun Country** (☎ 800/359-6786), **TWA** (☎ 800/221-2000), **United** (☎ 800/241-6522), **US Airways** (☎ 800/428-4322), and **Western Pacific** (☎ 800/930-3030).

THE LAS VEGAS AIRPORT
Las Vegas is served by **McCarran International Airport,** 5757 Wayne Newton Blvd. (☎ **702/261-5743** or TDD 702/ 261-3111), just a few minutes' drive from the southern end of the Strip. It's a big, modern airport, and rather unique in that it includes a casino area with more than 1,000 slot machines. Although these are reputed to offer lower paybacks than hotel casinos (the airport has a captive audience and doesn't need to lure repeat customers), it's hard to resist throwing in a few quarters while waiting for luggage to arrive.

Las Vegas & Environs

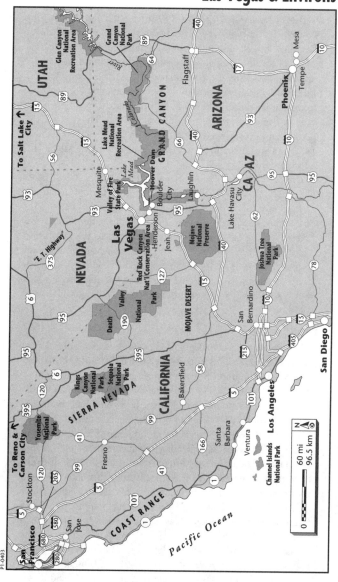

P1-0403

9

Bell Trans (☎ **702/739-7990;** fax 702/384-2283) runs 20-passenger minibuses daily between the airport and all major Las Vegas hotels and motels almost around the clock (4:30am to 2am). There are several other companies that run similar ventures—just stand outside on the curb and one will be flagged down for you. Buses from the airport leave about every 10 minutes. For departure from your hotel, call at least 2 hours in advance (though often you can just flag one down outside any major hotel). The cost is $3.50 per person each way to Strip and Convention Center area hotels, $4.75 to Downtown properties (any place north of the Sahara Hotel and west of I-15).

Even less expensive are **Citizen's Area Transit (CAT)** buses (☎ **702/CAT-RIDE**). The no. 108 bus departs from the airport and will take you to the Stratosphere, where you can transfer to the 301, which stops close to most Strip and Convention Center area hotels. The no. 109 bus goes from the airport to the Downtown Transportation Center at Casino Center Boulevard and Stewart Avenue. The fare is $1.50, 50¢ for seniors and children. *Note:* If you have heavy luggage, you should know that you might have a long walk from the bus stop to your door (even if it's right in front of your hotel).

RENTING A CAR

All of the major car-rental companies are represented in Las Vegas. We like **Allstate** (☎ **800/634-6147** or 702/736-6148), the least expensive of the airport-based car-rental agencies. Their fleet of more than 1,500 vehicles includes—besides the usual mix—an inventory of 15 passenger vans, four-wheel drives, Jeeps, minivans, sports cars, and convertibles. We've found this local, family-owned company (the largest independent operator in Las Vegas) friendly and competent, with an invariably charming staff at the airport. They're open 24 hours. And they've agreed to offer our readers a **20% discount off regular rental rates** at any Allstate location (just show the agent your copy of this book). In addition to McCarran Airport, there are Allstate car desks at the Aladdin, Riviera, Stardust, and Jackie Gaughan's Plaza hotels, and the company offers free pickup anywhere in Las Vegas.

National companies with outlets in Las Vegas include **Alamo** (☎ 800/327-9633), **Avis** (☎ 800/367-2847), **Budget** (☎ 800/922-2899), **Dollar** (800/842-2054), **Enterprise** (☎ 800/325-8007), **Hertz** (☎ 800/654-3131), **National** (☎ 800/227-7368) and **Thrifty** (☎ 800/367-2277)

Driving Distances to Las Vegas (in miles)			
Chicago	1,766	New York City	2,564
Dallas	1,230	Phoenix	286
Denver	759	Salt Lake City	421
Los Angeles	269	San Francisco	586

BY CAR

The main highway connecting Las Vegas with the rest of the country is I-15; it links Montana, Idaho, and Utah with Southern California. From the East Coast, take I-70 or I-80 west to Kingman, Arizona, and then U.S. 93 north to Downtown Las Vegas (Fremont Street). From the south, take I-10 west to Phoenix and then U.S. 93 north to Las Vegas. From San Francisco, take I-80 east to Reno and then U.S. 95 south to Las Vegas. If you're driving to Las Vegas be sure to read the driving precautions under "By Car" in "Getting Around," chapter 3.

PACKAGE DEALS

When you make reservations on any airline, also inquire about money-saving packages that include hotel accommodations, car rentals, tours, and so forth with your airfare.

For instance, at press time, a **Delta Dream Vacation** package leaving from New York could cost as little as $342.50 per person based on double occupancy, including round-trip coach air transportation, two nights at your choice of several major casino hotels, a rental car for 24 hours, airport transfers, and bonus discounts and admissions. At press time **Southwest Airlines** was offering round-trip airfare from Los Angeles with two nights at several different hotels complete with ground transportation; per person based on double occupancy, for the Mirage it was $174, and for the Golden Nugget $119. (Of course, this was midweek.) Similar packages are available from such companies as **American Airlines Fly Away Vacations, America West Vacations,** and **US Airways Vacations.** Prices vary according to the season, seat availability, hotel choice, whether you travel midweek or on the weekend, and other factors.

3

Getting to Know Las Vegas

*L*ocated in the southernmost precincts of a wide, pancake-flat valley, Las Vegas is the biggest city in the state of Nevada. Treeless mountains form a scenic backdrop to hotels awash in neon glitter. For tourism purposes, the city is quite compact.

1 Orientation

VISITOR INFORMATION

All major Las Vegas hotels provide comprehensive tourist information at their reception and/or sightseeing and show desks. Other good information sources are: the **Las Vegas Convention and Visitors Authority,** 3150 Paradise Rd., Las Vegas, NV 89109 (☎ **702/892-0711,** Monday to Friday 8am to 6pm, Saturday and Sunday 8am to 5pm); the **Las Vegas Chamber of Commerce,** 711 E. Desert Inn Rd., Las Vegas, NV 89109 (☎ **702/735-1616,** Monday to Friday 8am to 5pm), and, for information on all of Nevada, including Las Vegas, the **Nevada Commission on Tourism** (☎ **800/638-2328**).

FOR TROUBLED TRAVELERS

The **Traveler's Aid Society** is a social-service organization geared to helping travelers in difficult straits. Their services might include re-uniting families separated while traveling, feeding people stranded without cash, or even emotional counseling. If you're in trouble, seek them out. In Las Vegas there is a Traveler's Aid office at McCarran International Airport (☎ **702/798-1742**). It's open daily from 8am to 5pm. Similar services are provided by **Help of Southern Nevada,** 953–35B E. Sahara Ave. (suite 208), at Maryland Parkway in the Commercial Center (☎ **702/369-4357**). Hours are Monday to Friday 8am to 4pm.

CITY LAYOUT

There are two main areas of Las Vegas: the Strip and Downtown. Las Vegas Blvd. S. (the Strip) is Ground Zero for addresses; anything crossing it will start with 1 East and 1 West (and go up from there) at that point.

Las Vegas at a Glance

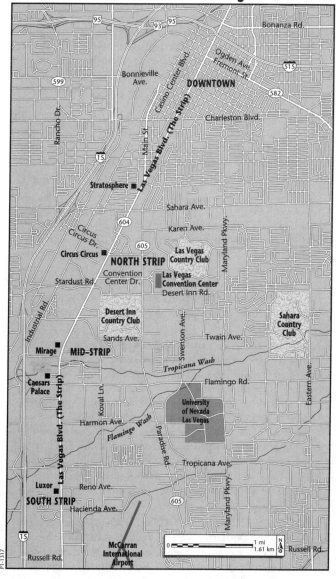

THE STRIP   The Strip is probably the most famous 3^1/$_2$-mile stretch of highway in the nation. Officially Las Vegas Boulevard South, it contains most of the top hotels in town and offers almost all of the major showroom entertainment. We divide the Strip into three sections: **South Strip** can be roughly defined as the portion of the Strip south of Harmon Avenue, including the MGM Grand, the Monte Carlo, the New York New York, and the Luxor hotels. **Mid-Strip** is a long stretch of the street between Harmon Avenue and Spring Mountain Road, including Caesars, the Mirage and Treasure Island, Bally's, the Flamingo Hilton, and Harrah's. **North Strip** stretches north from Stardust Road all the way to the Stratosphere Tower and includes the Stardust, Sahara, Riviera, Desert Inn, and Circus Circus.

CONVENTION CENTER   This area east of the Strip has grown up around the Las Vegas Convention Center. Las Vegas is one of the nation's top convention cities, attracting more than 2.9 million conventioneers each year. The major hotel in this section is the Las Vegas Hilton, but in recent years Marriott has built Residence Inn and Courtyard properties here, and the Hard Rock hotels have opened. You'll find many excellent smaller hotels and motels southward along Paradise Road. All of these offer close proximity to the Strip.

DOWNTOWN   Also known as "Glitter Gulch" (narrower streets make the neon seem brighter), Downtown Las Vegas, which is centered on Fremont Street between Main and 9th streets, was the first section of the city to develop hotels and casinos. With the exception of the Golden Nugget, which looks like it belongs in Monte Carlo, this area has traditionally been more casual than the Strip. But with the advent of the "Fremont Street Experience" (see chapter 6 for details), Downtown is experiencing a revitalization. The area is clean, the crowds low key and friendly, and the light show over head as silly as anything on the Strip. Don't overlook it. Las Vegas Boulevard runs all the way into Fremont Street Downtown (about a 5-minute drive from Stratosphere if traffic is good).

BETWEEN THE STRIP & DOWNTOWN   The area between the Strip and Downtown is a seedy stretch dotted with tacky wedding chapels, bail-bond operations, pawnshops, and cheap motels.

However, the area known as the **Gateway District** (roughly north and south of Charleston to the west of Las Vegas Boulevard South) is slowly but surely gaining a name for itself as an actual artists colony. Studios, small cafes, and other signs of life are springing up and one hopes this movement will last.

2 Getting Around

It shouldn't be too hard to navigate your way around. For the most part, you won't have to. The Strip is obvious (to put it mildly), Downtown is fairly obvious, and the other main streets should be as well.

BY CAR

We highly recommend a rental car for Vegas tourists. The Strip is too spread out for walking, Downtown is too far away for a cheap cab ride, and public transportation is ineffective at best. Plus, a car brings freedom. You should note that places with addresses some 60 blocks east or west from the Strip are actually a less than 10-minute drive, provided there is no traffic. However, if you plan to confine yourself to one part of the Strip (or one cruise down it) or to Downtown, your feet will suffice.

Note: If you can, avoid driving during peak rush hours, especially if you have to make a show curtain. Parking is usually a pleasure, since all casino hotels offer valet service. That means that for a mere $1 tip you can park right at the door. (Though the valet usually fills up on busy nights.) Furthermore, though bus tours are available to nearby attractions, a car lets you explore at your own pace rather than according to a tour schedule. See "Renting a Car" in chapter 2 for information and toll-free numbers of companies with offices in Las Vegas.

Since driving on the outskirts of Las Vegas—for example, coming from California—involves desert driving, you must take certain precautions. It's a good idea to check your tires, water, and oil before leaving. Take at least 5 gallons of water in a clean container that can be used for either drinking or the radiator. Pay attention to road signs that suggest when to turn off your car's air conditioner. And don't push your luck with gas—it may be 35 miles, or more, between stations. If your car overheats, do not remove the radiator cap until the engine has cooled, and then remove it only very slowly. Add water to within an inch of the top of the radiator.

BY TAXI

Since cabs line up in front of all major hotels, an easy way to get around town is by taxi. Cabs charge $2.20 at the meter drop and

30¢ for each additional ¹/₅ of a mile. A taxi from the airport to the Strip will run you $8 to $12, from the airport to Downtown $15 to $18, and between the Strip and Downtown about $7 to $10. You can often save money by sharing a cab with someone going to the same destination (up to five people can ride for the same fare).

If you want to call a taxi, any of the following companies can provide one: **Desert Cab Company** (☎ 702/376-2688), **Whittlesea Blue Cab** (☎ 702/384-6111), and **Yellow/Checker Cab/Star Company** (☎ 702/873-2000).

FAST FACTS: Las Vegas

Area Code   702.

Baby-Sitters   Contact **Around the Clock Child Care** (☎ 800/798-6768 or 702/365-1040). In business since 1985, this reputable company clears its sitters with the health department, the sheriff, and the FBI, and carefully screens references. Charges are $38 for 4 hours for one or two children, $7.50 for each additional hour, with surcharges for additional children and on holidays. Sitters are on call 7 days a week, 24 hours a day, and they will come to your hotel. Call at least 2 hours in advance.

Banks   Banks are generally open 9 or 10am to 3pm, and most have Saturday hours. See also "Cash and Credit," below.

Cash and Credit   It's extremely easy—too easy—to obtain cash in Las Vegas. Most casino cashiers will cash personal checks and can exchange foreign currency, and just about every casino has a machine that will provide cash on a wide variety of credit cards.

Convention Facilities   Las Vegas is one of America's top convention destinations. Much of the action takes place at the **Las Vegas Convention Center,** 3150 Paradise Rd., Las Vegas, NV 89109 (☎ **702/892-0711**). The largest single-level convention center in the world, its 1.3 million square feet includes 89 meeting rooms. And this immense facility is augmented by the **Cashman Field Center,** 850 Las Vegas Blvd. N., Las Vegas, NV 89101 (☎ **702/386-7100**). Under the same auspices, Cashman provides another 98,100 square feet of convention space.

Currency Exchange   Most Las Vegas hotels can exchange foreign currency. There's also a currency exchange desk run by Travelex in the ticketing area on the first level of McCarran International Airport.

Dentists and Doctors   Hotels usually have lists of dentists and doctors should you need one. In addition, they are listed in the Centel Yellow Pages.

For dentist referrals you can also call the **Clark County Dental Society** (☎ **702/255-7873**), weekdays 9am to noon and 1 to 5pm; when the office is closed, a recording will tell you whom to call for emergency service.

For physician referrals, call **Desert Springs Hospital** (☎ **800/ 842-5439** or 702/733-6875). Hours are Monday to Friday 8am to 5pm.

Drugstores   **Sav-on** is a large 24-hour drugstore and pharmacy close to the Strip at 1360 E. Flamingo Rd., at Maryland Parkway (☎ **702/731-5373** for the pharmacy, 702/737-0595 for general merchandise). **White Cross Drugs,** 1700 Las Vegas Blvd. S. (☎ **702/382-1733**), open daily 7am to 1am, will make pharmacy deliveries to your hotel during the day.

Emergencies   Dial ☎ **911** to contact the police or fire departments or to call an ambulance.

Emergency services are available 24 hours a day at **University Medical Center,** 1800 W. Charleston Blvd., at Shadow Lane (☎ **702/383-2661**); the emergency room entrance is on the corner of Hastings and Rose streets. **Sunrise Hospital and Medical Center,** 3186 Maryland Pkwy., between Desert Inn Road and Sahara Avenue (☎ **702/731-8080**), also has a 24-hour emergency room. For more minor problems, if you are on the Strip, the Imperial Palace has a 24-hour Urgent Care facility, the **Resorts Medical Center,** an independently run facility on the 8th floor, with doctors and X-ray machines. It's located at 3535 Las Vegas Blvd. S, between Sands and Flamingo (☎ **702/731-3311**).

Highway Conditions   For recorded information, call ☎ **702/ 486-3116.**

Hot Lines   The **Rape Crisis Center** (☎ **702/366-1640**), **Suicide Prevention** (☎ **702/731-2990**), **Poison Emergencies** (☎ **800/446-6179**).

Libraries   The largest in town is the **Clark County Library** branch at 1401 Flamingo Rd., at Escondido Street, on the southeast corner (☎ **702/733-7810**). Hours are Monday to Thursday 9am to 9pm, Friday and Saturday 9am to 5pm, Sunday 1 to 5pm.

Liquor and Gambling Laws   You must be 21 to drink or gamble. There are no closing hours in Las Vegas for the sale or consumption of alcohol, even on Sunday.

Newspapers and Periodicals   There are two Las Vegas dailies: the *Las Vegas Review Journal* and the *Las Vegas Sun*. The *Review Journal's* Friday edition has a helpful "Weekend" section with a comprehensive guide to shows and buffets. And at every hotel desk, you'll find dozens of free local magazines, such as *Vegas Visitor, What's On in Las Vegas, Showbiz Weekly,* and *Where To in Las Vegas,* that are chock-full of helpful information. The **International Newsstand** carries a vast selection of virtually every major U.S. city newspaper and many international ones; they probably don't have everything, but we tried and couldn't find one they had missed. 3900 Maryland Pkwy., in Citibank Plaza (☎ **702/ 796-9901**). It is open daily from 8:30am to 9pm.

Parking   Valet parking is one of the great pleasures of Las Vegas and well worth the dollar tip (given when the car is returned) to save walking a city block from the far reaches of a hotel parking lot, particularly when the temperature is over 100°. Another summer plus: The valet will turn on your air-conditioning, so you don't have to get in an "oven on wheels."

Police   For nonemergencies call ☎ **702/795-3111.** For emergencies call ☎ **911.**

Post Office   The most convenient post office is immediately behind the Stardust Hotel at 3100 Industrial Rd., between Sahara Avenue and Spring Mountain Road (☎ **800/297-5543**). It's open Monday to Friday 8:30am to 5pm. You can also mail letters and packages at your hotel, and there's a full-service U.S. Post Office in the Forum Shops in Caesars Palace.

Safety   In Las Vegas, vast amounts of money are always on display, and criminals find many easy marks. Don't be one of them. At gaming tables and slot machines, men should keep wallets well concealed and out of the reach of pickpockets, and women should keep handbags in plain sight (on laps). Outside casinos, popular spots for pickpockets and thieves are restaurants and outdoor shows, such as the volcano at the Mirage or at the Treasure Island pirate battle. Stay alert. Unless your hotel room has an in-room safe, check your valuables in a safety-deposit box at the front desk.

Taxes   Clark County hotel room tax is 8%; the sales tax is 7%.

Time Zone   Las Vegas is in the Pacific time zone, 3 hours earlier than the East Coast, 2 hours earlier than the Midwest.

Weather and Time   Call ☎ **702/248-4800.**

4

Accommodations in Las Vegas

*I*f there is one thing Vegas has, it's hotels. Big hotels: Here you'll find 19 of the 20 largest hotels in the world. And rooms: 105,000 rooms, to be exact—or at least exact at this writing. Every 5 minutes, or so it seems, someone is putting up a new giant hotel or adding another 1,000 rooms to an already existing one. So finding a place to stay in Vegas should be the least of your worries. Or is it?

When a convention, a fight, or some other big event is happening—and these things are always happening—darn near all of those 105,000 rooms are going to be sold out. (Over the course of last year, the occupancy rate for hotel rooms in Las Vegas ran at about 90%) A last-minute Vegas vacation can turn into a housing nightmare. If possible, plan in advance so you can have your choice.

But the bottom line is that with a few subtle differences, a hotel room is a hotel room. After you factor in location, price, and whether you have a pirate-loving kid, there isn't that much difference between rooms, except for perhaps size and the quality of their surprisingly similar furnishings. Price isn't even always a guideline; prices in Vegas are anything but fixed, so you will notice wild ranges (the same room can routinely go for anywhere from $60 to $250, depending on demand), and even that range is negotiable if it's a slow time. (Though such times are less and less common thanks to the influx of conventions.)

RESERVATIONS SERVICES   If you get harried when you have to haggle, use a free service offered by **Reservations Plus,** 2275 A Renaissance Dr., Las Vegas, NV 89119 (☎ **800/805-9528;** fax 702/795-8767). They'll find you a hotel room in your price range that meets your specific requirements. Because they book rooms in volume, they are able to get discounted rates. Not only can they book rooms, but they can arrange packages (including meals, transportation, tours, show tickets, car rentals, and other features) and group rates.

The **Las Vegas Convention and Visitors Authority** also runs a room reservations hot line (☎ **800/332-5334**), which can be helpful. They can apprise you of room availability, quote rates, contact a hotel for you, and tell you when major conventions will be in town.

1 Best Bets

- **Best for Conventioneers/Business Travelers:** The **Las Vegas Hilton,** 3000 Paradise Rd., adjacent to the Las Vegas Convention Center and the setting for many on-premises conventions, offers extensive facilities along with helpful services such as a full business center.

- **Best Elegant Hotel:** Country club elegance is the keynote of the **Desert Inn Country Club Resort and Casino,** 3145 Las Vegas Blvd. S. In its European-style casino, gaming tables are comfortably spaced, the glitzy glow of neon is replaced by the glitter of crystal chandeliers, and the scarcity of slot and video poker machines eliminates the usual noisy jangle of coins. Extensive facilities are complemented by attentive personal service. This is the most prestigious hotel address in town.

- **Best Archetypally Las Vegas Hotel:** By the end of 1998, there aren't going to be any. Las Vegas hotels are one and all doing such massive face lifts that the archetype is going to be but a memory. Still, despite some major face-lifts, **Caesars Palace,** 3570 Las Vegas Blvd. S., will probably continue to embody the excess and, well, down right silliness that used to characterize Vegas—and to a certain extent still does.

- **Best Swimming Pool:** The **Mirage,** 3400 Las Vegas Boulevard South, and the **Flamingo Hilton,** 3555 Las Vegas Blvd. S., probably tie for most stunning; both feature lushly landscaped areas, with trees galore, amorphously shaped pools with water slides and waterfalls, plus kiddie pools, Jacuzzis, and, in the case of the Flamingo, swan- and duck-filled ponds and islands of flamingos and African penguins. Far more Vegas, however, is the **Tropicana,** 3801 Las Vegas Blvd. S., where you'll also find a swim-up bar/blackjack table.

- **Best Health Club:** Like sumptuous swimming pools, deluxe state-of-the-art health clubs are the rule in Las Vegas hotels. Most exclusive (the fee is $18 per visit) and extensively equipped is the club at the **Mirage,** offering a full complement of machines—some with individual TVs (headphones are supplied), free weights, private whirlpool rooms as well as a large whirlpool and saunas, a thoroughly equipped locker room, and comfortable lounges in which to rest up after your workout. An adjoining salon offers every imaginable spa service. Steve Wynn works out here almost daily, as do many celebrity guests.

- **Best Hotel Dining/Entertainment:** Food aficionados will be thrilled with the nationally renowned celebrity chefs at the **MGM Grand,** 3799 Las Vegas Blvd. S. You'll find restaurants by Mark Miller, Emeril Lagasse, and Wolfgang Puck, as well as one of the best restaurants in Vegas: the Grand's gourmet room Gatsby's. There's also a re-creation of Hollywood's famed Brown Derby here.

- **Best for Twentysomethings Through Baby Boomers:** The **Hard Rock Hotel,** 4455 Paradise Rd., which bills itself as the world's "first rock 'n' roll hotel and casino" and "Vegas for a new generation." Aficionados of Hard Rock clubs won't mind the noise level, but we aren't sure about everyone else.

- **Best Interior:** For totally different reasons, it's a tie between **New York New York** 3790 Las Vegas Blvd. S. and the **Mirage.** The latter's tropical rain forest and massive coral-reef aquarium behind the registration desk may not provide as much relaxation as a Club Med vacation, but they're a welcome change from the general hubbub that is usual for Vegas. Speaking of hubbub, New York New York has cornered the market on it, but its jaw-dropping interior, with its extraordinary attention to detail (virtually every significant characteristic of New York City is re-created somewhere here) makes this a tough act to beat. Ever.

- **Best for Families:** It's a classic. **Circus Circus,** 2880 Las Vegas Blvd. S., has almost unlimited activities for kids—ongoing circus acts, a vast video-game arcade, a carnival midway, and a full amusement park.

- **Best Rooms:** On the strip, they're at the **Mirage;** downtown, they're at the **Golden Nugget,** 129 E. Fremont St. The rooms actually look almost identical, though the former are done in more earth tones, while golds are the hallmark of the latter. In both hotels, each room has a marble entryway, a half-canopy bed, a dressing table with lighted lamp, comfortable overstuffed chairs in the single-bed rooms, and a lush (if average size) marbled bathroom. You feel special in them.

- **Best Noncasino Hotel:** The very upscale **Alexis Park Resort,** 375 E. Harmon Ave., is the choice of many visiting celebrities and headliners. Many of its rooms have working fireplaces and/or Jacuzzis, and guests are cosseted with can-do concierge service.

- **Best Casinos:** Our favorite places to gamble are anywhere we might win. But we also like the **Mirage** (lively, beautiful, and not overwhelming), **Caesars Palace** (because the cocktail waitresses are dressed in togas), **New York New York** (because of the afore-mentioned attention to detail (it almost makes losing fun!), and **Main Street Station,** 200 N. Main St. (because it's about the most smoke-free casino in town, and because it's pretty).
- **Best Downtown Hotel:** It's a tie. The upscale **Golden Nugget** is exceptionally appealing in every aspect. The **Main Street Station,** which has done a terrific job of renovating an older space, now evokes turn-of-the century San Francisco, with great Victorian details everywhere, solidly good restaurants, and surprisingly nice rooms for an inexpensive price.
- **Best Views:** From high-floor rooms at the **Stratosphere,** 2000 Las Vegas Blvd. S., you can see the entire city.

2 South Strip

EXPENSIVE

✪ **MGM Grand Hotel/Casino.** 3799 Las Vegas Blvd. S., at Tropicana Ave., Las Vegas, NV 89109. ☎ **800/929-1111** or 702/891-7777. Fax 702/891-1112. 4,254 rms, 751 suites. A/C TV TEL. $69–$119 standard double, $79–$129 concierge floor double with breakfast, $99–$2,500 suite. Extra person $10. Children under 12 stay free in parents' room. AE, DC, DISC, MC, V. Free parking (self and valet).

The MGM Grand has recently completed one of the most amusing renovations in Vegas. When it first opened, the billion-dollar property, spread over 112 acres, had a Wizard of Oz theme. The outside was a shocking shade of emerald green, some door handles had "Oz" on them, rainbows were everywhere, and right in the center was a giant animatronic reenactment of MGM's most famous movie. Outside was a theme park, which initially charged an exorbitant entry fee.

That has changed. The outside is still green, but now the MGM Grand is The City of Entertainment, which means the theme is *all* MGM movies, not just one specific film beloved by children. Gone is the Oz attraction (though it may reappear at a later date in a different, less prominent part of the hotel), to be replaced by a Rain Forest Cafe—something more appealing to adults. The MGM did seem a bit cheesy (particularly if you contrast it to the even older, original MGM Grand, the elegant place that was destroyed in one of the worst hotel fires in history). As one of the world's largest hotels, it was also overwhelming and hard to navigate.

South Strip Accommodations

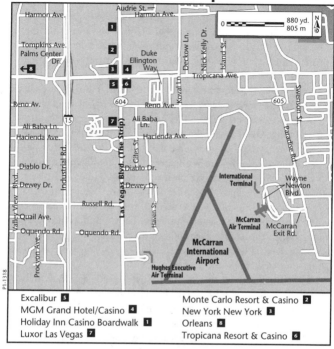

Excalibur **5**
MGM Grand Hotel/Casino **4**
Holiday Inn Casino Boardwalk **1**
Luxor Las Vegas **7**

Monte Carlo Resort & Casino **2**
New York New York **3**
Orleans **8**
Tropicana Resort & Casino **6**

The renovations are seeking to fix all that. The redesign will attempt to create some more intimate corners, and has already made navigating the still immense place somewhat easier. (It's actually kind of amusing how they are now backing away from bragging about their size and moving more toward trying to hide that fact.) And the staff, confirms a recent guest, couldn't be more helpful and friendly. Throughout, the theme of The City of Entertainment will be repeated, as old movies are evoked in the decor (though still considerably green, and the rainbows still remain). In certain areas (like the restaurant row), the look is meant to suggest a behind-the-scenes view of a film studio back lot. The rooms will give no cause for complaint. They are decorated in four distinct motifs. Most glamorous are the Hollywood rooms furnished in two-tone wood pieces (bird's-eye maple on cherry), with gold-flecked walls (hung with prints of Humphrey Bogart, Marilyn Monroe, and Vivien Leigh as Scarlett), gilded moldings, and beds backed by mirrors. Oz-themed rooms still have emerald-green rugs and upholstery, silver and gold star-motif wallpaper, bright poppy-print bedspreads, and tasseled green drapes; the walls are hung with paintings of Dorothy and friends. In the Casablanca rooms—decorated in earth tones with shimmery fabrics and pecan/walnut furnishings and moldings—artworks depict Moroccan scenes such as an Arab marketplace. And the cheerful Old South rooms feature 18th-century–style furnishings and faux-silk beige damask walls hung with paintings of southern belles and scenes from *Gone With the Wind*. All rooms offer gorgeous marble baths.

Dining: MGM houses the most prestigious assemblage of dining rooms of any hotel in town. Four cutting-edge stars in the Las Vegas culinary galaxy—the **Wolfgang Puck Café,** Emeril Lagasse's **Emeril's New Orleans Fish House, Gatsby's,** and Mark Miller's **Coyote Café**—along with buffet offerings, are described in chapter 5. Indeed, Emeril's New Orleans Fish House and Gatsby's vie for the honor of best restaurant in Vegas. The **Oz Buffet** is described in chapter 5. There are several other restaurants and lounges as well.

Services: 24-hour room service, foreign-currency exchange, guest-relations desk, shoeshine (in men's rooms).

Facilities: Casino, MGM Grand Adventures Theme Park, full-service health spa and health club; full-service unisex hair/beauty salon, four night-lit tennis courts with pro shop (lessons available), huge beach-entry swimming pool with waterfall, a 30,000-square-foot video arcade (including virtual-reality games), carnival midway with 33 games of skill, business center; florist, shopping arcade; two wedding chapels (in the theme park), show/sports event ticket desks; car-rental desk, sightseeing/tour desks, America West airline desk.

The **MGM Grand Youth Center** is a solid facility for children ages 3 to 16 (☎ **702/891-3200** for details and prices).

Monte Carlo Resort and Casino. 3770 Las Vegas Blvd. S., between Flamingo Rd. and Tropicana Ave., Las Vegas, NV 89109. ☎ **800/311-8999** or 702/730-7777. Fax 702/730-7250. 2,759 rms, 255 suites. A/C TV TEL. Sun–Thurs, $69–$199 double; Fri–Sat, $99–$269. Suites $139–$339. Extra person $15. Children under 12 stay free in parents' room. AE, CB, DC, DISC, MC, V. Free parking (self and valet).

The newest resort on the Strip, the massive Monte Carlo is the world's seventh-largest hotel. It's fronted by Corinthian colonnades, triumphal arches, splashing fountains, and allegorical (and slightly naughty) statuary, with an entranceway opening on a bustling casino. A separate entrance in the rear of the hotel leads to a splendid marble-floored, crystal-chandeliered lobby evocative of a European grand hotel. Palladian windows behind the registration desk overlook a salient feature: the hotel's 20,000-acre pool area, a lushly landscaped miniwater park with a 4,800-foot wave pool, a surf pond, waterfalls, and a "river" for tubing.

Spacious rooms with big marble baths exude a warmly traditional European feel. Striped tan wallpapers with fleur-de-lis friezes create a neutral backdrop for rich cherry wood furnishings and vivid floral-print fabrics and carpeting. Cable TVs are equipped with hotel-information channels, keno, and pay-movie options. A concierge level for VIPs is on the 32nd floor.

Dining: The restaurants include **Blackstone's,** the **Monte Carlo Pub and Brewery,** and the **Dragon Noodle Company.**

Services: 24-hour room service, foreign currency exchange, shoeshine, limo rental.

Facilities: Casino, car-rental desk, four tennis courts, sightseeing/tour/show desk, barber/beauty salon, vast swimming pool, kiddie pool, whirlpool, water attractions (see above), wedding chapel, full business center, large video-game arcade, large shopping arcade.

❍ **New York New York.** 3790 Las Vegas Blvd. S., at Tropicana Ave., Las Vegas, NV 89109. ☎ **800/693-6763** or 702/740-6969. Fax 702/740-6920. 2034 rms. AC TV TEL. Sun–Thurs from $89 double, Fri–Sat from $129 double. Extra person $20. AE, CB, DC, DISC, MC, V. Free parking (self and valet).

Just when you think Las Vegas has it all and has done it all, they go and do something like this. New York New York is just plain spectacular. Even the jaded and horrified have to admit it. You can't miss the hotel; it's that little (hah!) building on the corner of the Strip and Tropicana that looks like the New York City skyline: the Empire State Building, the Chrysler Building, the Public Library, down to the 150-foot Statue of Liberty and Ellis Island, all built to approximately one-third scale. And as if that isn't enough, they threw in a roller coaster running around the outside and into the hotel and casino itself. It's theme park as hotel.

And inside, it all gets better. There are details everywhere—so many, in fact, that the typical expression on the face of casino-goers is slack-jawed wonder. If you enter the casino via the Brooklyn Bridge (the walkway from the Strip), you find yourself in a replica of Greenwich Village, down to the cobblestones, the manhole covers, the tenement buildings, and the graffiti. (Yes, they even re-created that. You should see the subway station.) The main casino area is done as Central Park, complete with trees, babbling brooks, streetlamps, and footbridges. The change carts are little Yellow Cabs. The reception area and lobby are done in belle epoque, art deco, golden age of Manhattan style; you feel like breaking out into a 1930s musical number while standing there. It really is impossible to adequately describe the sheer mind-blowing enormity of the thing. So we are just going to leave it at: *Wow.* The word *subtle* was obviously not in the lexicon of the designers. It's hard to see how Vegas can ever top this, but then again that's been said before.

Rooms are housed in different towers, each with some New York–inspired name. There are 64 different styles of rooms, and they are all smashing. Each essentially is done up in a hard-core art deco style: various shades of inlaid wood, rounded tops to the armoires and headboards, usually shades of brown and wood colors. However, some of the rooms are downright tiny (just like New York again!), and in those all this massively detailed decoration could be overwhelming, if not suffocating. The bathrooms are also small, but with black, marble-topped sinks, which again lend a glamorous '20s image. And a mere 6 months after opening, the hotel announced they were doing so well they were commencing plans to add another 1,000 rooms.

Dining: Restaurants include **Il Fornaio, Chin Chin, Motown Cafe,** and **Gallagher's Steak House.**

Services: Concierge, courtesy limo, currency exchange, drycleaning, express checkout, laundry, newspaper delivery, room service, safety deposit boxes, video rentals, valet, and self-parking.

Facilities: Beauty salon, car rental, arcade, pool, tour desk. The spa is smaller than average and merely adequate, but at $15 a day it is slightly cheaper than other major hotels.

Tropicana Resort and Casino. 3801 Las Vegas Blvd. S., at Tropicana Ave., Las Vegas, NV 89109. ☎ **800/634-4000** or 702/739-2222. Fax 702/739-2469. 1,884 rms, 130 suites (for high rollers only). A/C TV TEL. Sun–Thurs from $75 double, Fri–Sat from $129. Extra person $15. Children under 18 stay free in parents' room. AE, CB, DC, DISC, MC, V. Free parking (self and valet).

This long-time denizen of the Strip is looking great since a major renovation in 1995. The entranceway is now a colorful Caribbean-village facade; there are nightly laser light shows on the Outer Island corner facing the Strip; pedestrian skywalks across the Strip link the Trop with the MGM Grand, the Excalibur, and the Luxor; and the resort's resident bird and wildlife population has dramatically increased. The Trop today comprises a lush landscape of manicured lawns, towering palms, oleanders, weeping willows, and crepe myrtles. There are dozens of waterfalls, thousands of exotic flowers, lagoons, and koi ponds. Many birds live on the grounds. There's even a wildlife walk (home to pygmy marmosets, boa constrictors, and others) inside the resort itself.

Rooms in the Paradise Tower are traditional, with French provincial furnishings and turn-of-the-century-look wallpapers. Island Tower rooms are more befitting a tropical resort, and some have beds with mirrored walls and ceilings. Motel rooms out back can be tiny and oddly shaped. All Trop rooms have sofas and safes; TVs offer Spectravision movies, account review, video checkout, and channels for in-house information.

Dining: Restaurants include **Mizuno's, El Gaucho,** and **Papagayo's.**

Services: 24-hour room service, shoeshine.

Facilities: Casino, health club (a range of machines, treadmills, exercise bikes, steam, sauna, Jacuzzi, massage, and tanning room), video-game arcade, tour and show desks, wedding chapel, car-rental desk, beauty salon and barbershop, business center, travel agent, shops (jewelry, chocolates, women's footwear, logo items, women's fashions, sports clothing, gifts, newsstand) and three swimming pools, including one with a swim-up blackjack table.

MODERATE

Excalibur. 3850 Las Vegas Blvd. S., at Tropicana Ave., Las Vegas, NV 89109. ☎ **800/937-7777** or 702/597-7777. Fax 702/597-7040. 4,032 rms. A/C TV TEL. For up to 4 people: $49–$119. Children under 17 stay free in parents' room; children over 17 pay $12. Rates are higher during holidays and convention periods. AE, CB, DC, DISC, MC, V. Free parking (self and valet).

Now this is kitsch. One of the largest resort hotels in the world, Excalibur is a gleaming white, turreted castle complete with moat, drawbridge, battlements, and lofty towers. And it's huger than huge. Apparently, the creators thought there were a lot of Arthur and Guenevere wannabes out there. And probably they are right; but do we really need a medieval, forest-themed, knights-running-amok hotel in which to act out our fantasies?

And it is hilarious. What it is not, is comfortable, which is actually historically accurate since big castles were not traditionally warm, cozy, inviting places. Excalibur is just too darn big, a chaotic frenzy at all times. Even the must-see factor fades quickly.

The rooms maintain the Arthurian motif with walls papered to look like stone castle interiors. Guests who have stayed in Tower 2 have complained about the noise from the roller coaster across the street at New York New York. It shuts down at 11pm, so early birds should probably stay in a different part of the hotel.

Dining: Restaurants include **Camelot, Sir Galahad's, Wild Bill's,** and **Lance-a-Lotta Pasta.**

Services: 24-hour room service, free gaming lessons, shoeshine, foreign-currency exchange.

Facilities: Casino, tour and show desks, state-of-the-art video-game arcade, wedding chapel (you can marry in medieval attire), unisex hairdresser, car-rental desk, a parking lot that can accommodate RVs, shops and two large pools.

Holiday Inn Casino Boardwalk. 3750 Las Vegas Blvd. S., between Harmon and Tropicana aves., Las Vegas , NV 89109. ☎ **800/HOLIDAY,** 800/635-4581, or 702/735-2400. Fax 702/730-3166. Web site www.hiboardwalk.com. 641 rms, 12 suites, 2 executive suites. A/C TV TEL. $39–$109 double, $250–$495 1-bedroom suite, $495–$895 2-bedroom suite. Extra person $15. Rates may be higher during special events. Children 19 and under stay free in parents' room. AE, DC, DISC, JCB, MC, V. Parking (free self and valet).

This is just like a Holiday Inn, only in Vegas you *gotta* have a theme, and the hotel just finished an extensive renovation to give it a more attractive Coney Island and Boardwalk flavor, both inside and especially out. Being a Holiday Inn means you know what you are getting in terms of quality, and the Strip location is a good one. Also, you don't have to walk through the casino to get to the lobby, which is a plus. On the other hand, it's a bit pricey—at the high end for what are standard Holiday Inn hotel rooms. The ones in the new 16-story tower are perhaps a bit nicer than the older units. All offer cable TVs with pay-movie options. Irons and ironing boards are in the rooms.

Dining: Cyclone Coffee Shop, a 24-hour facility has some of the best bargain meals in town (see chapter 5 for details).

Services: 24-hour room service, shoeshine.

Facilities: Casino, two small swimming pools, shops, coin-op washers/dryers, video-game arcade and shooting gallery, sightseeing/show/tour desk, car rental desk. Guests can use health club facilities nearby.

✪ Luxor Las Vegas. 3900 Las Vegas Blvd. S., between Reno and Hacienda aves., Las Vegas, NV 81119. ☎ **800/288-1000** or 702/262-4000. Fax 702/262-4452. 4,500 rms, 488 suites. Sun–Thurs, $49–$259 double; Fri–Sat, $99–$299 double; $179–$279 concierge level; $99–$329 Jacuzzi suite; $500–$800 for other suites. Extra person $10. Children under 12 stay free in parents' room. AE, CB, DC, DISC, MC, V. Free parking (self and valet).

By the time this book comes out, Luxor will have completed a $300 million renovation and expansion. Cheese fans will be disappointed to learn that the Egyptian fantasma that set the pace for all others isn't all that tacky anymore. Oh sure, the main hotel is still a 30-story bronze pyramid, complete with really tall, 315,000-watt light beam at the top. (The Luxor says that's because the Egyptians believed their souls would travel up to heaven in a beam of light; we think it's really because it gives them something to brag about: "The most powerful beam on earth!") Sure, replicas of Cleopatra's Needle and the Sphinx still grace the outside, but the interior redesign has been made much more inviting, classier, and functional.

The rooms have had a freshening up in the pyramid. High-speed "inclinator" elevators run on a 39° angle, making the ride up to your room a bit of a thrill. Sloped, window walls remind you you're in a pyramid. *Note:* In the pyramid, most baths have showers only, no tubs. The rooms are probably better in the new tower. Featuring fine art deco and Egyptian furnishings, they are full of nice touches. Huge armoires house not only the TV but closet space. The marble bathrooms have phones, vanity mirrors, and hair dryers. These are one of the few rooms in Las Vegas that stand out. You know you are in the Luxor when you are in these rooms, as opposed to the cookie-cutter decor usually found in town. Especially desirable is a group of suites with glamorous art deco elements, private sitting rooms, refrigerators, and—notably—Jacuzzis by the window (enabling you to soak under the stars at night).

Dining: Restaurants include **Isis** and the **Sacred Sea Room.**

Services: 24-hour room service, foreign-currency exchange, shoeshine.

Facilities: Casino, full-service unisex hair salon, complete spa and health club (with massage, facials, herbal wraps, and other beauty treatments available), VirtuaLand, an 18,000-square-foot video arcade that showcases Sega's latest game technologies, car-rental desk, tour/show/sightseeing desks, five swimming pools.

INEXPENSIVE

✪ **Orleans.** 4500 W. Tropicana Ave., west of Strip and I-15, Las Vegas, NV 89103. ☎ **800/ORLEANS** or 702/365-7111. Fax 702/365-7505. AOL Keyword: Coast Casinos. 840 rooms, 30 suites. $39–$79 standard double, $89–$125 1-bedroom suite. A/C TV TEL. AE, DC, DISC, MC, V. Free parking (self and valet).

Just opened in December 1997, the Orleans is owned by the same company that owns the Barbary and Gold Coast casinos. It's a little out of the way, but as construction is completed on an upcoming 12-screen movie complex, complete with food court and day-care center, this becomes an increasingly attractive option to staying on the hectic Strip.

♟ Family-Friendly Hotels

Most of the hotels are backing away from being perceived as a place for families. Still, anything with a serious theme and/or outlets for kids, as the following all have, is probably better than a regular hotel.

Circus Circus *(see p. 44)*   Centrally located on the Strip, this is our first choice if you're traveling with the kids. The hotel's mezzanine level offers ongoing circus acts daily from 11am to midnight, dozens of carnival games, and an arcade with more than 300 video and pinball games. And behind the hotel is a full amusement park.

Excalibur *(see p. 27)*   Also owned by Circus Circus, Excalibur features a whole floor of midway games, a large video-game arcade, crafts demonstrations, free shows for kids (puppets, jugglers, magicians), and thrill cinemas. It has child-oriented eateries and shows (details in chapter 8).

Luxor Las Vegas *(see p. 28)*   Another Circus Circus property. Kids will enjoy VirtuaLand, an 18,000-square-foot video-game arcade that showcases Sega's latest game technologies. Another big attraction here is the "Secrets of the Luxor Pyramid," a high-tech adventure/thrill ride utilizing motion simulators and IMAX film.

The MGM Grand Hotel, Casino, and Theme Park *(see p. 22)*   This MGM movie–themed resort is backed by a 33-acre theme park and houses a state-of-the-art video-game arcade and carnival midway. A unique offering here is a youth center for hotel guests ages 3 to 16, with separate sections for different age groups. Its facilities range from a playhouse and tumbling mats for toddlers to extensive arts and crafts equipment for the older kids.

If the prices hold true (as always, quotes vary), this hotel is one of the best bargains in town, despite the location. The rooms are particularly nice—the largest in town, so the hotel claims, next to Rio's. They all have a definite New Orleans French feel. They are L-shaped with a seating alcove by the windows and come complete with slightly turn-of-the-century style overstuffed chair and sofa. The one drawback is that the many furnishings and the busy floral decorating theme, make the rooms, particularly down by the seating area in front of the bathrooms, seem crowded. Still, it's meant to evoke a cozy, warm Victorian parlor, which traditionally is very overcrowded, so maybe it's successful after all.

Dining: Still to come are a number of restaurants, but right now the offerings include **Canal St. Grill** and **Don Miguel's.**

Services: Room service, safety deposit boxes, courtesy bus to/from airport and the Strip.

Facilities: Beauty salon, business center, game room/arcade, 70-lane bowling alley, wedding chapel, 40,000 square feet of meeting space (with more on the way), two swimming pools.

3 Mid-Strip

VERY EXPENSIVE

Bally's Las Vegas. 3645 Las Vegas Blvd. S., at Flamingo Rd., Las Vegas 89109. ☎ **800/634-3434** or 702/739-4111. Fax 702/794-2413. 2,549 rms, 265 suites. A/C TV TEL. $95–$135 double, $35 more for concierge floor (including breakfast), $300–$2,500 suite. Extra person $15. Children 18 and under stay free in parents' room. AE, CB, DC, JCB, MC, V. Free parking (self and valet).

Bally's recently completed a $72 million renovation, which included the construction of a monorail that whisks passengers from its downstairs shopping level (a bit of a hike from the casino) to the MGM Grand. More noticeable is its elaborate new facade, a plaza containing four 200-foot people movers that transport visitors to and from the Strip via a neon-lit arch surrounded by cascading waters and lush landscaping. Light, sound, and water shows take place here every 20 minutes after dark.

The large rooms all have sofas. TVs offer video checkout, not to mention cash-advance capability for your credit card. The 22nd floor is a concierge level.

Dining: Restaurants include **Seasons, Bally's Steakhouse, Al Dente,** and **Las Olas.**

Services: 24-hour room service, guest-services desk, shoeshine, foreign-currency exchange.

Facilities: Casino, tour and show desks, car-rental desk, small video-game arcade, shopping arcade, wedding chapel, men's and women's hair salons, state-of-the-art health spa and fitness center, eight night-lit tennis courts and pro shop (lessons available), two basketball courts and a pool.

Bellagio. Corner of Las Vegas Blvd. S. and Flamingo Rd.

Steve Wynn's latest amazing upscale resort is due to open in late 1998, on the site of the legendary Dunes Hotel. The Bellagio is inspired by the eponymous Italian village that overlooks Lake Como.

The front of the property will feature a 12-acre lake, the setting for water-ballet extravaganzas (more free shows!) and a replica of an Italian Village. The grounds will be some of the most lushly landscaped, with classical gardens, fountains, and pools. The hotel will have 3,000 rooms and 270 suites. All this comes with a hefty price tag: $1.3 billion. For that price, it better be good. Knowing Wynn, it will be.

✪ **Caesars Palace.** 3570 Las Vegas Blvd. S., just north of Flamingo Rd., Las Vegas, NV 89109. ☎ **800/634-6661** or 702/731-7110. Fax 702/731-6636. 3,200 rms. A/C TV TEL. From $99 standard double, $109–$500 "run of house deluxe" double, $549–$1,000 suite. Extra person $20. Children under 12 stay free in parents' room. AE, CD, DC, DISC, MC, V. Free parking (self and valet).

Since 1966, Caesars has stood as simultaneously the ultimate in Vegas luxury and the nadir (or pinnacle, depending on your values) of Las Vegas cheese. It's the most Vegasey of hotels you can find. Or at least it was. By the end of 1997, most of that will have changed. Caesars is undergoing a massive, $300 million renovation, inside and out. Don't worry, the Roman theme will remain. But as with everything else in Vegas, it has been upgraded to, let's say, a nicer neighborhood in Rome.

Past or future, Caesars remains spectacular. From the Roman temples, heroic arches, golden charioteers, and 50-foot Italian cypresses at its entrance, to the overwhelming interiors, it's the spectacle a good Vegas hotel should be.

Caesars is also known for its luxurious rooms and service. (Long lines at the reservation desk are sometimes relieved by gratis champagne.) You'll likely enjoy a lavish bath with marble floor, European fixtures, and an oversized marble tub (about half are Jacuzzis). (*Note:* Some of the rooms have said lavish tubs in the middle of the room, which can be uncomfortable if you want to bathe and don't want this to turn into a spectator sport.) Furnishings tend to be neoclassic styles; Roman columns, pilasters, and pediments are common. Many rooms have four-poster beds with mirrored ceilings, and all are equipped with three phones (bedside, bath, and desk), cable TVs with HBO, a gaming instruction channel (with cameo appearances by hotel headliners like Natalie Cole and Johnny Mathis), and in-house information stations. All rooms have private safes, hair dryers, irons and ironing boards, and lighted closets.

Dining: Caesars has a well-deserved reputation for superior in-house restaurants. There are nine in the hotel, plus dining facilities in The Forum shopping area. All are highly recommended.

Mid-Strip Accommodations

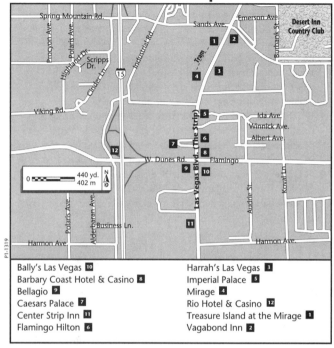

Bally's Las Vegas **10**
Barbary Coast Hotel & Casino **8**
Bellagio **9**
Caesars Palace **7**
Center Strip Inn **11**
Flamingo Hilton **6**

Harrah's Las Vegas **3**
Imperial Palace **5**
Mirage **4**
Rio Hotel & Casino **12**
Treasure Island at the Mirage **1**
Vagabond Inn **2**

Services: 24-hour room service, shoeshine, complimentary gaming lessons, valet and dry cleaning services.

Facilities: Three casinos, two extensive shopping arcades, state-of-the-art video arcade, American Express office, full-service unisex salon, show desks, car-rental desk, swimming pool, health spa.

EXPENSIVE

Flamingo Hilton. 3555 Las Vegas Blvd. S., between Sands Ave. and Flamingo Rd., Las Vegas, NV 89109. ☎ **800/732-2111** or 702/733-3111. Fax 702/733-3353. 3,642 rms, 176 suites, 201 time-share units. A/C TV TEL. $69–$205 double, $250–$580 suite. Extra person $16. Children 18 and under stay free in parents' room. Inquire about packages and time-share suites. AE, CB, DC, DISC, JCB, MC, V. Free parking (self and valet).

The Flamingo has changed a great deal since Bugsy Siegel opened his 105-room oasis "in the middle of nowhere" in 1946. It was so luxurious for its time that even the janitors wore tuxedos. Jimmy Durante was the opening headliner, and the wealthy and famous flocked to the tropical paradise of swaying palms, lagoons, and waterfalls. While the Flamingo is a senior citizen on the Strip with a colorful history, a fresh, new look, enhanced by a recent $130 million renovation and expansion, has made Siegel's "real class joint" better than ever. Still, reaching the outside world (the Strip and Flamingo competitors) can be difficult; there is a lot of casino between you and the lobby, and then again between you and the street.

For those planning some leisure time outside the casino, the Flamingo's exceptional pool area, spa, and tennis courts are a big draw. The pool is smashing, one of the two best in Vegas, with countless trees and foliage, live birds, two water slides, waterfalls and so forth. Rooms occupy six towers and are variously decorated.

Dining: Restaurants include **Beef Baron, Alta Villa, Peking Market, Hamada of Japan,** and **Lindy's Deli.**

Services: 24-hour room service, guest services desk, translation services (interpreters are available for more than 35 languages; gaming guides are available in 6 languages).

Facilities: Casino, car-rental desk, tour and show desks, full-service beauty salon/barber shop, wedding chapel, four night-lit championship tennis courts with pro shop and practice alley (tennis clinics and lessons are available), shopping arcade, and a health club.

✪ **Harrah's Las Vegas.** 3475 Las Vegas Blvd. S., between Flamingo and Spring Mountain rds., Las Vegas, NV 89109. ☎ **800/HARRAHS** or 702/369-5000. Fax 702/369-5008. 2,600 rms, 45 suites, 55 executive suites. A/C TV TEL. $75–$289 standard double, $99–$329 deluxe double, $195–$1000 suite. Extra person $15. Children 12 and under stay free in parents' room. AE, CB, DC, DISC, MC, V. Free parking (self and valet).

A recent radical face-lift has completely transformed Harrah's. It's more elegant with a European carnival theme. Over all, Harrah's has done a terrific job with their remodeling, creating a comfortable and fun environment while somehow eschewing both kitsch and the haughtiness that follows in the wake of other hotel conversions to more upscale images.

The rooms are also light and festive, with marble fixtures and light wood accents. All the rooms are larger than average; the points that emerge from both the old and the new tower wings translate inside into an extra triangle of space for a couch and table. In all rooms, TVs offer hotel information and keno channels, pay movies, Nintendo, and video account review and checkout.

Dining: Restaurants include **Claudine's, Range Steakhouse,** and **Asia.**

Services: 24-hour room service (including a special pizza and pasta menu), complimentary gaming lessons.

Facilities: Casino, car-rental desk, tour and show desks, nice size video-game arcade, coin-op laundry, shops, unisex hair salon, health club, and swimming pool.

✪ **Mirage.** 3400 Las Vegas Blvd. S., between Flamingo Rd. and Sands Ave., Las Vegas, NV 89109. ☎ **800/627-6667** or 702/791-7111. Fax 702/791-7446. 3,044 rms, 279 suites. A/C TV TEL. Sun–Thurs, $79–$399 double; Fri–Sat and holidays, $159–$399; $250–$3,000 suite. Extra person $30. AE, CB, DC, DISC, MC, V. Free parking (self and valet).

We really like this place. Actually, ask around; most visitors and locals agree. Even if they haven't stayed here, the majority consider it the most beautiful hotel in Vegas. From the moment you walk in and breathe the faintly tropically perfumed air (we think it's vanilla) and enter the lush rain forest, you just know that you are on vacation. It's a totally different experience from most Vegas hotels, where you step inside the door and are immediately the victim of a sensory assault.

Occupying 102 acres, the Mirage is fronted by more than a city block of cascading waterfalls and tropical foliage centering on a very active "volcano," which, after dark, erupts every 15 minutes, spewing fire 100 feet above the lagoons below. (In passing, that volcano cost $30 million, which is equal to the entire original construction cost for Caesars next door.) The lobby is dominated by a 53-foot, 20,000-gallon simulated coral reef aquarium stocked with more than 1,000 colorful tropical fish, including six sharks.

To get to the casino and the rooms, you walk through the rain forest, which occupies a 90-foot domed atrium—a path meanders through palms, banana trees, waterfalls, and serene pools. The formerly tropical-themed rooms have been redone in varying neutrals, with liberal use of muted gold. A marble entry way, mirrors, vanity table, and canopy over the bed's headboard give even the standards a luxurious appearance. The bathrooms are marble and slightly on the small size, depending on the room. Oak armoires house 25-inch TVs, and phones are equipped with fax and computer jacks. Further up the price scale are super-deluxe rooms with whirlpool tubs.

Off the casino is a habitat for Siegfried and Roy's white tigers, a plaster enclosure that allows for photo taking and "aaaahhhs." Out back is the pool, one of nicest in Vegas (it has a 1/4-mile shoreline), a tropical paradise of waterfalls, trees, water slides, and so forth.

Behind the pool is the dolphin habitat and the new Siegfried and Roy's Secret Garden, which has a separate admission.

Dining: Restaurants include **The Noodle Kitchen, Kokomo's, Mikado, Moongate, Restaurant Riva,** and a **California Pizza Kitchen.**

Services: 24-hour room service, overnight shoeshine on request, morning newspaper delivery.

Facilities: Casino, car-rental desk, shops, unisex hairdresser and salon offering all beauty services, video arcade, business-services center. A free tram travels between the Mirage and Treasure Island almost around the clock. **The Mirage Day Spa** is highly recommended.

Rio Hotel and Casino. 3700 W. Flamingo Rd., at I-15, Las Vegas, NV 89103. ☎ **800/752-9746** or 702/252-7777. Fax 702/252-0080. 2,582 suites. A/C TV TEL. $95 Sun–Thurs, $149 Fri–Sat. Extra person $15. Inquire about golf packages. AE, CB, DC, MC, V. Free parking (self and valet).

The Rio Hotel confounded expectations by not only succeeding in a somewhat removed area away from the Strip, but by thriving there. They recently completed an immediately popular $200 million addition: a new 41-story tower and the Masquerade Village. Totally not in keeping with the rest of the tropically themed hotel, this latter simulates a European village, complete with shops, restaurants, and a bizarre live action show in the sky. The addition is actually quite nice—not only is the architecture, in its faux way, aesthetically pleasing, but this part of the casino is much more airy, thanks to the very tall ceilings.

The rooms are touted because of their size; everyone is a "suite," which does not mean two separate rooms, but rather one large one with a sectional, corner sofa, and coffee table at one end. The dressing areas are certainly larger than average and feature a number of extra amenities, such as refrigerators (unusual for a Vegas hotel room), coffeemakers, and small snacks. Windows, running the whole length of the room, are floor to ceiling, with a pretty impressive view. The furniture does not feel like hotel room standard, but otherwise, the decor (shades of green) is fairly bland and nothing to get excited about.

Dining: Restaurants include **Fiore** (the Rio's premier restaurant described in chapter 5), **Antonio's, Napa, Mask,** and the **Voodoo Cafe.**

Services: 24-hour room service, guest-services desk, foreign-currency exchange, shoeshine, complimentary shuttle bus to/from the MGM and the Forum Mall.

Facilities: Casino, tour and show desks, unisex hair salon (all beauty services, including massage and facials), small video-game arcade, fitness room, shops (gifts, clothing for the entire family, logo merchandise), three swimming pools.

✪ **Treasure Island at the Mirage.** 3300 Las Vegas Blvd. S., at Spring Mountain Rd., Las Vegas, NV 89177-0711. ☎ **800/944-7444** or 702/894-7111. Fax 702/894-7446. Web site www.treasureislandlasvegas.com. 2,679 rms, 212 suites. A/C TV TEL. From $69 double, from $109 suite. Extra person $30. Inquire about packages. AE, DC, DISC, JCB, MC, V. Free parking (self and valet).

They will deny it now if you ask them, but Treasure Island was originally conceived (more or less) as the family alternative to the more grown-up Mirage. Why else would you build a hotel that is essentially a blown up version of Disneyland's Pirates of the Caribbean? But that's all behind them; sure, the pirate theme remains, with a vengeance, complete with plenty of skulls, crossbones, treasure chests, pirate ships' figure heads, animatronic skeletons and pirate nautical paraphernalia. But a $25 million face-lift has added more marble and gilded the bones, so to speak (actually, literally in some cases). And let's not forget that free pirate show out front during the evening. It's still Pirates of the Caribbean, but with lots and lots of money thrown at it. Despite this renovation, it still remains a top family choice and has many kids running about, which some vacationers may not find desirable.

The rooms continue the Caribbean theme; in other words, expect a lot of sand. And parchment. It's not quite as opulent as the Mirage, but comfortable. (Anything done by the Mirage organization is done well.) Best of all, Strip-side rooms have a view of the pirate battle—views are best from the sixth floor on up.

Dining: The hotel's premier restaurant, the **Buccaneer Bay Club,** is described in chapter 5. Other restaurants include **Madame Ching's**, **The Plank,** and the **Black Spot Grille.**

Services: 24-hour room service, limo rental, foreign currency exchange, shoeshine (in men's room in the lobby and casino).

Facilities: Casino, tour and sightseeing desks, car-rental desk, travel agency, Mutiny Bay (an 18,000-square-foot, state-of-the-art video game arcade and carnival midway; one highlight is a full-size Mazda Miata motion-simulator ride), two wedding chapels, full-service unisex salon (full days of beauty are an option), shopping arcade, pool and health spa. A free tram travels between Treasure Island and the Mirage almost around the clock.

MODERATE

Barbary Coast Hotel and Casino. 3595 Las Vegas Blvd. S., at Flamingo Rd., Las Vegas, NV 89109. ☎ **800/634-6755** or 702/737-7111. Fax 702/ 737-6304. 200 rms. A/C TV TEL. Sun–Thurs, $39–$75 double; Fri–Sat and holidays, $100. Extra person $10. Children under 12 stay free in parents' room. AE, CB, DC, DISC, JCB, MC, V. Free parking (self and valet).

Evoking the romantic image of turn-of-the-century San Francisco but not quite as nicely as Main St. Station Downtown, the Barbary Coast enjoys a terrific Strip location. The casino is adorned with $2 million worth of magnificent stained-glass skylights, and the extremely charming, Victorian-style rooms make for an opulent setting. All accommodations include little sitting parlors with entrances framed by floral chintz curtains.

Dining: There are two restaurants in the hotel.

Services: 24-hour room service, shoeshine.

Facilities: Casino, Western Union office, tour and show desks, gift shop.

Imperial Palace. 3535 Las Vegas Blvd. S., between Sands Ave. and Flamingo Rd., Las Vegas, NV 89109. ☎ **800/634-6441** or 702/731-3311. Fax 702/ 735-8328. Web site www.imperial-palace.com. 2,400 rms, 300 suites, 15 executive suites. A/C TV TEL. $29–$99 double; $59–$129 "luv tub" suite, $89–$199 other suites. Extra person $15. Inquire about packages. AE, CB, DC, DISC, MC, V. Free parking (self and valet).

Though appearing even older than its 17 years, the Imperial Palace has much more going for it than first impression might give. The Strip location, right in the middle of the action, can't be beat. The standard rooms are just that, but they all have balconies, which is exceeding rare in Vegas. The "luv tub" rooms are a great deal; for the price, you get a larger bedroom (with a mirror over the bed!) while the larger than usual bathroom features a 300-gallon sunken "luv tub" (with still more mirrors). A perfect Vegas hoot. Given the slightly larger size of the "luv tub" rooms, that $59 low-end fee plus the location make them one of the best bargains on the Strip. And the hotel also has a well-appointed 24-hour Urgent Care clinic, open to the public, which, given the location—in the middle of the afore-mentioned action—is well worth knowing about.

Dining: The hotel has several restaurants and 10 bars/lounges.

Services: 24-hour room service, free gaming lessons, shoeshine in casino.

Facilities: Casino, health club (machines, free weights, sauna, steam, massage, tanning, TV lounge), show and tour desks, car-rental desk, travel agency, unisex hairdresser, wedding chapel, shopping arcade, swimming pool.

INEXPENSIVE

Center Strip Inn. 3688 Las Vegas Blvd. S., at Harmon Ave., Las Vegas, NV 89109. ☎ **800/777-7737** or 702/739-6066. Fax 702/736-2521. 105 rms, 51 suites. A/C TV TEL. Sun–Thurs, $39.95–$49.95 double; Fri–Sat and holidays, from $79.95 double. Suites (for up to 4): $79.95 Sun–Thurs, higher Fri–Sat, and special events. Rates include continental breakfast. Mention you read about the Center Strip in Frommer's for a $5 discount Sun–Thurs. AE, DC, DISC, MC, V. Free parking at your room door.

This centrally located little motel is owned and operated by Robert Cohen, who is usually on the premises making sure guests are happy. He's a bit of an eccentric, and his hotel doesn't fit into any expected budget-property pattern. For example, the rooms have video-cassette players, and a selection of about 1,000 movies can be rented for just $2 each. Local calls and use of a fax machine are free. There is a free continental breakfast and free coffee is available in the lobby all day. A free pasta dinner is offered daily (subject to availability). There is no restaurant in the hotel. Facilities include a swimming pool and a car-rental desk; the front desk can arrange tours.

Vagabond Inn. 3265 Las Vegas Blvd. S., just south of Sands Avenue, Las Vegas, NV 89109. ☎ **800/828-8032,** 800/522-1555, or 702/735-5102. Fax 702/735-0168. 126 rms. A/C TV TEL. Sun–Thurs, $42–$95 standard double; $65–$125 king room; Fri–Sat, $52–$110, $72–$150. Rates include continental breakfast. AE, CB, DC, DISC, MC, V. Free self parking.

A central location just across the street from Treasure Island (a cool place from which to watch the pirate battle —drag out a lawn chair), plus clean, nicely decorated basic motel rooms, makes this a viable choice. One-third of the rooms have patios or balconies, and all offer cable TVs with pay-movie options. King rooms have wet bars and refrigerators. A wide selection of complimentary bath amenities is available at the front desk, and free coffee is served in the lobby around the clock, as is a daily continental breakfast. Facilities include coin-op washers and dryers. There's a swimming pool but no restaurant. A gratis airport shuttle and free local calls are pluses.

4 North Strip

VERY EXPENSIVE

✪ Desert Inn Country Club Resort and Casino. 3145 Las Vegas Blvd. S., between Desert Inn Rd. and Sands Ave., Las Vegas, NV 89109.

☎ **800/634-6906** or 702/733-4444. Fax 702/733-4744. 566 rms, 136 suites/ mini-suites. A/C TV TEL. $175–$185 double, $215–$225 minisuite, $350–$555 suite. Extra person $35. Children under 12 stay free in parents' room. AE, CB, DC, DISC, JCB, MC, V. Free parking (self and valet).

The Desert Inn has long been the most glamorous and gracious of Vegas hotels; coming here means leaving the hectic Strip action behind. They consider themselves more a resort than a hotel, and the property and prices reflect this. The property has just undergone a serious renovation. The look now reflects a turn-of-the-century Palm Beach resort, with elegant, clean, and spare lines. (Frankly, the time period of the decor is not turn-of-the-century in many parts, but let's not be picky.) As with most Vegas renovations, the look of everything is lighter, brighter, and cleaner—apparently, in the '90s, sand tone, rather than dark, means glamour. The clientele this attracts is middle to upper class, with a large convention crowd, thanks to their close proximity to the Sands Convention Center. Since this is more resort than hotel, expect first-rate service all the way.

The newly redone rooms (in light golds and greens) feel spacious, with comfortable armchairs and matching hassocks. Rooms have views of either the Strip or the golf course (the latter helps really give the feel of a getaway), and some even have small balconies. Each room has a very big closet with an iron and ironing board. Business travelers will be pleased that the phone lines have modem connections. Cable TVs feature pay-movie options as well as gaming instruction and hotel-information channels. The bathrooms are perhaps the best in Vegas: beautiful and large, done in black and gray granite with double sinks, a separate enclosure for the toilet, and a glass shower separate from the tub. Amenities include a big basket of Neutrogena products, a phone, and hair dryer.

Dining: See chapter 5 for details on the opulent **Monte Carlo Room.** There are five other restaurants, all better than average.

Services: 24-hour room service, concierge, shoeshine.

Facilities: Golf course, five tennis courts, swimming pool (some suites have private swimming pools), day spa, casino, tour and show desks, car-rental desk, beauty salon/barbershop, business center, shops, including golf and tennis pro shops.

EXPENSIVE

Riviera Hotel and Casino. 2901 Las Vegas Blvd. S., at Riviera Blvd., Las Vegas, NV 89109. ☎ **800/634-6753** or 702/734-5110. Fax 702/794-9451. 1,978 rms, 158 suites. A/C TV TEL. $59–$95 double, $125–$500 suite. Extra person $20. Inquire about "Gambler's Spree" packages. AE, CB, DC, MC, V. Free parking (self and valet).

North Strip Accommodations

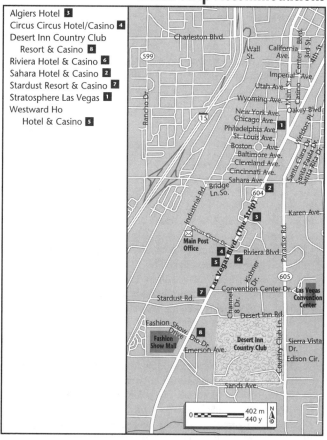

Algiers Hotel **3**
Circus Circus Hotel/Casino **4**
Desert Inn Country Club
   Resort & Casino **8**
Riviera Hotel & Casino **6**
Sahara Hotel & Casino **2**
Stardust Resort & Casino **7**
Stratosphere Las Vegas **1**
Westward Ho
   Hotel & Casino **5**

Opened in 1955 (Liberace cut the ribbon and Joan Crawford was official hostess of opening ceremonies), the Riviera is styled after the luxurious casino resorts of the Côte d'Azur. Its original nine stories made it the first "high-rise" on the Strip. Several towers later, the present-day Riviera is as elegant as ever.

Accommodations are richly decorated with handsome mahogany furnishings and burgundy or teal bedspreads with matching gold-tasseled drapes. Half the rooms offer pool views. Amenities include in-room safes and cable TVs with pay-movie options and in-house information stations.

Dining: There are five restaurants plus a food court.

Services: 24-hour room service, shoeshine.

Facilities: Casino (one of the world's largest), large arcade with carnival and video games, well-equipped health club, Olympic-size swimming pool, wedding chapel, beauty salon/barbershop, comprehensive business-services center, America West airlines desk, tour and show desks, car-rental desk, shops, two Har-Tru tennis courts lit for night play. A unique feature here: a wine-tasting booth operated by Nevada's only winery.

MODERATE

Sahara Hotel and Casino. 2535 Las Vegas Blvd. S., at E. Sahara Ave., Las Vegas, NV 89109. ☎ **800/634-6666** or 702/737-2111. Fax 702/737-2027. 1,945 rms, 90 suites, A/C TV TEL. $35–$55 standard double, $55–$85 deluxe double, $200–$600 suite. Extra person $10. Children under 14 stay free in parents' room. AE, CB, D, DC, MC, V. Free parking (self and valet).

One of the few venerable hotel casinos remaining in Vegas (it's come a long way since it opened in 1952 on the site of the old Club Bingo), the Sahara is in the process of undergoing a major facelift. The two-part process should be completed by 1998; certainly by then over half the rooms will have been redecorated, and the hotel's front will be completely different—think onion domes and other Eastern-type detailing. The point is not only to keep up with the Joneses—as the newer, glitzy hotels make the old ones seem not just quaint but shabby—but also to attempt to unify the theme.

The rooms suffer from decoration overkill, with stars and stripes assaulting the eyes and not looking terribly Moroccan (but then again, neither does Morocco). The boldly striped bedspreads on the otherwise comfortable beds are a particular mistake. The windows open, which is unusual for Vegas. It should be noted that the Sahara feels it is not as well equipped as other hotels for children and discourages you from bringing yours.

Dining: Restaurants and bars were in the process of changing at press time.

Services: 24-hour room service.

Facilities: Casino, beauty salon/barbershop, car-rental desk, tour and show desks, shops, video-game arcade. A tiled swimming pool is still under construction at press time.

Stardust Resort and Casino. 3000 Las Vegas Blvd. S., at Convention Center Dr., Las Vegas, NV 89109. ☎ **800/634-6757** or 702/732-6111. Fax 702/732-6257. Web site www.vegas.com./hotel/star. 2,335 rms, 160 suites. A/C TV TEL. Tower rooms and suites, $60–$1,000; Motor Inn rooms, $36–$200

(2-person max). Extra person $10. Children 12 and under stay free in parents' room. AE, CB, D, DC, JCB, MC, V. Free parking (self and valet).

Opened in 1958, the Stardust is a longtime resident of the Strip, its 188-foot starry sign one of America's most recognized landmarks. Today, fronted by a fountain-splashed exterior plaza, the Stardust has kept pace with a growing city. In 1991, it added a 1,500-room tower and a 35,000-square-foot state-of-the-art meeting and conference center, part of a comprehensive $300 million expansion and renovation project. It's a likable hotel, but has no personality, despite being the only star of *Showgirls*. (It was probably chosen for it's oh-so-Vegas lightbulb-intensive facade.)

Rooms in the Towers are perfectly adequate, nice even, but frankly, completely forgettable. There are also Villa rooms in two-story buildings surrounding a large swimming pool. The least expensive rooms are in the Stardust's Motor Inn set far back on the property. In the past, they were rundown motel rooms, but have been redecorated in more cheerful colors. A suite can be better, but it is a long walk to your hotel. Motor Inn guests can park at their doors. All Stardust accommodations offer in-room safes, and TVs have Spectravision movie options and in-house information channels.

Dining: Restaurants include **William B's, Tres Lobos, Ralph's Diner,** and a branch of **Tony Roma's.**

Services: 24-hour room service, shoeshine, free ice on every floor.

Facilities: Casino, beauty salon/barbershop, video-game arcade, car-rental desk, show desk, shops (gifts, candy, clothing, jewelry, logo items, liquor). There are two large swimming pools.

Stratosphere Las Vegas. 2000 Las Vegas Blvd. S., between St. Louis St. and Baltimore Ave., Las Vegas, NV 89104. ☎ **800/99-TOWER** or 702/380-7777. Fax 702/383-5334. 1,278 rms, 222 suites. A/C TV TEL. Sun–Thurs, $39–$93 double; Fri–Sat, $59–$129; $69–$400 suites. Extra person $15. Children 18 and under stay free in parents' room. Rates may be higher during special events. AE, CB, DC, DISC, JCB, MC, V. Free parking (self and valet).

At 1,149 feet, this is the tallest building west of the Mississippi. In theory, this should have provided yet another attraction for visitors; climb (okay, elevator) to the top and gaze at the stunning view. But location—it's a healthy walk from anywhere—and the hefty price charged for the privilege of going up have conspired to keep the crowds away.

But in an effort to lure crowds back, prices have dropped, and some changes have been made. The casino has been toned down (previously it was a World's Fair theme; now it's more temperate and adult looking). The shopping arcade, again with a "major cities" theme, has been expanded slightly. You can still ride the incredible thrill rides (provided the wind isn't blowing too hard that day) on top of the tower, including the world's highest roller coaster. Indoor and outdoor observation decks do offer the most stunning city views you will ever see, especially at night.

The rooms are furnished in handsome, Biedermeier-style cherry-wood pieces with black lacquer accents. Ask for a high floor when you reserve to optimize your view.

Dining: Three restaurants, including the revolving **Top of the World**, plus some fast-food outlets.

Services: 24-hour room service, foreign currency exchange.

Facilities: Casino, guest services desk, tour and show desk, video-game arcade, shopping arcade, three wedding chapels (offering incredible views from the 103rd floor), car-rental desk. An exercise facility, child care center, and vast resort-style pool and sundeck are in the works.

INEXPENSIVE

Algiers Hotel. 2845 Las Vegas Blvd. S., between Riviera Blvd. and Sahara Ave., Las Vegas, NV 89109. ☎ **800/732-3361** or 702/735-3311. Fax 702/792-2112. 105 rms, 1 suite. A/C TV TEL. Sun–Thurs from $40 double; Fri–Sat & holidays from $55 double. Extra person $10. Children under 12 stay free in parents' room. AE, CB, DC, DISC, MC, V. Free self parking at your room door.

A venerable denizen of the Strip, the Algiers opened in 1953. However, a recent multimillion dollar renovation—including landscaping (note the lovely flower beds out back) and a new facade with a 60-foot sign—brought rooms and public areas up-to-date. There's no casino here, though you can play video poker in the bar. Neat two-story, aqua-trimmed peach stucco buildings house nice sized rooms (with dressing areas) that are clean and spiffy looking. Free local calls are a plus. Facilities include a medium-size pool and palm-fringed sundeck.

✪ Circus Circus Hotel/Casino. 2880 Las Vegas Blvd. S., between Circus Circus Dr. and Convention Center Dr., Las Vegas, NV 89109. ☎ **800/444-CIRC,** 800/634-3450, or 702/734-0410. Fax 702/734-2268. 3,744 rms. A/C TV TEL. Sun–Thurs, $39–$79 double; Fri–Sat, $59–$99. AE, CB, DC, DISC, MC, V. Free parking (self and valet).

Perhaps the strongest evidence that things are changing in Las Vegas is the massive remodeling and renovation of this classic hotel and casino. The circus theme remains, but Jumbo the Clown has been replaced by commedia dell'arte harlequins. In other words, like everyone else, even the venerable Circus Circus, once the epitome of kitsch, is trying to be taken more seriously. But don't come expecting an adult atmosphere; the circus theme remains and the kid appeal along with it. The midway level features dozens of carnival games, a large arcade (more than 300 video and pinball games), trick mirrors, and ongoing circus acts under the big top from 11am to midnight daily. According to the *Guinness Book of World Records,* it's the world's largest permanent circus.

The thousands of rooms here occupy sufficient acreage to warrant a free Disney World–style aerial shuttle (another kid pleaser) and minibuses connecting its many components. Tower rooms, especially those in the new 35-story tower, are just slightly better than average, brand-spanking new hotel room furnishings and offer safes, and TVs are equipped with in-house information and gaming-instruction stations. The Manor section comprises five white, three-story buildings out back. These rooms are usually among the least expensive in town, but you get what you pay for.

Dining: Several different restaurants and seven casino bars.

Services: 24-hour room service (continental breakfast and drinks only), shoeshine.

Facilities: Three casinos, wedding chapel, tour and show desks, car-rental desk, unisex hairdresser, two swimming pools, two video-game arcades, shops, Grand Slam Canyon Theme Park (see chapter 6).

Adjacent to the hotel is **Circusland RV Park,** with 384 full-utility spaces and up to 50-amp hookups. It has its own 24-hour convenience store, swimming pools, saunas, Jacuzzis, kiddie playground, fenced pet runs, video-game arcade, and community room. The rate is $12 Sunday to Thursday, $16 Friday and Saturday, $18 holidays.

Westward Ho Hotel and Casino. 2900 Las Vegas Blvd. S., between Circus Circus Dr. and Convention Center Dr., Las Vegas, NV 89109. ☎ **800/ 634-6803** or 702/731-2900. 656 rms, 121 suites. A/C TV TEL. $36.90– $56 double, $76 suite. Extra person $10. MC, V. Free parking at your room door.

Located next door to Circus Circus, the Westward Ho is fronted by a vast casino, with rooms in two-story buildings that extend out back for several city blocks. In fact, the property is so large that a free bus shuttles regularly between the rooms and the casino 24 hours a day. There are three swimming pools. The rooms are adequately furnished motel units. A good buy here: two-bedroom suites with 1¹/₂ baths, living rooms with sofa beds, and refrigerators; they sleep up to six people.

There's a 24-hour restaurant in the casino under a stained-glass skylight dome. Other facilities include a tour desk, free airport shuttle, a gift shop, a casino lounge.

5   Convention Center & Paradise Road

VERY EXPENSIVE

Alexis Park Resort. 375 E. Harmon Ave., between Koval Lane and Paradise Rd., Las Vegas, NV 89109. ☎ **800/582-2228** or 702/796-3300. Fax 702/796-4334. 500 suites. A/C MINIBAR TV TEL. $99–$139 1-bedroom suite, $175–$250 1-bedroom loft suite, $350–$1,500 larger suite. Extra person $15. Children 18 and under stay free in parents' room. AE, CB, DC, DISC, JCB, MC, V. Free parking (self and valet).

A low-key atmosphere, luxurious digs, and superb service combine to make Alexis Park the hotel choice of many showroom head-liners and visiting celebrities.

Spacious suites are decorated in light resort colors with taupe lacquer furnishings. Loft suites have cathedral ceilings. All are equipped with refrigerators, wet bars, two-line phones (one in each room of your suite) with computer jacks, and TVs (also one in each room) with HBO and pay-movie options. More than a third of the suites have working fireplaces and/or Jacuzzi tubs.

Dining: There are two restaurants.

Services: 24-hour room service, concierge.

Facilities: Gift shop, unisex hair salon, health club, swimming pool.

Courtyard Marriott. 3275 Paradise Rd., between Convention Center Dr. and Desert Inn Rd., Las Vegas, NV 89109. ☎ **800/321-2211** or 702/791-3600. Fax 702/796-7981. 137 rms, 12 suites. A/C TV TEL. Sun–Thurs, $109 double; Fri–Sat, $119; $119–$129 suite. Convention rates can be higher. AE, CB, DC, DISC, MC, V. Free parking at your room door.

The Courtyard is a welcome link in the Marriott chain. Although the services are limited, don't picture a no-frills establishment. This is a beautiful hotel, with a pleasant, plant-filled lobby and very nice rooms indeed.

Like its public areas, the rooms—most with king-size beds—still look spanking new. Decorated in shades of gray-blue, mauve, and burgundy, with sofas and handsome mahogany furnishings (including large desks), they offer TVs with multiple On-Command movie options. All rooms have balconies or patios.

Accommodations East of the Strip

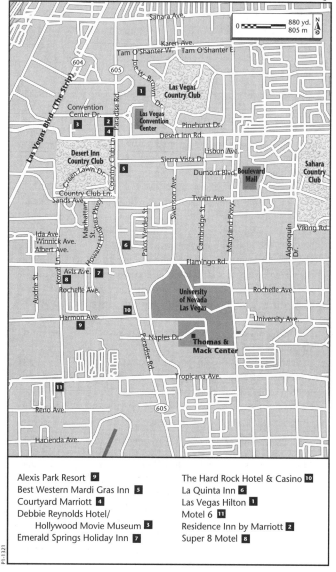

Alexis Park Resort **9**
Best Western Mardi Gras Inn **5**
Courtyard Marriott **4**
Debbie Reynolds Hotel/
    Hollywood Movie Museum **3**
Emerald Springs Holiday Inn **7**

The Hard Rock Hotel & Casino **10**
La Quinta Inn **6**
Las Vegas Hilton **1**
Motel 6 **11**
Residence Inn by Marriott **2**
Super 8 Motel **8**

Dining: One restaurant and one lounge.

Services: Room service 4 to 10pm, complimentary airport shuttle.

Facilities: Small exercise room, medium-size swimming pool with adjoining whirlpool, picnic tables and barbecue grills, coin-op washers/dryers.

✪ **The Hard Rock Hotel and Casino.** 4455 Paradise Rd., at Harmon Ave., Las Vegas, NV 89109. ☎ **800/473-ROCK** or 702/693-5000. Fax 702/693-5010. 311 rms, 24 suites, 4 executive suites. A/C TV TEL. Sun–Thurs, $75–$250 double; Fri–Sat, $145–$300; from $250 suite. Extra person $25. Children 12 and under stay free in parents' room. AE, CB, DC, DISC, MC, V. Free parking (self and valet).

Everything here is rock-themed, from the Stevie Ray Vaughan quote over the entrance ("When this house is a rocking, don't bother knocking, come on in") to the vast collection of music memorabilia displayed in public areas. The casino features piano-shaped roulette tables and guitar-neck-handle slot machines. Even the walls of the bell desk are lined with gold records.

Large, attractive rooms, with photographs of rock stars adorning the walls, have beds with leather headboards and French windows that actually open to fresh air (a rarity in Las Vegas). Uncharacteristically large 27-inch TVs offer pay-movie options and special music channels.

Dining: The hotel has three restaurants, including the **Hard Rock Cafe.**

Services: 24-hour room service, concierge.

Facilities: Small video-game arcade, gift/sundry shop and immense Hard Rock retail store, show desk (for **The Joint** only; tickets to other shows can be arranged by the concierge), health club, swimming pool.

✪ **Las Vegas Hilton.** 3000 Paradise Rd., at Riviera Blvd., Las Vegas, NV 89109. ☎ **800/376-7917** or 702/732-7111. Fax 702/732-5790. 3,174 rms, 305 suites, A/C TV TEL. $95–$279 double. Extra person $25. Children of any age stay free in parents' room. Inquire about attractively priced golf and other packages. CB, DC, DISC, MC, V. Free parking (self and valet).

Elvis played here. Do you really need to know anything more?

Oh, all right. This is really quite a classy hotel, which is probably why so many business travelers prefer it. (That, and the location next to the convention center.) There are quite a few terrific restaurants, plus the largest hotel convention and meeting facilities in the world. A serious renovation is adding a number of new shops, plus **Star Trek: The Experience,** a themed attraction, which should be open in late 1997 (the available details are in chapter 6). They want to start attracting more of a leisure crowd, but you do have to wonder how all these additions might change the otherwise high-rent atmosphere.

The rooms are undergoing a remodeling. Though nothing particularly special in terms of decor, they are very comfortable. Some have views of the adjacent 18-hole golf course. They do feature automatic checkout on the TV and a hotline number on the phone that sends you directly to housekeeping.

Dining: The hotel has a number of terrific restaurants, including **Bistro Le Montrachet, the Seafood Grille, Benihana,** and **Andiamo.**

Services: 24-hour room service, foreign-currency exchange.

Facilities: Casino, car-rental desk, tour desk, travel agency, shops, small video-game arcade, business service center (faxing and express mail), multiservice beauty salon/barbershop, jogging trail, 18-hole golf course, swimming pool, tennis courts and health club.

EXPENSIVE

La Quinta Inn. 3970 Paradise Rd., between Twain Ave. and Flamingo Rd., Las Vegas, NV 89109. ☎ **800/531-5900** or 702/796-9000. Fax 702/796-3537. 176 rms, 5 suites. A/C TV TEL. $85–$95 standard double, $89–$99 executive double, $115–$125 suite. Rates include continental breakfast; inquire about seasonal discounts. AE, CB, DC, DISC, MC, V. Free parking (self).

This La Quinta offers a tranquil alternative to the razzle-dazzle of Strip hotels. Although you're just a minute (and a gratis shuttle ride) from major casinos, you'll feel like you're staying in a countryside retreat. Lovely grounds, with manicured lawns, lovingly tended flower beds, and a charming stone fountain, offer rustic benches, lawn games (croquet, badminton, volleyball), barbecue grills, and picnic tables.

Accommodations are immaculate and attractive. Most accommodations have patios or balconies, and all feature baths with oversized whirlpool tubs. TVs offer satellite channels and HBO.

Dining: The restaurant is called the **Patio Cafe,** which offers complimentary continental breakfast.

Facilities: Car rentals/tours arranged at the front desk, coin-op washers/dryers, medium-size swimming pool and adjoining whirlpool. A free 24-hour shuttle offers pickup and return to and from the airport and several Strip casino hotels.

✪ Residence Inn by Marriott. 3225 Paradise Rd., between Desert Inn Rd. and Convention Center Dr., Las Vegas, NV 89109. ☎ **800/331-3131** or

702/796-9300. 144 studios, 48 penthouses. A/C TV TEL. $89–$169 studio, $109–$219 penthouse. Rates include continental breakfast. AE, CB, DC, DISC, MC, V. Free parking (self).

Staying here is like having your own apartment in Las Vegas. The property occupies 7 acres of perfectly manicured lawns, tropical foliage, and neat flower beds. It's a great choice for families and business travelers. Monday through Friday, they offer a free light dinner with beer, wine, and soda.

Accommodations, most with working fireplaces, are housed in condo-like, two-story wood and stucco buildings, fronted by little gardens.

Dining/Entertainment: A big continental buffet breakfast is served each morning. Weekday evenings from 5:30 to 7pm, complimentary buffets with beverages are also served.

Services: Local restaurants deliver food, and there's also a complimentary food-shopping service. Maids wash your dishes.

Facilities: Car-rental desk, barbecue grills, coin-op washers/dryers, sports court (paddle tennis, volleyball, basketball), swimming pool.

MODERATE

Best Western Mardi Gras Inn. 3500 Paradise Rd., between Sands Ave. and Desert Inn Rd., Las Vegas, NV 89109. ☎ **800/634-6501** or 702/731-2020. Fax 702/733-6994. 315 minisuites. A/C TV TEL. $40–$125 double. Extra person $8. Children 18 and under stay free in parents' room. AE, CB, DC, DISC, JCB, MC, V. Free parking at your room door.

Opened in 1980, this well-run little casino hotel is a block from the convention center and close to major properties.

Accommodations are all spacious, queen-bedded minisuites with sofa-bedded living room areas and eat-in kitchens, the latter equipped with wet bars, refrigerators, and coffeemakers. All are attractively decorated and offer TVs with HBO and pay-movie options. Staying here is like having your own little Las Vegas apartment.

Dining: A pleasant restaurant/bar off the lobby serves typical coffee-shop fare.

Services: Free transportation to/from airport and major Strip hotels.

Facilities: Small casino (64 slots/video poker machines), small video-game arcade, car-rental desk, tour and show desks, coin-op washers/dryers, unisex hairdresser, gift shop, RV parking, swimming pool.

Debbie Reynolds Hotel/Hollywood Movie Museum. 305 Convention Center Dr., between Las Vegas Blvd. S. and Paradise Rd., Las Vegas, NV 89109. ☎ **800/633-1777** or 702/734-0711. Fax 702/734-7548. 153 rms, 39 suites, 39 executive suites. A/C TV TEL. Standard $75–$99, $129–$200 suites. Extra person $10. AE, CB, DC, DISC, MC, V. Free parking (self and valet).

Note: At press time, in addition to having lost its gaming license (so the hotel currently has no casino), the Debbie Reynolds Hotel has filed for bankruptcy. An attempt to sell the hotel has fallen through, but Ms. Reynolds and her organization insist that the hotel will stay open and that Ms. Reynolds will continue to perform there. But obviously, under the circumstances, the future of the place must remain in some doubt.

In 1993, America's sweetheart, musical-comedy star Debbie Reynolds, took over the 12-story Paddlewheel Hotel, transforming its signature paddlewheel facade into a neon-lit revolving film reel. The lobby is a minimuseum of Hollywood memorabilia.

Large rooms offer great views of the Strip from picture windows. Some accommodations also offer refrigerators, hair dryers, and coffeemakers. In keeping with the hotel's Hollywood theme, walls are hung with large black-and-white photographs of movie legends (perhaps Gable and Lombard will be watching over you).

Dining: The 24-hour **Celebrity Café** serves as both a hotel coffee shop and a lounge where Debbie and her Strip entertainer friends can hang out and perform.

Services: 24-hour room service.

Facilities: Large swimming pool with bilevel sundeck, whirlpool, saunas, gift shop, sightseeing/show/tour desk. A large shopping center with a drugstore/pharmacy, post office, dry cleaner, and coin-op laundry, is just across the street.

Emerald Springs Holiday Inn. 325 E. Flamingo Rd., between Koval Lane and Paradise Rd., Las Vegas, NV 89109. ☎ **800/732-7889** or 702/732-9100. Fax 702/731-9784. 132 rms, 18 suites. A/C TV TEL. $69–$99 studio, $99–$129 Jacuzzi suite, $129–$175 hospitality suite. Extra person $15. Children 18 and under stay free in parents' room. AE, CB, DC, DISC, MC, V. Free parking (self).

Emerald Springs offers a friendly, low-key alternative to the usual glitz and glitter. Typical of the inn's hospitality is a bowl of apples for the taking at the front desk. And weeknights from 10:30pm to midnight you can "raid the icebox" at the Veranda Café, which offers complimentary cookies, peanut butter and jelly sandwiches, and coffee, tea, or milk. Although your surroundings here are serene, you're only 3 blocks from the heart of the Strip.

Even the smallest accommodations (studios) offer small sofas, desks, and armchairs with hassocks. You also get two phones (desk and bedside), an in-room coffeemaker (with gratis coffee), and a wet bar with refrigerator.

Dining: The hotel has a coffee shop and bar.

Services: Concierge, complimentary limousine transportation to and from the airport and nearby casinos between 6:30am and 11pm (van service available 11pm to 6:30am), room service, business services, gratis newspapers available at the front desk.

Facilities: Fitness room, swimming pool.

INEXPENSIVE

✪ **Motel 6.** 195 E. Tropicana Ave., at Koval Lane, Las Vegas, NV 89109. ☎ **800/4-MOTEL-6** or 702/798-0728. Fax 702/798-5657. 602 rms. A/C TV TEL. Sun–Thurs, $34 single; Fri–Sat, $52 single. Extra person $6. Children under 17 stay free in parents' room. AE, CB, DC, DISC, MC, V. Free parking at your room door.

Las Vegas's Motel 6 is the largest in the country, and it happens to be a great budget choice, quite close to major Strip casino hotels (the MGM is nearby). The rooms, in two-story cream stucco buildings, are clean and attractively decorated. Some rooms have showers only, others, tub/shower baths. Local calls are free and your TV offers HBO.

Three restaurants (including a pleasant 24-hour family restaurant called **Carrows**) adjoin. On-premises facilities include a large, well-stocked gift shop, vending machines, a tour desk, two swimming pools, a whirlpool, and coin-op washers/dryers.

Super 8 Motel. 4250 Koval Lane, just south of Flamingo Rd., Las Vegas, NV 89109. ☎ **800/800-8000** or 702/794-0888. 290 rms. A/C TV TEL. Sun–Thurs, $41–$43 double; Fri–Sat, $56–$58 double. Extra person $8. Children 12 and under stay free in parents' room. Pets $8 per night (one pet only). AE, CB, DC, DISC, MC, V. Free parking (self).

"The world's largest Super 8 Motel." Coffee is served gratis in a pleasant little lobby furnished with comfortable sofas and wing chairs. Rooms are clean and well maintained. Some have safes, and TVs offer free movie channels.

Dining: Ellis Island Restaurant, open 24 hours, offers typical coffee-shop fare.

Services: Limited room service via Ellis Island, free airport transfer.

Facilities: Casino (actually located next door at Ellis Island, race book and 50 slot/poker/21 machines), small pool/sundeck and adjoining whirlpool, car-rental desk, coin-op washers/dryers.

6 Downtown

EXPENSIVE

✪ **Golden Nugget.** 129 E. Fremont St., at Casino Center Blvd., Las Vegas, NV
89101. ☎ **800/634-3454** or 702/385-7111. Fax 702/386-8362. 1,805 rms,
102 suites. A/C TV TEL. $49–$299 double, $275–$500 suite. Extra person $20.
AE, CB, DC, DISC, MC, V. Free parking (self and valet).

The Golden Nugget opened in 1946, the first building in Las
Vegas constructed specifically for casino gambling. Steve Wynn took
it over as his first major project in Vegas, in 1973. He gradually
transformed the Old West/Victorian interior (typical for Downtown) into something more high rent. The whole package seems
considerably more resortlike and genuinely luxurious, especially for
Downtown Vegas.

If the decor of the Mirage sounded appealing to you and you
want to stay Downtown, come here, since the same people own
them and the rooms look almost identical.

Dining: Five restaurants, including **California Pizza Kitchen.**

Services: 24-hour room service, shoeshine, concierge.

Facilities: Casino, car-rental desk, full-service unisex hair salon,
shops (gifts, jewelry, designer fashions, sportswear, logo items),
video-game arcade, swimming pool, health club.

MODERATE

✪ **Fitzgeralds Casino Holiday Inn.** 301 Fremont St., at 3rd St., Las Vegas,
NV 89101. ☎ **800/274-LUCK** or 702/388-2400. Fax 702/388-2181. 638 rms,
14 suites. A/C TV TEL. $40–$85 double, $60–$105 suite. Extra person $10.
Children under 19 stay free in parents' room. AE, CB, DC, DISC, MC, V. Free
parking (self and valet).

Fitzgeralds recently became a Holiday Inn franchise and has up-
graded all their rooms to fit said chain's code. The result is attractive and received an award for Best Redesign from the Governor's
Conference. Fitzgerald's has the only balcony in Downtown from
which you can watch the Fremont Street Experience.

The look in the rooms is clean and comfortable, standard hotel
room decor, done in shades of green (no, the leprechaun theme does
not follow in here). Because this is the tallest building in downtown
(34 stories), you get excellent views; either snow-capped mountains,
downtown lights, or the Strip. Jacuzzi tub rooms are $20 more and
are slightly larger with wraparound windows. All offer safes and
25-inch TVs with pay-movie options.

Dining: Limericks is an upscale Irish pub. There are two other
restaurants, a **McDonald's,** and three bars.

Services: 24 hour room service, complimentary gaming lessons.

Facilities: Casino, tour and show desks, car-rental desk, gift shop, jewelry shop.

✪ **Four Queens.** 202 Fremont St., at Casino Center Blvd., Las Vegas, NV 89101. ☎ **800/634-6045** or 702/385-4011. Fax 702/387-5122. 662 rms, 38 suites. A/C TV TEL. $59–$179 double, $119–$350 suite. Extra person $10. Children under 2 stay free in parents' room. AE, CB, DC, DISC, MC, V. Free parking (self and valet).

Opened in 1966 with a mere 120 rooms, the Four Queens (named for the owner's four daughters) has evolved over the decades into a major Downtown property occupying an entire city block. You just know you are in old Las Vegas. And are glad. As the staff says, this is the place to stay if you just want to gamble.

Notably nice rooms—in a basic hotel room kind of way—are located in 19-story twin towers. Especially lovely are the North Tower rooms, decorated in a southwestern motif and, in most cases, offering views of the Fremont Street Experience. Some rooms are equipped with small refrigerators and coffeemakers.

Dining: Hugo's Cellar is described in chapter 5. There are three other restaurants and two bars.

Services: 24-hour room service.

Facilities: Gift shop, car-rental desk, tour and show desks, small video-game arcade, plus a basic workout room that is free.

INEXPENSIVE

California Hotel/Casino and RV Park. 12 Ogden Ave., at 1st St., Las Vegas, NV 89101. ☎ **800/634-6255** or 702/385-1222. Fax 702/388-2660. 781 rms, 74 suites. A/C TV TEL. Sun–Thurs, $50 double; Fri–Sat, $60; holidays, $70. Extra person $5. Children 12 and under stay free in parents' room. AE, CB, DC, DISC, MC, V. Free parking (self and valet).

This is a hotel with a unique personality. California-themed, it markets mostly in Hawaii, and since 85% of the guests are from the "Aloha State," it offers Hawaiian entrees in several of its restaurants and even has an on-premises store specializing in Hawaiian foodstuff.

The rooms, however, reflect neither California nor Hawaii. Decorated in contemporary-look burgundy/mauve or apricot/teal color schemes, they have mahogany furnishings and attractive marble baths. In-room safes are a plus, and TVs offer pay-per-view movies and keno channels.

Dining: Four restaurants and two bars.

Accommodations Downtown

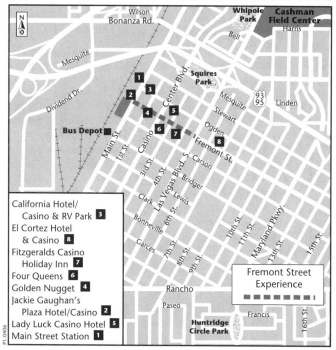

California Hotel/
  Casino & RV Park **3**
El Cortez Hotel
  & Casino **8**
Fitzgeralds Casino
  Holiday Inn **7**
Four Queens **6**
Golden Nugget **4**
Jackie Gaughan's
  Plaza Hotel/Casino **2**
Lady Luck Casino Hotel **5**
Main Street Station **1**

Services: Room service (breakfast only).

Facilities: Casino, car-rental desk, car wash, small rooftop pool, small video-game arcade, shops (gift shop, chocolates). A food store carries items popular with Hawaiians.

El Cortez Hotel and Casino. 600 Fremont St., between 6th and 7th sts., Las Vegas, NV 89101. ☎ **800/634-6703** or 702/385-5200. 404 rms, 14 minisuites. A/C TV TEL. $32 double, $40 minisuite. Extra person $3. AE, CB, DC, DISC, JCB, MC, V. Free parking (self and valet).

This small hotel is popular with locals for its casual, "just-folks" Downtown atmosphere and its frequent big-prize lotteries. The nicest accommodations are the enormous minisuites in the newer, 14-story tower. Some are exceptionally large king-bedded rooms with sofas; others have separate sitting areas with sofas, armchairs, and tables, plus small dressing areas. The rooms in the original building are furnished more traditionally and with less flair, and they cost less. There are two restaurants.

On-premises facilities include a small video-game arcade, beauty salon, gift shop, and barbershop.

Jackie Gaughan's Plaza Hotel/Casino. 1 Main St., at Fremont St., Las Vegas, NV 89101. ☎ **800/634-6575** or 702/386-2110. Fax 702/386-2378. 876 rms, 161 suites. A/C TV TEL. $40–$120 double, $80–$150 suite. Extra person $8. Children under 12 stay free in parents' room. AE, DC, DISC, MC, V. Free parking (self and valet).

Built in 1971 on the site of the old Union Pacific Railroad Depot, the Plaza, a double-towered, 3-block-long property, permanently altered the Downtown skyline. Las Vegas's Amtrak station (currently unused) is right in the hotel, and the main Greyhound terminal adjoins it.

Accommodations are spacious and attractively decorated, with king rooms offering plush sofas.

Dining: The **Center Stage Restaurant,** offering fabulous views of Glitter Gulch and the Fremont Street Experience. Also two other restaurants.

Services: Guest-services desk (also handles in-house shows), tour desk.

Facilities: Casino, car-rental desk, shops, a wedding chapel, beauty salon/barbershop, swimming pool, a quarter-mile outdoor jogging track, and four Har-Tru tennis courts.

Lady Luck Casino Hotel. 206 N. 3rd St., at Ogden Ave., Las Vegas, NV 89101. ☎ **800/523-9582** or 702/477-3000. Fax 702/382-2346. 649 rms, 143 suites. A/C TV TEL. $40–$155 double; junior suite, $55–$75 Sun–Thurs, $70–$105 Fri–Sat. Extra person $8. AE, CB, DC, DISC, JCB, MC, V. Free parking (self and valet). Web site www.lady-luck.com/ladyluck/.

Lady Luck opened in 1964 as Honest John's, but today is a major Downtown player taking up an entire city block. What it retains from earlier times is a friendly atmosphere, one that has kept customers coming back for decades. Eighty percent of Lady Luck's clientele is repeat business.

Tower rooms (one of the towers is actually across the street, accessible by an over-the-street enclosed walkway) are larger, brighter, and lighter than you might expect (though again, a variation on familiar hotel room decor). Rooms also have full length mirrors. The bathroom amenities come in a red plastic, heart-shaped container. All rooms are equipped with small refrigerators and TVs with pay-per-view movie options. The original Garden Rooms are a little smaller and less spiffy-looking in terms of decor; on the plus side, they're right by the pool, which is not heated, by the way (but there aren't a lot of pools in Downtown).

Dining: Three restaurants.

Services: 24-hour room service, multilingual front desk, and complimentary airport shuttle.

Facilities: Casino, tour and show desks, car-rental desk, gift shop, unheated swimming pool and sundeck.

✪ **Main Street Station.** 200 N. Main St., between Fremont and I-95, Las Vegas, NV 89101. ☎ **800/465-0711** or 702/387-1896. Fax 702/388-2660. 392 rms, 14 suites. A/C TV TEL. Sun–Thurs, $45 double; Fri–Sat, $55; holidays and conventions, $65. AE, CB, DC, DISC, MC, V. Free parking (valet and self).

Though not actually on Fremont Street, the Main Street Station is just two short blocks away—barely a 3-minute walk. Considering how terrific it is, this is hardly an inconvenience. In our opinion, this is one of the nicest hotels in Downtown and one of the best bargains in the city. The overall look is, admittedly as usual for Downtown, turn-of-the-century San Francisco. Outside, gas lamps flicker on wrought iron railings and stained glass windows. Inside are (faux, but still) hammered tin ceilings, ornate antique style chandeliers, and lazy ceiling fans. The small lobby is filled with wood panels, long wooden benches, and a front desk straight out of the Old West with an old-timey key cabinet with beveled glass windows. Even the cashier cages look like antique brass bank teller's cages. Over the casino bar, rattan blade fans rotate horizontally rather than vertically. It's all very Victorian, and even though faux it feels authentic. It's also incredibly appealing and just plain pretty.

The long and narrow rooms are possibly the largest in Downtown. The simple but not unattractive furniture is vaguely French provincial, done in medium tone neutrals. It's all clean and in good taste. It should be noted that rooms on the north side overlook the freeway, and the railroad track is nearby. The soundproofing seems quite strong—we couldn't hear anything when inside. A few guests have complained about noise in these rooms, but the majority have had no problems. If you are concerned, request a room on the south. Each room has Nintendo for a charge and movies for free.

Dining: The excellent buffet is described in chapter 5. Two other restaurants, including one with a cigar club.

Services: Dry cleaning and laundry service, in-room massage, safety deposit boxes.

Facilities: Gift shop, show desk, shopping and game room arcade at California Hotel accessible via connecting walkway.

5

Dining in Las Vegas

*A*mong the many images that people have of Las Vegas is cheap food deals, bargains so good the food is practically free. They think of the buffets—all a small country can eat, only $3.99!

All that is true, but frankly, eating in Las Vegas is no longer something you don't have to worry about budgeting for. The buffets are certainly there—no good hotel would be without one—as are the cheap meal deals, but you get what you pay for. Some of the cheaper buffets, and even the more moderately priced ones, are mediocre at best, ghastly and inedible at worst. And we don't even want to think about those 69¢ cup of beef stew specials. We found two notable food courts: the Monte Carlo Food Court and La Piazza Food Court at the Forum Shops at Caesars Palace.

As for quality restaurants, little by little they have been sneaking into Las Vegas. Wolfgang Puck's Spago, Emeril Lagasse's Emeril's New Orleans Fish House (serving stunning Creole seafood), Gatsby's (the MGM Grand's gourmet restaurant, which even hardcore foodie snobs say serves some of the best food they've ever eaten), the Fog City Diner, and Mark Miller's Coyote Cafe all would be standouts in any other major city. Reliable chains such as Lawry's and Il Fornaio have crept in during the last year. The Enigma Cafe, located in the slowly burgeoning Gateway artists district (right between the Strip and Downtown so it's accessible to both), offers up healthy interesting food at prices comparable to some of the best hotel meal deals in town.

There are tricks to surviving dining in Vegas. You should make restaurant reservations in advance, particularly for the better restaurants. Eat as much as you can during off hours, which admittedly are hard to find. But you know that noon to, say, 1:30 or 2 is going to be prime for lunch and 5:30 to 8:30 (and just after the early shows get out) for dinner. And give yourself plenty of it, particularly if you have to catch a show.

1 Best Bets

- **Best Splurge:** It's a toss-up between **Gatsby's** and **Emeril's New Orleans Fish House,** both located in the MGM Grand, and both of which vie for the unofficial "Best Restaurant in Vegas" title. It's apples and oranges: Emeril's features creole seafood, while Gatsby's is nouvelle and slightly Asian influenced. Both are superb dining experiences.

- **Best Buffet:** For the Strip, it's **The Mirage.** Not at all the cheapest in town, but the quality goes up accordingly. In Downtown, the new **Main Street Station** has an incredible buffet; all live-action stations, wood-fired brick-oven pizzas, fresh lovely salsas and guacamole in the Mexican section, and better than average desserts. Nowhere else in Downtown comes even close.
- **Best Sunday Champagne Brunch: Bally's** lavish **Sterling Sunday Brunch,** where display tables embellished with floral arrangements and ice sculptures are laden with everything from mounds of fresh shrimp to sushi and sashimi, and fancy entrees include the likes of roast duckling with black-currant and blueberry sauce.
- **Best Graveyard Dinner Deal: Binion's Horseshoe** offers a complete New York steak dinner served with potato, roll, and salad for just $3 from 10pm to 5:45am.
- **Best Cheap Breakfast:** Make your first stop of the day the **Cyclone Coffee Shop** at the Holiday Inn Casino Boardwalk, where a $1.29 breakfast includes two eggs, bacon or sausage, hash browns, and toast. It's served around the clock.
- **Best Spot for a Romantic Dinner:** The warmly elegant **Fiore,** with its gorgeous interior and arched windows overlooking the palm-fringed pool, is the most simpatico setting for a leisurely romantic dinner. Brilliant cuisine, a great wine cellar, and superb service combine to create a memorable evening.
- **Best Spot for a Celebration: Mizuno's** teppanyaki grills are ideal for small parties, with the chef's theatrics comprising a tableside show. Additionally, the elegant **Gatsby's** with its superlative food would make a fine spot for a wedding supper.
- **Best Free Show at Dinner:** At Treasure Island's **Buccaneer Bay Club** everyone rushes to the window when the ship battle begins.
- **Best Wine List:** The distinguished cellar at **Gatsby's** houses 600 wines in all price ranges and has a friendly master sommelier on hand to guide you in your selections. Trust him; he knows his stuff.
- **Best View:** See all of Las Vegas from the revolving **Top of the World,** at the Stratosphere, 106 stories up.
- **Best California Cuisine:** Wolfgang Puck's **Spago** didn't invent California cuisine (or did it?), but it might as well have.

- **Best Chinese Cuisine: Chin's**—where piano bar music enhances an ambience of low-key elegance—offers scrumptious and authentic Cantonese fare, including some original creations such as deep-fried battered chicken served with strawberry sauce and fresh strawberries.
- **Best Deli:** The **Stage Deli** in Caesars will give no cause for complaints. You might also try the new deli in **New York New York,** which has been winning raves.
- **Best Healthy/Veggie Conscious:** The **Enigma Cafe** in the Gateway District, which makes it convenient for both the Strip and Downtown, offers a large selection of really cheap sandwiches, salads, and smoothies, all fresh and interesting.
- **Best Italian Cuisine: Il Fornaio** in New York New York is the best for a moderately priced meal, and **Fiore** in the Rio for something quite a bit more dear.
- **Best New Orleans Cuisine:** One of Las Vegas's newest celebrity chef venues, **Emeril's New Orleans Fish House** at the MGM Grand, offers total authenticity combined with culinary brilliance.
- **Best Southwestern Cuisine:** The fact that it's the only notable southwestern restaurant in town doesn't make the **Coyote Cafe** any less impressive. Superstar Santa Fe chef Mark Miller brings contemporary culinary panache to traditional southwestern cookery, and the results are spicy and spectacular.
- **Best Steak and Seafood: Lawry's The Prime Rib** has such good prime rib, it's hard to ever imagine having any better.
- **Best Barbecue: Ware's T Bones Texas BBQ** is a bit out of the way, but the second that meat falls off the bone, or falls apart under your fork, you will be glad you made the drive.

2 Restaurants by Cuisine

AMERICAN

All Star Cafe (South Strip, Showcase Mall, *M*)

Binion's Coffee Shop (Downtown, Binion's Horseshoe, *I*)

Bucaneer Bay Club (Mid-Strip, Treasure Island, *VE*)

Carson Street Café (Downtown, Golden Nugget, *I*)

Dive! (North Strip, Fashion Show Mall, *M*)

Fog City Diner (East Las Vegas, *M*)

Hard Rock Cafe (Convention Center/ Paradise Road, *M*)

Key to Abbreviaitons: *VE*=Very Expensive; *E*=Expensive; *M*=Moderate; *I*= Inexpensive

Hippo and the Wild Bunch
(Convention Center/
Paradise Road, *M*)
Top of the World
(North Strip, Strato-
sphere, *VE*)

BARBECUE

Big Sky (North Strip,
Stratosphere, *I*)
Country Star (South Strip, *M*)
Ware's T Bones Texas
Style Bar-B-Que
(West Las Vegas, *M*)

BUFFETS/BRUNCHES

Bally's Big Kitchen Buffet
(Mid-Strip, *M*)
Bally's Sterling Sunday
Brunch (Mid-Strip, *E*)
Caesars Palace Palatium
Buffet (Mid-Strip, *M*)
Excalibur's Round Table
Buffet (South Strip, *I*)
Flamingo Hilton Paradise
Garden Buffet (Mid-
Strip, *I*)
The Golden Nugget Buffet
(Downtown, *M*)
Lady Luck Buffet
(Downtown, *I*)
Las Vegas Hilton Buffet of
Champions (Convention
Center/Paradise Road, M)
The Luxor Pharoah's Feast
Buffet (South Strip, *I*)
Main Street Station Garden
Court (Downtown, *I*)
Mirage Buffet (Midstrip, *M*)
Rio's Carnival World Buffet
(Midstrip, *I*)
Sam Boyd's Fremont Paradise
Buffet (Downtown, *I*)

Tropicana Island Buffet
(South Strip, *M*)
Tropicana Sunday Brunch
Buffet (South Strip, *E*)

CALIFORNIA

Enigma Cafe (West Las
Vegas, *I*)
Planet Hollywood (Mid-Strip,
Caesars Palace, *M*)
Spago (Mid-Strip, Caesars
Palace, *VE*)
Wolfgang Puck Cafe
(South Strip, MGM
Grand, *E*)

CHINESE

Cathy House (West Las
Vegas, *M*)
Chin's (North Strip, Fashion
Show Mall, *E*)
The Noodle Kitchen (Mid-
Strip, Mirage, *M*)

CONTEMPORARY CREOLE

Emeril's New Orleans Fish
House (South Strip, MGM
Grand, *VE*)

CONTINENTAL

Bacchanal (Mid-Strip, Caesars
Palace, *VE*)
Buccaneer Bay Club (Mid-
Strip, Treasure Island, *VE*)
Pegasus (Convention Center/
Paradise Road, Alexis Park
Resort, VE)
Top of the World
(North Strip, Strato-
sphere, *VE*)

CUBAN

Rincon Criollo (North
Strip, *I*)

DELI

Stage Deli (Mid-Strip, Caesars Palace, *M*)

DINER

Liberty Cafe at the Blue Castle Pharmacy (North Strip, *I*)

EURASIAN

Gatsby's (South Strip, MGM Grand, *VE*)

FRENCH

Andre's (Downtown, *VE*)
Bistro Le Montrachet (Convention Center/ Paradise Road, Las Vegas Hilton, *VE*)
Monte Carlo Room (North Strip, Desert Inn, *VE*)
Palace Court (Mid-Strip, Caesars Palace, *VE*)
Pamplemousse (Convention Center/Paradise Road, *VE*)

GERMAN/AMERICAN

The Rathskeller (Convention Center/ Paradise Road, *I*)

INDIAN

Shalimar (Convention Center/Paradise Road, Citibank Plaza, *M*)

INTERNATIONAL

The Garlic Cafe (West Las Vegas, *E*)
Hugo's Cellar (Downtown, Four Queens, *VE*)

ITALIAN

Fiore (Mid-Strip, Rio, *VE*)

JAPANESE

Ginza (Convention Center/ Paradise Road, *M*)
Mizuno's (South Strip, Tropicana, *E*)

MEDITERRANEAN

Enigma Cafe (West Las Vegas, *I*)
Mediterranean Cafe and Market (East Las Vegas, *I*)

MEXICAN

Ricardo's (East Las Vegas, *M*)
Viva Mercados (West Las Vegas, *M*)

MOROCCAN

Mamounia (Convention Center/ Paradise Road, *M*)
Marrakesh (Convention Center/ Paradise Road, *M*)

PROVENÇALE

Fiore (Mid-Strip, Rio, *VE*)

PUB FARE

Monte Carlo Pub and Brewery (South Strip, Monte Carlo, *I*)

SOUTHWESTERN

Country Star (South Strip, *M*)
Coyote Cafe (South Strip, MGM Grand, *VE*)
Motown Cafe (South Strip, New York New York, *M*)

STEAK/SEAFOOD

Lawry's The Prime Rib (Convention Center/ Paradise Road, *E*)

Limerick's (Downtown,
 Fitzgeralds, *E*)
The Palm (Mid-Strip, Caesars
 Palace, *VE*)
The Tillerman
 (East Las Vegas, *VE*)

SWISS/GERMAN
 Alpine Village Inn
  (Convention Center/
  Paradise Road, *M*)

TEX-MEX
 Z Tejas Grill (Convention
  Center/Paradise Road, *M*)

3 South Strip

VERY EXPENSIVE

✪ **Coyote Cafe.** The MGM Grand, 3799 Las Vegas Blvd. S. ☎ **702/ 891-7349.** Reservations recommended for the Grill Room, not accepted for the Cafe. Grill Room main courses $15–$32. Cafe main courses $7.50–$17.50 (many are under $10). AE, CB, DC, DISC, JCB, MC, V. Grill Room daily 5:30– 10pm. Cafe daily 8am–11pm. SOUTHWESTERN.

In a town where restaurant cuisine often seems stuck in a 1950s time warp, Mark Miller's Coyote Cafe evokes howls of delight. His robust regional cuisine combines elements of traditional Mexican, Native American, Creole, and Cajun cookery with cutting-edge culinary trends. The main dining room is fronted by a lively cafe/ bar, in which an exhibition-cooking area houses a *cazuela* (casserole) oven and *comal* grill under a gleaming ceramic tile hood. The adobe-walled Grill Room offers a more tranquil setting.

The Grill Room menu changes monthly. If you're lucky, you might find the heavenly "painted soup"—half garlicky black bean, half beer-infused smoked Cheddar—"painted" with chipotle cream and garnished with salsa fresca and de árbol chili powder. A reliable main course is the salmon fillet crusted with ground pumpkin seeds and corn tortillas topped with roasted chile/pumpkin-seed sauce and presented on a bed of spinach-wrapped spaghetti squash studded with pine nuts, corn kernels, scallions, and morsels of sun-dried tomato. Desserts include chocolate banana torte served on banana crème anglaise and topped with a scoop of vanilla ice cream. The wine list includes many by-the-glass selections, including champagnes and sparkling wines, which nicely complement spicy southwestern fare; Brazilian daiquiris are a house specialty.

The Cafe menu offers similar but somewhat lighter fare. Southwestern breakfasts ($5.95 to $9.50) range from *huevos rancheros* to blue-corn pancakes with toasted pine nuts, honey butter, and real maple syrup.

✪ **Emeril's New Orleans Fish House.** The MGM Grand, 3799 Las Vegas Blvd. S. ☎ **702/891-7374.** Reservations suggested. Main courses $12–$18 lunch, $18–$28 dinner (more for lobster). AE, CB, DC, DISC, MC, V. Daily 11am–3pm, 5:30–10:30pm. CONTEMPORARY CREOLE.

Tucked into an almost unseen corner of the MGM Grand is one of the very finest restaurants in the city. Chef Emeril Lagasse of New Orleans's Emeril's and NOLA (and an extremely popular TV chef on cable's Food Network) has brought his cuisine to town. The restaurant's quiet and comforting decor provides the stage for creative, exciting, "BAM!" food.

Although Lagasse caters to the tastes of everyone from poultry lovers to vegetarians, seafood is the specialty here, flown in from Louisiana or from anywhere that the chef finds the quality of the ingredients to be the very finest. We started off with the most recent edition of Lagasse's legendary savory "cheesecakes," the Lobster Cheesecake with tomato-tarragon coulis, topped with a dollop of succulent Louisiana choupique caviar. It's a heady, rich appetizer that may be completely unlike anything you've ever had before. Oysters on the half-shell is also a favorite. And try the barbecue shrimp, which come in a garlic, herb butter sauce that will have you mopping your plate with bread in a most embarrassing, un-artery-conscious manner.

Our entrees did not fail to elicit a "Wow!" from everyone at the table. A Creole-seasoned, seared ahi steak was stuffed with Hudson Valley foie gras and served in a bed of Lagasse's famous "smashed" potatoes, creamy and rich, with roasted shallots and a part-shallot reduction—absolutely luxurious. A medley of seafood, from caviar to shrimp to mussels and clams, came over pasta in a delicious and very spicy broth. And in a dish that bordered on the sinful, there was a marvelously seasoned filet mignon stuffed with a crawfish dressing and topped with Bordelaise sauce with crawfish tails and sliced andouille sausage. Meat eaters will also be very happy with the utterly tender and flavorful fillet of beef with tasso Hollandaise sauce and homemade Worcestershire.

It would be difficult to recommend one particular dessert from the vast menu since they're all fabulous, but if it's your first visit, a slice of the Banana Cream Pie with banana crust and caramel drizzle is one of the finest desserts you will ever have. And if your capacity for rich food is depleted by the end of your meal, try one of the house-made sorbets, which provide a lovely, lighter finish to your meal. If you're feeling adventurous, don't miss Chef's Degustation, a seven-course tasting menu. It usually features smaller portions

South Strip Dining

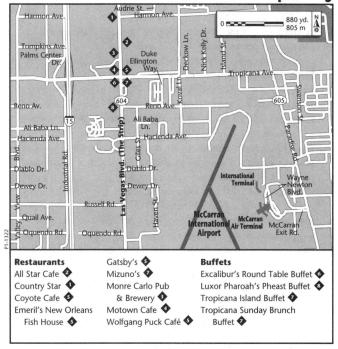

Restaurants
All Star Cafe ❷
Country Star ❶
Coyote Cafe ❺
Emeril's New Orleans
   Fish House ❺

Gatsby's ❺
Mizuno's ❼
Monre Carlo Pub
   & Brewery ❸
Motown Cafe ❹
Wolfgang Puck Café ❺

Buffets
Excalibur's Round Table Buffet ❻
Luxor Pharoah's Pheast Buffet ❽
Tropicana Island Buffet ❼
Tropicana Sunday Brunch
   Buffet ❼

(thank heavens) of the most exciting dishes from the regular menu, plus some specials of the evening.

✪ **Gatsby's.** The MGM Grand, 3799 Las Vegas Blvd. S. ☎ **702/891-7337.** Reservations suggested. Jackets suggested for men. Main courses $28.95–$58. Degustation (tasting) menu $75, $95 with selected wines accompanying each course. AE, CB, DC, DISC, MC, V. Wed–Mon 6–10:30pm. EURASIAN.

This is a very expensive restaurant but on par with the swankiest establishments in more food-oriented cities. Gatsby's chef de cuisine, Terence Fong, has quite a conundrum to solve: How do you please the generally food-conservative Las Vegas customer and offer an innovative, exciting dining experience that invigorates everyone involved? Provide the expected but don't let it dictate preparation; combine familiar ingredients with more unusual ones to subtly educate the unadventurous; use only fresh, lovely, seasonal items. This means, for example, that Fong's lobster bisque, a rich soup you'll find on many a local menu, presented here with perhaps two lumps of divinely sweet meat and a few bites of equally sugar-rich roasted corn, awakens one to the difference between the ordinary and the extraordinary. It means starting with aromatic yet familiar jasmine and basmati rice, but adding toasted orzo, wheat berries, and quinoa (a rather trendy but very healthful and tasty grain) to produce a delicious confetti of flavors rather than a safe side dish. It means that the gracious wait staff brings unexpected treats to tease diners into anticipation, such as tiny cilantro crêpe purses of beluga caviar and vodka crème fraîche, or perfectly smoked salmon on 50¢-sized blini.

Anything from this kitchen that includes foie gras is worth ordering. This delicacy might show up on the menu in more than one guise, accompanied with pan-roasted stuffed quail and a lentil-corn salad, or with Perigourd truffles and organic greens dressed in a port wine vinaigrette that will leave you surreptitiously wiping up any stray drops with a bit of bread. Maine lobster might be simply sautéed and served with lobster-ginger butter to gild the already sumptuous meat; ahi tuna gets an Asian preparation with a sesame seed crust and a spicy wasabi butter. Fans of exotic meats, or anyone curious to try ostrich or buffalo, are in the right place. The grilled domestic ostrich, bathed in a red wine–shallot reduction and served with wild mushroom risotto, is a lovely dish, tender and not the least bit gamey. Duck is well treated here, as well. It's slow roasted, so the slices are as tender and lean as possible, garnished with an Asian-style sauce and pretty little vegetables. Vegetarians will find dinner just as lush. Along with the chef's vegetable plate, replete with couscous or risotto or that wonderful rice confetti and lots of recently plucked delicacies, vegetable broth-based soups, a couple of salads, and appetizers such as the vegetable spring rolls will profoundly satisfy your appetite and expectations.

It's painful to recall the dessert menu, living so far from the source. Melanie Bonnano, the pastry chef, takes great delight in whimsical presentations like a Cup of Java, a treat that fulfills coffee and chocolate lovers on a number of levels. Her coffee-and-cream granita-laden chocolate cup will have you examining your freezer in a new light. Soufflés available in five flavors are a house specialty, but chocolate cake mysteriously filled with fresh raspberries and wrapped in filo pastry is a feast for the eyes and tongue.

Everything, from the lavish crackers and bread to the sorbets presented in the center of ice flowers, is made in-house. It's also possible to request a special tasting menu ($75), which will truly give you a sense of the restaurant's possibilities. For an extra $30, the enthusiastic sommelier will pair wines from the luxuriously stocked cellar with each course.

EXPENSIVE

Mizuno's. Tropicana Resort and Casino, 3801 Las Vegas Blvd. S. ☎ **702/ 739-2222.** Reservations suggested. Full Samurai dinners mostly $14.95–$19.95, Shogun combination dinners $24.95–$38.95. AE, CB, DC, MC, V. Daily 5– 10:30pm. JAPANESE.

This stunning, marble-floored restaurant is filled with authentic Japanese artifacts. A meandering glass "stream" is lit by tiny twinkling lights to suggest running water, and cut-glass dividers are etched with graceful cherry blossoms, irises, and plum trees. Food is prepared at marble teppanyaki grill tables where you're seated with other patrons. This being Las Vegas, the chef's dazzling display of dexterity is enhanced by a flashing light show over the grill.

Entrees comprised of tasty morsels of steak, shrimp, lobster, chicken, or shrimp and vegetable tempura come with miso soup or consommé (get the tastier miso), salad with ginger dressing, an array of crispy flavorful vegetables stir-fried with sesame seeds and spices, steamed rice, and tea. Though it's a lot of food, an appetizer of shrimp and mushrooms sautéed in garlic butter with lemon soy sauce merits consideration. And a bottle of warm sake is recommended. Ginger or red bean ice cream make for a fittingly light dessert. A great bargain here: a full early bird dinner served from 5 to 6pm for just $9.95.

MODERATE

All Star Cafe. 3785 Las Vegas Blvd. S., at Tropicana Ave. (in the showcase mall, right next to the MGM Grand). ☎ **702/795-8326.** Reservations only for parties of 10 or more. Main courses $6–$18. DC, DISC, JCB, MC, V. Sun–Thurs 11am–midnight, Fri–Sat 11am–1am. AMERICAN.

This is the sports theme restaurant, filled with memorabilia from "hundreds of different sports legends, "covering just about every sport you can imagine. Buffs should be pleased. The co-owners are Vegas resident Andre Agassi, Monica Seles, Wayne Gretsky, Ken Griffey Jr., Joe Montana, Shaquille O'Neal, and new wunderkind Tiger Woods (who recently joined as an investor). The menu is "All American" and includes pasta specialties, salads, and the usual hamburgers and hot dogs.

Country Star. 3724 Las Vegas Blvd. S., at Harmon Ave. ☎ **702/740-8400.** Reservations for large parties only. Main courses $5.95–$21.95 (most under $14). AE, CB, DC, DISC, MC. V. Sun–Thurs 11am–10pm, Fri–Sun 11am–11pm. BARBECUE/SOUTHWESTERN.

This would be the country music entry, attempting to cash in on the success of the Hard Rock. Restaurant principals include Reba McEntire and Vince Gill. It's more low key and friendly than, say,

Hard Rock or Planet Hollywood. Dozens of video monitors, including several embedded in the entranceway floor, play nonstop C&W music videos. Actually, the food here is pretty good. The barbecue sauce is terrific (bottles are on the tables).

Motown Cafe. New York New York Hotel, 3790 Las Vegas Blvd. S, at Tropicana. ☎ **702/740-6440.** Reservations not accepted. $6–$17. AE, DISC, MC, V. Sun–Thurs 7am–11pm, Fri–Sat 7am–12am. SOUTHWESTERN.

Okay, this is a salute to Motown greats (who are not involved in the operation), who heralded in an era when timeless hits kept coming out every five minutes from Berry Gordy's place. The menu features "light southwestern cuisine—jambalya, shrimp Creole—probably because no one could figure out what the indigenous cuisine of Detroit was. (This is in addition to the basic burgers and so forth). They also offer a breakfast buffet. And as we all know, Motown music is just about the best there is for dancing, and so the Cafe stays open until 3am on weekdays and 4am on weekends for dancing.

✪ **Wolfgang Puck Café.** MGM Grand, 3799 Las Vegas Blvd. S. ☎ **702/895-9653.** Reservations not accepted. Main courses $9–$14.95. AE, MC, V. Sun–Thurs 8am–11pm, Fri–Sat 8am–midnight. CALIFORNIA.

A brightly colored riot of mosaic tiles and other experiments in geometric design, the Wolfgang Puck Cafe stands out in the MGM Grand. It's more or less Spago Lite: downscaled salads, pizzas, and pastas, all showing the Puck hand; and while perhaps a little more money than your average cafe, the food is comparably better, if sometimes not *that* special. However, it's all very fresh nouvelle cuisine, which makes a nice change of pace. The specialty pizzas are fun; constructed on crusts topped with fontina and mozzarella cheeses, they're brushed with pesto and layered with embellishments such as spicy jalapeño-marinated sautéed chicken, leeks, and cilantro. (And no, it's not just like eating the Puck brand sold in the frozen food section.) It's always a thrill to get a good salad in Vegas, and there are quite a few on this menu. Worth noting is the signature Chinois chicken salad tossed with crispy fried wontons, julienned carrots, cabbage, and green onions in a Chinese honey-mustard sauce. For something cheap, try the surprisingly large baby greens salad with goat cheese toast—that and the very fine herb bread that comes gratis is $4.95 and fills you up in a fairly healthy way for not a lot of money. Desert highlights include a caramel cheesecake, a warm chocolate soufflé, and a hot chocolate truffle cake with chocolate sauce. There does tend to be a line, particularly after EFX lets out just across the casino.

INEXPENSIVE

Monte Carlo Pub and Brewery. Monte Carlo Resort, 3770 Las Vegas Blvd. S., between Flamingo Rd. and Tropicana Ave. ☎ **702/730-7777.** Main courses $5.95–$7.95. AE, CB, DC, DISC, MC, V. Sun–Thurs 11am–1am, Fri–Sat 11am–3am. PUB FARE.

This is a favorite lunch spot and after-work hangout for local business people. A working microbrewery (you can view the copper holding tanks and vats through large windows), it has a high-ceilinged warehouse/industrial interior, with exposed-brick and rusty corrugated-tin walls, track lighting, and a network of exposed pipes overhead. An ornate mahogany bar adds a note of elegance. The Pub is cigar-friendly (maintaining a humidor), and rock videos blare forth from a large screen and 40 TV monitors around the room.

The menu features somewhat sophisticated versions of pub fare, doled out in enormous portions. We like the pizza topped with lamb, grilled eggplant, and goat cheese. Other choices include penne pasta with wild mushrooms in garlic cream sauce, a sample platter of sausages served with warm potato salad and whole-grain mustard, sandwiches, burgers, and barbecued baby back ribs. A microbrew with your meal (or a sampler of five) is de rigueur. Desserts include bread pudding with butterscotch rum sauce and creamy peanut butter pie. After 9pm, only pizza is served, and dueling pianos provide dance music and entertainment.

4 Mid-Strip

VERY EXPENSIVE

Bacchanal. Caesars Palace, 3570 Las Vegas Blvd. S., just north of Flamingo Rd. ☎ 702/731-7110. Reservations essential. Fixed-price $69.50, plus tax and gratuity. AE, CB, DC, DISC, MC, V. Tues–Sat 6–11pm with seatings at 6pm, 6:30, 9 and 9:30pm. CONTINENTAL.

Its pedimented doorways guarded by golden lions, Bacchanal is an archetypal Las Vegas experience—an imperial Roman feast with comely "wine goddesses" performing sinuous belly dances, decanting wine from shoulder height into ornate silver chalices, and, believe it or not, massaging male diners and feeding them grapes! When not performing, the goddesses repose gracefully around a fountained pool. The setting is palatial: White-columned walls are backed by murals of ancient Rome; an azure ceiling suggests an open sky, with a grape arbor looping from beam to beam and crystal torches provide romantic lighting. You'll be greeted by "Caesar," then he and "Cleopatra" tour the room greeting diners. Abandon all reality, ye who enter here.

Dinner is a sumptuous multicourse feast, including unlimited wine and champagne. The menu changes a bit seasonally. Dinner begins with a selection of crudités served with creamy roasted garlic-chive dip. This is followed by a smoked roma tomato soup and a salad of field greens with champagne vinaigrette dressing. A choice of five entrees might range from roast rack of lamb to oven-roasted wild salmon fillet. The dramatic finale—a flaming dessert of vanilla ice cream topped with liqueur-soaked fresh fruits—will be accompanied by petits fours and tea or coffee. The food falls short of haute gourmet standards, but there's plenty of it, and the elaborate presentation (not to mention the wine) justifies the price.

✪ **Buccaneer Bay Club.** Treasure Island, 3300 Las Vegas Blvd. S. ☎ **702/ 894-7350.** Reservations required. Main courses $16–$26. AE, CB, DC, DISC, JCB, MC, V. Nightly 5–10:30pm. AMERICAN/CONTINENTAL.

This is a little-known gem (at least, outside of Treasure Island guests) that features a laudable menu more innovative than the standard found at other equivalent hotel restaurants. And it's considerably cheaper. Plus, they stage a pirate battle right outside, just for you! (Just kidding.)

A meandering layout creates a serious of intimate dining nooks (perfect for quiet conversations, preferably with someone else) all done in a posh pirate theme with a low-beamed ceiling and stucco walls adorned with daggers and pistols. The whole thing overlooks the hotel's "bay" where a pirate battle is waged every ninety minutes. This probably isn't the best place to view it (the windows are small-ish, and you're behind the action), but the wait staff does notify you at show time and will hold your food service until it's through if you have chosen to watch. It's fun to watch everyone rush to the windows when they announce, "Pirates are on!"

Speaking of the service, it is among the best we've experienced, with an efficient team of friendly, knowledgeable, and almost prescient servers at every table (they anticipated a woman's desire for another glass of wine before she even had finished wistfully vocalizing it).

Appetizers come in both hot (shrimp Jamaica, escargot brioche) and cold (shrimp cocktail, Parma prosciutto) varieties with the savory celery root flan and the quail being the true standouts. Regarding the latter, it was not on the menu, so be sure to inquire about specials. Entrees run the gamut from poultry (chicken, duck, pheasant) to beef (filet mignon, prime rib, steak) to seafood (sea bass, lobster, salmon). Favorites here are the Pheasant Charles, which comes with pan-seared, thyme-roasted wild mushroom risotto and is served

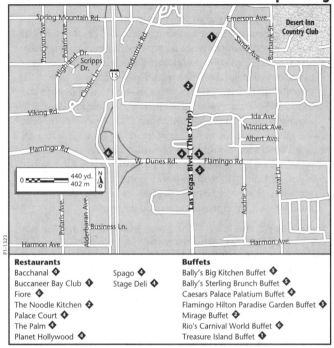

Restaurants

Bacchanal ◆
Buccaneer Bay Club ❶
Fiore ◆
The Noodle Kitchen ❷
Palace Court ◆
The Palm ◆
Planet Hollywood ◆

Spago ◆
Stage Deli ◆

Buffets

Bally's Big Kitchen Buffet ◆
Bally's Sterling Brunch Buffet ❺
Caesars Palace Palatium Buffet ◆
Flamingo Hilton Paradise Garden Buffet ❸
Mirage Buffet ◆
Rio's Carnival World Buffet ◆
Treasure Island Buffet ◆

in a Merlot lingonberry sauce. There's also Colorado Buffalo Prime Rib, which is roasted and grilled over mesquite wood and served with creamy horseradish potatoes. It's hard to get over the thought of eating buffalo at first, but if you can, it'll be one of the best pieces of cow-based meat you'll ever taste. Desserts include apple binets, white chocolate cheesecake with raspberry sauce, and the house specialty apricot or harlequin (Grand Marnier, white and dark chocolate) minisoufflés.

Fiore. Rio Suite Hotel, 3700 W. Flamingo Rd., at I-15. ☎ **702/252-7702.** Reservations recommended. Main courses $26–$48. AE, CB, DC, DISC, MC, V. Nightly 5–11pm. ITALIAN/PROVENCÇALE.

Fiore offers a deliciously simpatico setting for the brilliantly innovative cuisine of chef Kolachai Ngimsangaim. We love the interior space, but it's also tempting to dine alfresco on the flower-bordered flagstone terrace (heated in winter, mist-cooled in summer).

Ngimsangaim's seasonally changing menus complement the culinary elegance of northern Italy with the earthy exuberance of southern France. For an appetizer we've had the sautéed herb-crusted prawns in a buttery mustard/anise sauce. This was followed by an entree of barbecued Atlantic salmon in honeyed hickory sauce, served with grilled polenta, Portobello mushrooms, roasted roma tomatoes, and grilled asparagus spears. Fiore's thoughtful list of more than 400 wines, in several price ranges, is international in scope and includes 45 premium by-the-glass selections. Consult knowledgeable sommelier Barrie Larvin for suggestions. Dine slowly, and consider including a cheese course—excellent cheeses are served with seasonal fruits. But do save room for dessert—perhaps a warm chocolate torte on crème anglaise embellished with raspberry stars and chocolate hearts. In addition to an extensive listing of cognacs, ports, and dessert wines, hand-rolled cigars—elegantly presented in a mahogany humidor—are a postprandial option on the terrace.

Palace Court. Caesars Palace, 3570 Las Vegas Blvd. S., just north of Flamingo Rd. ☎ **702/734-7110.** Reservations essential. Main courses $29–$55. AE, MC, V. Nightly 6, 6:30, 9, 9:30. FRENCH.

The Palace Court has long been considered one of the best restaurants in town, but word from those who know is that it has declined somewhat in quality. While alumni are cooking up delicious storms at other restaurants, the Palace Court recently (as of this writing) had lost both its long-time chef and pastry chef. This doesn't bode well for improvements; on the other hand, once the new staff is settled in, a recovery might follow. It would be worth asking around before spending a bundle here.

But if you do go, here is what you can expect. Menus change seasonally. A recent one offered appetizers of poached champagne-glazed Long Island oysters (embellished with beluga caviar, smoked salmon, and julienned leeks) and ravioli stuffed with minced pink prawns, mushrooms, and truffles in lobster bisque sauce. Sorbets are served between courses in frosted glass lilies. Among the entrees, Maine lobster was served with coral (lobster roe) butter and steamed broccoli, and chateaubriand came with peppery red wine/game sauce, a mousseline of spinach, poached pears, and dauphinois potatoes.

There's an extensive wine list, with 12 by-the-glass selections; consult the sommelier for assistance.

Petit-fours and chocolate truffles are served gratis at the conclusion of your meal. However, that doesn't mean you should forgo dessert. Choices include ambrosial soufflés and a totally satisfying flourless chocolate truffle cake topped with homemade hazelnut ice cream. *Note:* A fixed-price pretheater special (soup or salad, entree, and dessert) is served Sunday to Thursday from 6 to 7pm; it costs $34.50.

End your evening over après-dinner drinks in the romantic adjoining piano bar/lounge.

The Palm. The Forum Shops at Caesars Palace, 3500 Las Vegas Blvd. S. ☎ **702/732-7256.** Reservations recommended. Main courses $8.50–$14 lunch, $15–$35 dinner. AE, CB, DC, MC, V. Daily 11:30am–11pm. STEAK/ SEAFOOD.

Grandsons of New York's original Palm owners John Ganzi and Pio Bozzi have parlayed the family business into a nationwide restaurant empire. Hence, this Las Vegas branch. In the Palm tradition, signature pine-wainscoted ecru walls are plastered with celebrity caricatures of everyone from Wayne Newton to Walt Kelly's Pogo. Diners are comfortably seated in roomy mahogany booths upholstered in dark green leather.

Another Palm tradition is a bare-bones menu that austerely offers up appetizers (such as shrimp cocktail, clams casino, melon and prosciutto) and entrees (filet mignon, lamb chops, salmon fillet, broiled crab cakes, linguine with clam sauce, prime rib of beef) without descriptive frills. By contrast, a listing for string beans *aglio e olio* (in garlic and oil) seems positively lyrical. Food preparation is simple (nothing is drizzled, infused, or nuanced here). Rather, the emphasis is on fresh fish and seafood, top-quality cuts of meat, and salads using the ripest, reddest, and juiciest tomatoes—all served up in satisfying, good-sized portions. Side dishes of cottage fries and creamed spinach are recommended. The wine list nicely complements the menu, and desserts include big wedges of cheesecake and chocolate pecan pie. At lunch you can choose a $12 fixed-price meal, which includes an entree (perhaps prime rib or batter-fried shrimp), salad, cottage fries, and tea or coffee.

✪ **Spago.** The Forum Shops at Caesars Palace, 3500 Las Vegas Blvd. S. ☎ **702/369-6300.** Reservations recommended for the dining room; not accepted at the cafe. Dining Room: main courses $14–$28. Cafe: main courses $8.50–$16.50. AE, CB, DC, DISC, MC, V. Dining Room: Sun–Thurs 6–10:30pm, Fri–Sat 5:30–11pm. Cafe: Daily 11am–1am. CALIFORNIA.

Wolfgang Puck's landmark L.A. restaurant provides a rare foodie oasis in Vegas. However, though one of the few truly innovative restaurants in Vegas, Spago has been riding a bit on its reputation. While anything you get here is going to be better, and more interesting, than the vast majority of Vegas restaurants, you get the feeling they've been far ahead of the pack for just long enough to get comfortable. Which is not to say Spago is not worth the splurge—it just means that others have caught up with them (and in some cases, though it may be considered heresy to say it, may have surpassed Puck's baby), and they are no longer the only foodie game in town.

But it's still an experience going there—call it California casual elegance. The postindustrial interior is the very model of a modern major restaurant, while the exterior cafe on the Forum Shops is more relaxed and provides an opportunity for people watching as fine as at any European sidewalk cafe (if said European cafe were under a roof with a fake sky painted on it.) It's probably not as star-heavy as the celebrated L.A. original, but it's safe to say that any Hollywood high-muck-a-muck in town would probably be inclined to eat here.

When, in the film *Showgirls,* Nomi Malone came to eat at the cafe, she peevishly said she didn't "know what any of this stuff is." She must not get out much; the cafe menu features such familiar items as meat loaf and pizza, although glamorized versions—this isn't Country Kitchen, and so this pizza features smoked salmon. Not to mention crème fraîche. It sounds like an unholy hybrid of Italian and deli, but it's sublime. Other cafe specialties include Puck's signature Chinois chicken salad and a superb mesquite-fried salmon served with a tangy toss of soba noodles and cashews in a coconut-sesame-chili paste vinaigrette nuanced with lime juice and Szechuan mustard. The inside menu changes seasonally; examples of potential choices include scallops with a divine basil risotto, an appetizer of tuna sashimi in hot olive oil and sesame or porcini mushrooms with a truffle sauce. The "signature" dish is a Chinese style duck, moist but with a perfectly crispy skin. It's about as good as duck gets. It was served with a doughy steamed bun and Chinese vegetables. Deserts range from fresh fruit sorbets in surprising flavors (cantaloupe, honeydew), to a luscious brownie topped with homemade chocolate, whipped cream, and ice cream. The wine list is impressive, but the house wine was a disappointment and possibly not worth the cost.

MODERATE

The Noodle Kitchen. Mirage, 3400 Las Vegas Blvd. S., between Flamingo Rd. and Sands Ave. ☎ **800/456-4564.** Reservations not accepted. Main courses $7.95–$22.75 (many under $10). AE, CB, DC, DISC, MC, V. Daily 11am–4am. CHINESE.

The Mirage designed The Noodle Kitchen to serve its sizable clientele of Asian high rollers—a clientele desirous of authentic, non-Americanized Chinese fare. Most of the diners here are Asian, but

American and European food aficionados will also appreciate the Kitchen's high-quality cuisine. It's really not so much a separate establishment as a section of the hotel's lushly tropical Caribe Café.

Start off with clear soup, flavored with Chinese parsley and replete with thin egg noodles and dumplings filled with minced shrimp and ear mushrooms. A combination plate of soy chicken slices, roast pork, and tender crisp-skinned roast duck with plum sauce makes a marvelous entree choice, especially when accompanied by delicious al dente steamed vegetables (Chinese broccoli or choy sum) in oyster sauce. If you like to spice things up, you'll find three hot sauces on the table. There are Asian desserts (such as red bean ice delight), but as these are an acquired taste, you might prefer fresh-baked cakes and pies from the Caribe Café menu. Or skip dessert altogether in favor of sweet Vietnamese iced coffee mixed with condensed milk, coconut milk, and shaved ice. All bar drinks, including Chinese and Japanese beers, are available.

Planet Hollywood. Forum Shops at Caesars Palace, 3500 Las Vegas Blvd. S. ☎ **702/791-STAR.** Reservations not accepted. Main courses $7.95–$19.95 (most under $13). AE, DC, MC, V. Sun–Thurs 11am–midnight, Fri–Sat 11am–1am. CALIFORNIA.

Arnold, Sly, Bruce, and Demi joined forces with some finance buddies to create a movie version of the Hard Rock. It was an instant success and a sure sign of the decline of western civilization. Some of the objects displayed are worthless, others are sort of amusing—Barbara Eden's genie bottle, chariot wheels from *Ben Hur,* the side of beef Stallone sparred with in *Rocky,* the *Star Trek* control tower. Video monitors are everywhere. Further reluctant credit is given for the more imaginative than average theme-restaurant menu; blackened shrimp served with Creole mustard sauce; linguine tossed with Thai shrimp, peanuts, and julienned vegetables in spicy sweet chili sauce; white chocolate bread pudding drenched in whiskey sauce and topped with white chocolate ice cream. There's a walkway here directly from the Strip.

Stage Deli. Forum Shops at Caesars Palace, 3500 Las Vegas Blvd. S. ☎ **702/893-4045.** Reservations accepted for large parties only. Main courses $9.95–$13.95, sandwiches $5.95–$13.95. AE, DC, DISC, JCB, MC, V. Sun–Thurs 7:30am–10:30pm, Fri–Sat 7:30am–midnight. DELI.

This is a branch of the New York City institution, which has been around for more than half a century. The deli is often not crowded. In addition to being handy for Caesars guests, if you are staying next door at the Mirage, it's easy to pop over, making it a satisfying breakfast alternative (too often overcrowded, overpriced, and not very good hotel breakfast joints in the area). The huge (we mean it) menu means finding something for even the pickiest of eaters.

Most of the fare—including fresh-baked pumpernickel and rye, meats, chewy bagels, lox, spicy deli mustard, and pickles—comes in daily from New York. (It's the water, you know.) The Stage dishes up authentic 5-inch-high sandwiches stuffed with pastrami, corned beef, brisket, or chopped liver. Maybe overstuffed is a better description. Unless you have a hearty appetite, are feeding two, or have a fridge in your room for leftovers, you might want to try the half sandwich and soup or salad combos. Other specialties here include matzo ball soup, knishes, kasha varnishkes, cheese blintzes, kreplach, pirogen, and smoked fish platters accompanied by bagels and cream cheese. Or you might prefer a full meal consisting of pot roast and gravy, salad, homemade dinner rolls, potato pancakes, and fresh vegetables. Desserts run the gamut from rugelach cheesecake to Hungarian-style apple strudel, and available beverages include wine and beer, milk shakes, Dr. Brown's sodas, and chocolate egg creams.

5 North Strip

VERY EXPENSIVE

The Monte Carlo Room. Desert Inn, 3145 Las Vegas Blvd. S., between Desert Inn Rd. and Sands Ave. ☎ **702/733-4444.** Reservations recommended. Jackets required. Main courses $28–$80. AE, CB, DC, DISC, JCB, MC, V. Thurs–Mon 6–11pm. FRENCH.

The delightful Monte Carlo Room is equally renowned for its sublime setting and fine French cuisine. Excellent appetizer choices include seafood ravioli with champagne-caviar sauce or a terrine of fresh goose liver. We also love the thick, velvety, cognac-laced lobster bisque, full of rich flavor, served in a scooped-out round loaf of bread. For your entree, consider a classic French entrecôte au poivre or duck à l'orange served with apple- and pine nut–studded wild rice. A mélange of vegetables and a potato dish (perhaps pommes soufflés) accompany entrees. There's an extensive wine list; consult the sommelier for suggestions. Flaming tableside preparations are a specialty, including desserts such as crêpes Suzette and cherries jubilee.

Top of the World. Stratosphere Las Vegas Hotel, 2000 Las Vegas Blvd. S., between St. Louis St. and Baltimore Ave. ☎ **702/380-7711.** Reservations required. Main courses $13–$21 lunch, $21–$29 dinner. AE, CB, DC, DISC, JCB, MC, V. Daily 11am–3:45pm; Sun–Thurs 4–11pm, Fri–Sat 4pm–midnight. AMERICAN/CONTINENTAL.

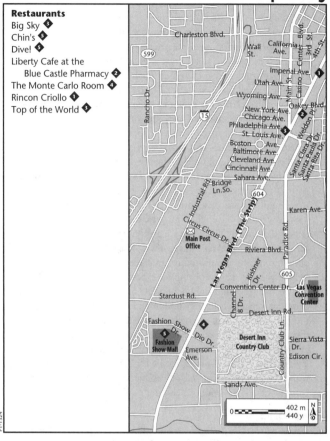

Restaurants
Big Sky ◆
Chin's ◆
Dive! ◆
Liberty Cafe at the
    Blue Castle Pharmacy ◆
The Monte Carlo Room ◆
Rincon Criollo ◆
Top of the World ◆

Okay, revolving restaurants are the very definition of kitsch. But you know what? We like 'em. And when you've got views like these, well, there is a difference between having good taste and being made of stone.

Because you are 869 feet in the air, Vegas is stretched out before you in a glittering palette. Who knew this town could be so beautiful? This proves the Stratosphere is good for something. The Top of the World restaurant may not have the best food in Vegas (though some things are actually pretty good), but it has hands down the best view. You will be so busy admiring the Strip, noticing that Vegas goes on much farther than you thought, wondering which casino that particular cluster of lights is, and trying to spot your hotel, that you won't even notice what you are eating. It's one of the most romantic spots in town to dine.

But it's expensive, and the entrees, at least, are not worth the cost. Having anticipated that customers might want to fill up tables just ordering a small snack, there is a $15 per person minimum. Here's what you do: Order the generous sized appetizers and desserts— only. You won't be disappointed, and you can easily make the minimum. The menu changes, but recent appetizers included southwestern spring rolls (think of a cross between an egg roll and a fajita) filled with chicken and veggies, slightly deep fried to a nice crunch, and served with a fine guacamole. It's tart, crunchy, messy, and fattening, which means it has to be good. There was also an oversized (to the point of silliness) bruschetta (chopped tomato, basil, and garlic covered in olive oil on huge toasted slices of bread) that was tasty if hard to eat. The salads are overpriced and overly fussy, while the entrees are not terribly imaginative. (The fillet of almond-crusted salmon did get a thumbs up on an earlier visit.) The desserts were stellar, with the standout being the expensive ($9), but easily shared by two (it's huge and rich), Chocolate Stratosphere Tower. Yep, a chocolate replica of the very building in which you are sitting; the top part is filled with a terrific chocolate mousse, and the whole thing gets covered in chocolate sauce, poured by your waiter with great ceremony. Additional happiness came with towering *vacherin:* layers of hazelnut meringue filled with Bavarian cream, garnished with fresh berries, and served with crème anglaise and kiwi and raspberry sauces. The service was also impeccable.

EXPENSIVE

✪ **Chin's.** 3200 Las Vegas Blvd. S., in the Fashion Show Mall (turn at the Frontier sign). ☎ **702/733-8899.** Reservations recommended. Main courses $9.95–$11.95 lunch, $10–$29.50 dinner. AE, MC, V. Mon–Sat 11:30am–10pm, Sun noon–10pm. CHINESE.

Chin's has been a Vegas fixture for nearly 20 years and is consistently voted by locals in the *Las Vegas Review* as their favorite Chinese restaurant. It is certainly a surprise for anyone who knows Chinese food solely through take-out or strip malls. The simple, stark decor produces an ambience of low-key elegance. The prices will surprise you, too. This is not cheap Chinese food. But as convivial owner Mr. Chin points out, Chinese food takes so much time to prepare (all that chopping, dicing, splicing, and what not) and to present in the traditionally stylish way (no steam trays here) that it's a wonder anyone would ever charge just a couple dollars for a dish.

Chin is justly proud of his achievements, but he adds as much to his restaurant as the food. You will see him moving from table to table, greeting regulars by name; do try to have him visit with you, if you can. He's full of stories, like how Jerry Lewis and Neil Sedaka are regulars, with a special dish created just for the latter (shrimp with lobster in lobster sauce—no vegetables).

However, anyone whose experience with Chinese food is more broad than the aforementioned take-out and strip malls won't find anything terribly surprising here. Experiments with more radical dishes failed (too timid tourists?), and so the menu is on the safe side. Which is not to say it isn't good. Standouts include strawberry chicken (think lemon chicken but with a different fruit; Chin's created this twist on a familiar dish, and other local restaurants have copied it); an appetizer of sinful deep-fried shrimp puffs (stuffed with minced shrimp and mildly curried cream cheese); splendid spring rolls; and barbecue pork fried rice that strikes that tricky, careful balance between dry and greasy.

MODERATE

Dive! 3200 Las Vegas Blvd. S., in the Fashion Show Mall. ☎ **702/369-DIVE.** Reservations for large parties only. $6.95–$13.95. AE, CB, DC, DISC, MC. V. Sun–Thurs 11:30am–10pm, Fri–Sat 11:30am–11pm. AMERICAN.

Notable for being one of the few theme restaurants not devoted to memorabilia, DIVE! was partly created by Steven Spielberg and movie exec Jeffrey Katzenberg. The outside is admittedly quite fun: yellow submarine crashing through a 30-foot wall of water that cascades into an oversized pool erupting with depth-charge blasts. Its gunmetal-gray interior replicates the hull of a submarine with vaulted cylindrical ceilings, porthole-shaped (albeit neon-accented since this is Vegas) windows, exposed conduits that burst with steam, sonar screens, and working periscopes. Every hour a high-tech show projected on a 16-cube video wall (and 48 additional monitors throughout the restaurant) simulates a fantasy submarine dive. And overhead, a luxury ocean liner, a manta ray research vessel, exotic fish, a fighting shark, and model subs circumnavigate the room on a computerized track. It's all whimsical and imaginative; they even serve submarine sandwiches (among other choices). Kids should love it, and adults will find it slightly less annoying than, say, Chuck E. Cheese (and with somewhat more sophisticated food).

INEXPENSIVE

Big Sky. Stratosphere Las Vegas Hotel, 2000 Las Vegas Blvd. S., between St. Louis St. and Baltimore Ave. ☎ **702/780-7777.** All-you-can-eat dinner $12.99,

free for children under 6. AE, CB, DC, DISC, JCB, MC, V. Sun–Thurs 5–11pm,
Fri–Sat 5pm–midnight. BARBECUE.

Food bargains abound in Las Vegas, and this is one of the best. Big
Sky offers a suitably rustic setting for hearty all-you-can-eat family-
style feasts. Country music helps set the tone, and service is down-
home and friendly.

Entree choices include prime rib with creamed horseradish sauce
and a barbecue combination (beef brisket, St. Louis ribs, Carolina
pulled pork, and fried chicken). At press time, there was talk of adding steaks as well. Whatever you select, it will come with a huge
salad, scrumptious corn muffins (don't fill up on them; there's lots
more food coming), corn on the cob, seasoned steak fries, coleslaw,
Texas toast, and baked beans with pork. And when you've eaten
your fill, you can waddle over to the dessert table and help yourself
to apple cobbler, fresh berries and cream, and bread pudding with
rum sauce. There's a full bar.

☻ Liberty Cafe at the Blue Castle Pharmacy. 1700 S. Las Vegas Blvd.
☎ 702/383-0101. Reservations not accepted. Nothing over $6.50. Cash only.
24 hours. DINER.

You can go to any number of retro soda fountain replicas (Johnny
Rockets and so on) and theme restaurants that pretend to be cheap
diners, but why bother when the decidedly unflashy real thing is just
past the end of the Strip? The soda fountain/lunch counter at the
Blue Castle Pharmacy was Las Vegas's first 24-hour restaurant, and
it has been going strong for 60 years. Plunk down at the counter,
and watch the cooks go nuts trying to keep up with the orders. The
menu is basic comfort food: standard grill items (meat loaf, ground
round steak, chops), fluffy cream pies, and classic breakfasts served
"anytime"—try the biscuits and cream gravy at 3am. They also serve
gyros and the like. But the best bet is a $1/3$-pound burger and "thick
creamy shake," both the way they were meant to be and about as
good as they get. At around $5, this is half what you would pay for
a comparable meal at the Hard Rock Cafe. And as waitress Beverly
says, "This is really real." Places like this are a vanishing species—
it's worth the short walk from the Stratosphere.

Rincon Criollo. 1145 Las Vegas Blvd. So. **☎ 702/388-1906.** Reservations not
accepted. Main courses $6.50–$9.95, paella (for 3) $20. AE, DISC, MC, V.
CUBAN.

Located beyond the wedding chapels on Las Vegas Boulevard,
Rincon Criollo has all the right details for a good, cheap ethnic joint:
full of locals and empty of frills. It's not the best Cuban food ever,

🏃 Family-Friendly Dining

Buffets *(see p. 100)*   Cheap meals for the whole family. The kids can choose what they like, and there are sometimes make-your-own sundae machines.

DIVE! *(see p. 79)*   Housed in a submarine and featuring a zany high-tech show every hour projected on a video wall, this is the most fun family-oriented spot of all.

Hard Rock Cafe *(see p. 86)*   Kids also adore this restaurant, which throbs with excitement and is filled with rock memorabilia.

Hippo and the Wild Bunch *(see p. 87)*   A cartoonlike decor and wild party atmosphere (sometimes balloon artists are on hand making hats and animals for diners) makes this a favorite with kids. Adults will be thrilled with the high food quality.

Planet Hollywood *(see p. 75)*   This popular chain houses a veritable museum of movie memorabilia, and the action on numerous video monitors keeps kids from getting bored.

---

but it gets the job done. The main courses (featuring Cuban pork and chicken specialties) are hit and miss; try the marinated pork leg or, better still, ask your server for a recommendation. Paella is offered, but only for parties of three or more (and starts at $20). The side-course *chorizo* (a spicy sausage) is excellent, and the Cuban sandwich (roast pork, ham, and cheese on bread, which is then pressed and flattened out) is huge and tasty. For only $3.50, the latter makes a fine change of pace meal.

6 Convention Center/Paradise Road/ Sahara Avenue

VERY EXPENSIVE

Bistro Le Montrachet. Las Vegas Hilton, 3000 Paradise Rd. ☎ **702/ 732-5111.** Reservations suggested. Main courses $23–$46. AE, CB, DC, DISC, JCB, MC, V. Wed–Mon 6–10:30pm. FRENCH.

Dishes are exquisitely presented and prepared at this ultraelegant French restaurant. You might begin with chilled duck foie gras served on toast points. Also noteworthy are creamy lobster bisque and the salad "Le Montrachet," a refreshing mélange of Belgian endive, watercress, julienned beets, and enoki mushrooms in a Gorgonzola/walnut oil dressing. Entree choices range from roasted breast of Muscovy duck (served with white and black beans and currants in a crème de cassis sauce) to broiled live Maine lobster removed from the shell and served atop herbed Moroccan couscous with crab dressing and drawn butter. Among desserts, we're partial to the rich crème brûlée complemented by seasonal fruits, berries, and petits fours. The restaurant's wine cellar stocks more than 400 wines from vineyards spanning the globe.

Pegasus. Alexis Park Resort, 375 E. Harmon Ave., between Koval Lane and Paradise Rd. ☎ **702/796-3300.** Reservations recommended. Main courses $13.50–$39. AE, DC, MC, V. Nightly 6–11pm. CONTINENTAL.

This low-key luxury resort attracts many visiting celebrities and Strip headliners, and its premier restaurant is a fitting venue for such an upscale clientele. Its splashing fountains and mist of diffused lighting playing on etched mirrors make us feel like we're dining in an underwater kingdom.

Flambé dishes are featured, and sorbets are served between courses. You might begin with a quail egg and mandarin orange salad tossed with sweet mustard dressing. Among the soups, a splendid choice is the velvety cognac-laced lobster bisque. And fresh-shucked oysters Rockefeller here elevate this dish to its delicate apogee. The featured entree is Maine lobster sautéed with black truffles in a Madeira/bordelaise sauce; crowned with almond meringue baked to a golden brown, it is dramatically presented in a flaming veil of fire. A daily game special is offered each evening— perhaps ostrich with fresh seared foie gras. Desserts include bananas Foster and cherries jubilee along with pastries and cakes from the cart. There's an extensive wine list (mostly French and Californian) with choices in varying price ranges.

EXPENSIVE

✪ **Lawry's The Prime Rib.** 4043 Howard Hughes Pkwy. at Flamingo (between Paradise and Koval). ☎ **702/893-2223.** Reservations recommended. Main courses $18.95–$29.95. AE, DC, DISC, JCB, MC, V. Sun–Thurs 5–10pm, Fri–Sat 5–11pm. STEAK/SEAFOOD.

If you love prime rib, come here, because Lawry's does only one thing, and it does it better than anyone else. Lawry's first opened in Los Angeles in 1938 and still remains an always packed tradition. Over the years, it has added three branches, the most recent landing in Las Vegas at the beginning of 1997. Yes, you can get prime rib all over town for under $5. But that's tuna fish sandwiches to Lawry's caviar (if one might mix food metaphors).

Eating at Lawry's is a ceremony, with all the parts played the same for the last 60 years. Waitresses in brown and white English maid

Dining East of the Strip

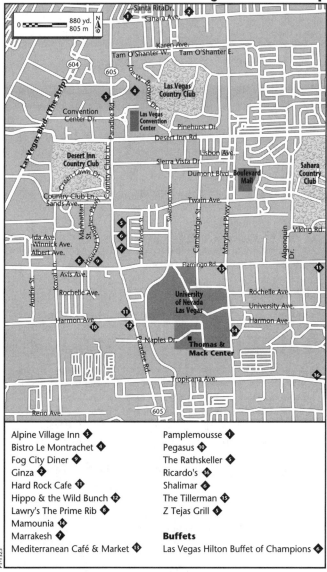

Alpine Village Inn **3**
Bistro Le Montrachet **4**
Fog City Diner **9**
Ginza **2**
Hard Rock Cafe **11**
Hippo & the Wild Bunch **12**
Lawry's The Prime Rib **8**
Mamounia **14**
Marrakesh **7**
Mediterranean Café & Market **13**

Pamplemousse **1**
Pegasus **10**
The Rathskeller **5**
Ricardo's **16**
Shalimar **6**
The Tillerman **15**
Z Tejas Grill **5**

Buffets
Las Vegas Hilton Buffet of Champions **6**

uniforms come up and take your order. For side dishes, that is. The real decision—what cut of rib (or fresh fish) you are going to have—comes later. Anyway, you tell the waitress what side dishes you might want (sublime creamed spinach, baked potato) for an extra price. Later, she returns with a spinning salad bowl (think salad preparation as Busby Berkeley musical number). The bowl, resting on crushed ice, spins as she pours Lawry's special dressing in a stream from high over her head. Tomatoes garnish. Applause follows. Eventually, giant metal carving carts (designed after the original ones) come to your table, bearing the meat. You name your cut (the regular Lawry's, the extra large Diamond Jim Brady—only for serious carnivores, the wimpy thin English cut), rare, medium, well. It comes with terrific Yorkshire pudding (nicely browned and not soggy) and some creamed horseradish that is combined with fluffy whipped cream, simultaneously sweet and tart. You eat.

And it's so good. This will be the best prime rib you will ever have. Flavorful, tender, perfectly cooked, lightly seasoned; it's enough to make a meat eater swoon with ecstasy. It just has to be tasted to be believed. You can finish off with a rich dessert (English trifle is highly recommended), but it almost seems pointless.

Pamplemousse. 400 E. Sahara Ave., between Santa Paula and Santa Rita drives, just east of Paradise Rd. ☎ **702/733-2066.** Reservations essential. Main courses $17.50–$24.50. AE, CB, DC, DISC, MC, V. Two seatings nightly at 6–6:30pm and 9–9:30pm. FRENCH.

Evoking a cozy French countryside inn, Pamplemousse is a catacomb of low-ceilinged rooms and intimate dining nooks with rough-hewn beams. It's all very charming and un-Vegasy. There's additional seating in a small garden sheltered by a striped tent. The restaurant's name, which means grapefruit, was suggested by the late singer Bobby Darin, one of the many celebrity pals of owner Georges La Forge.

The menu, which changes nightly, is recited by your waiter. The meal always begins with a large complimentary basket of crudités, a big bowl of olives, and a basket of hard-boiled eggs (a nice country touch). From there, you might proceed to an appetizer of lightly floured bay scallops sautéed in buttery grapefruit sauce, followed by an entree of crispy duck breast and banana in a sauce of orange honey, dark rum, and crème de banane. Filet mignon, New York steak, and rack of lamb are always featured. For dessert, perhaps there'll be homemade dark chocolate ice cream with pralines in a sabayon sauce. An extensive, well-rounded wine list complements the menu.

MODERATE

Alpine Village Inn. 3003 Paradise Rd., between Riviera Blvd. and Convention Center Dr. ☎ **702/734-6888.** Reservations recommended. Fixed-price dinners $9.95–$19.50; children's portions (under 12 only) about half price. AE, CB, DC, DISC, MC, V. Sun–Thurs 5–10pm, Fri–Sat 5–11pm. SWISS/GERMAN.

A Las Vegas tradition since 1950, this extremely popular family restaurant doesn't subscribe to the less-is-more theory of interior design. Walls are painted with murals of snowy Alpine scenery, an effect echoed by snow-covered chalet roofing, twinkling Christmas tree lights, and miniature ski lifts on cables strung across the ceiling. There are Swiss and Austrian cowbells, mounted deer heads, and window boxes filled with geraniums. And the very efficient wait staff is in Tyrolean costume.

Dinner is a multicourse feast beginning with a big pewter bowl of crudités served with herbed cottage cheese dip. A steaming bowl of savory Bavarian chicken soup is followed by a salad, and a basket of fresh-baked breads includes scrumptious hot cinnamon rolls. For your entree, try the roast duckling with sausage stuffing served over wild and brown rice (it comes with orange and cherry sauces) or roast tender chicken with chestnut stuffing. These are accompanied by an array of vegetables and choice of crisp potato pancakes, a baked potato, or Swiss *Rösti* potatoes (shredded potato mixed with onion, bacon, eggs, and spices, fried in a pancake, and garnished with grated Parmesan). If you'd like more than one of the above selections, the waiters generally comply. The finale: homemade apple or peach strudel, served warm (topped with vanilla ice cream if you so desire). Tea or coffee is included. The wine list offers wines by the glass and a large selection of beers, 19 varieties of schnapps, and exotic cocktails.

Ginza. 1000 E. Sahara Ave., between State St. and Maryland Pkwy. ☎ **702/732-3080.** Reservations for large parties only. Main courses $12.55–$17.50. AE, MC, V. Tues–Sun 5pm–1am. JAPANESE.

For almost 2 decades, this charming little restaurant has attracted a devoted clientele of local Japanese and Japanese food aficionados.

You might begin with a shared appetizer of tempura shrimp and vegetables. Entrees—such as beef, chicken, or salmon sprinkled with sesame seeds in a thick teriyaki sauce—come with soup (miso or egg flower), salad, and green tea. Sushi is a highlight, and there are about 30 à la carte selections from which to choose. Be sure to try an appetizer or entree portion of Ginza's unique Vegas rolls—salmon, tuna, yellowtail, and avocado rolled with seaweed in sesame-studded rice and quickly deep-fried so the sesame seeds form a

Have You Heard the One About the Belly Dancer?

If you have never tried Moroccan food, you should. Not only are you in for some new taste treats, but the action-packed presentation and gluttonous portions are very appropriate to Vegas. Vegas has two notable Moroccan establishments. One is **Marrakesh,** 3900 Paradise Rd., at Howard Hughes Drive (☎ 702/737-5611), where a six-course meal will cost you $23.95 per person (reservations recommended; AE, DISC, DC, MC, V accepted; open Monday to Sunday 5:30 to 11pm). The other is **Mamounia,** 4632 S. Maryland Pkwy., between Harmon and Tropicana avenues (☎ 702/597-0092), where a Moroccan feast will set you back $22.95 per person (reservations recommended; AE, DISC, MC, V accepted; open Monday to Sunday 5pm to 11pm).

Both rooms are covered, floor to ceiling, with Moroccan (or Moroccan-style) rugs, furnished with low tables made of intricately inlaid wood (from the town of Essaouria). There is some simple tile work on the walls at Marrakech. It all adds up to that Arabian nights den of thieves feel. Diners sit on cushions on the floor or on very low cushioned benches.

Oh, and you eat with your fingers. Yep, that's part of the fun. A waiter comes out and pours water into a brass bowl so you can wash your hands and passes out huge towels for your lap. You then start a multicourse feast, beginning with a trio of cold salads: marinated carrots, eggplant, and tomato, and cucumber. Use the

crunchy crust. It's served with lemon soy sauce. Also delicious are seaweed-wrapped California rolls. The fish is extremely fresh, and everything here is made from scratch. A bottle of sake is recommended. For dessert there's lemon sherbet or ginger and green tea ice creams.

MODERATE

Hard Rock Cafe. 4475 Paradise Rd., at Harmon Ave. ☎ **702/733-8400.** Reservations not accepted. Main courses $8.95–$13.95; burgers and sandwiches $5.50–7.95. AE, DC, MC, V. Sun–Thurs 11am–11:30pm, Fri–Sat 11am–midnight. AMERICAN.

The original Hard Rock Cafe opened in London as a meeting place for American expatriates and homesick exchange students dying for a good burger. Now Hard Rocks are everywhere. But this is the only Hard Rock (so far) attached to a hotel and a truly extraordinary casino, so let's cut this branch some slack. The menu offers some good bread supplied from a big basket to scoop it up. The salads are relatively simple and supremely tasty. This is followed by shrimp in a garlic sauce that seems more Italian than Moroccan (peculiarly, both restaurants feature this out-of-place item). But if you like garlic and shrimp, you won't complain too much. Next is *b'stilla,* a truly amazing dish if done right. Layers of filo are interspersed with chicken, eggs, and nuts; the whole thing is topped by powdered sugar and cinnamon. The uninitiated raise their eyebrows at it, while their more informed companions dig in. The final course is some kind of fowl (chicken or Cornish game hen), usually in a wonderful lemon and olive sauce. You finish up with some sweet mint tea, poured with great ceremony. Then the belly dancer comes out to dazzle you with her gravity defying shimmy skills, get the crowd going in a conga line (or, unfortunately, the Macarena), and accept a tip or two.

This experience is roughly the same at the two restaurants, but the food at Marrakech is considerably better. However, they found that the b'stilla was too strange for many patrons, so they turned it into a dessert with a fruit filling; they will make it with chicken if you ask when ordering; trust us and do. In its favor, the Mamounia offers à la carte items (Marrakech is considering this), so you can try other Moroccan specialties such as tajines, which are delicious stews cooked in clay pots.

salads in addition to the burgers. An inexpensive children's menu is a plus for families. Don't be frightened by the line outside—it's usually not for the restaurant but the on-premises Hard Rock merchandise store. The Hard Rock Hotel and Casino is next door (see chapter 4).

✪ **Hippo and the Wild Bunch.** 4503 Paradise Rd., at Harmon Ave., just across from the Hard Rock Hotel. ☎ **702/731-5446.** Main courses $5.95–$13.95; children's menu $1.75–$2.95. AC, CB, DC, DISC, MC, V. Sun–Thurs 11am–3am, Fri–Sat 11am–5am. AMERICAN.

Georges La Forge, owner of the cozily romantic Pamplemousse (see description above), surprised everyone when he opened this wildly whimsical restaurant in 1995. Its kooky-cluttery interior includes cartoonlike animal sculptures (such as a hippo in a tree house), a tangle of vines strung overhead, and walls painted with bright jungle foliage. There are balloons tied to many chairs, and often a balloon artist is on the scene creating twisty animals and hats for guests. There are usually several exuberant parties going on (only some of them children's parties), and the chaotic ambience is exacerbated by loud rock music, a wait staff on roller skates, a bustling exhibition kitchen, and TV monitors over the bar airing sporting events. Tuesday to Sunday from 8pm to 3am, a DJ plays music for dancing.

Hippo's "party-on" atmosphere notwithstanding, the food is superb. Come at lunch to enjoy it without all the hoopla; at dinner, weather permitting, you might sit out on the quieter, tree-bordered patio. Noteworthy items on La Forge's eclectic menu include delicious potstickers with chili oil/soy dipping sauce, a classic salad Niçoise, pizzas, and spicy southwestern ravioli in a red pepper sauce topped with diced vegetables. Burgers here are as good as burgers get, charcoal grilled and served on fresh-baked buns (ask for garlic mashed potatoes instead of fries). There's a dynamite tiramisu for dessert, and beverages, including a full bar, range from fresh-squeezed juices to coffee specialties.

✪ **Shalimar.** 3900 S. Paradise Rd. (in the Citibank Plaza). ☎ **702/796-0302.** Reservations suggested. Lunch buffet $6.95; dinner main courses $10.50–$15.95. AE, DISC, MC, V. Mon–Fri 11:30am–2:30pm, 5:30–10:30pm; Sat–Sun 5:30–10:30pm. INDIAN.

In a town full of buffet deals, it's hard to get excited about another one; but on the other hand, all those other buffet deals offer pretty much the identical food: carving stations, various cafeteria hot dishes, and so forth. Here at Shalimar, a lunch buffet means about two dozen different North Indian–style dishes. All for about $7. It's not as colorful or huge (in fact, it's just a table covered with steam trays) as those buffets up the street, but it is far more interesting and different. It's also a great deal and one of the first places to run to if you are sick of Strip food. Just ask the locals who vote it their favorite ethnic restaurant in the *Las Vegas Review Journal's* annual poll.

The buffet usually includes *tandoori* (chicken marinated in spiced yogurt cooked in a clay oven), *marsala* (tandoori in a curry sauce), *naan* (the flat Indian bread), and various vegetable dishes. (Vegetarians will find plenty to eat here—they offer special veggie dishes daily.) One standout at a recent visit was the *Bengan Bharta* (eggplant diced fine and cooked with onions, tomatoes, and spices). There was also a yellow squash curry that was outrageously good. The tandoori chicken was perfect, tender, and moist. (Tandoori, by the way, is a very low-fat way of preparing chicken.) In the evening, a full Indian menu, with *vindaloo* (an especially hot curry where the meat is marinated in vinegar), flavored naans (try the garlic or onion), and other Indian specialties are offered à la carte. They will spice to order: mild, medium, hot, or very hot. If you make a mistake, you can always order *raita* (yogurt mixed with mild spices and cucumber); it cools your mouth nicely.

Z Tejas Grill. 3824 Paradise Road, between Twain Ave. and Corporate Dr. ☎ **702/732-1660.** Reservations recommended. Main courses $7.25–$ll.95 at lunch, $9.75–$16.95 at dinner. AE, CB, DC, DISC, JCB, MC, V. Daily 11am–11pm. TEX-MEX.

This Austin, Texas–based restaurant's rather odd name came about because its original chef, a Frenchman, kept referring to it as "zee" Tejas Grill.

A unique, and very tasty, appetizer here is the Navajo roll—crisp-fried Mexican cheeses, seasoned fresh lump crabmeat, and vegetables wrapped in herb bread and topped with fried spinach and cornmeal crumbs. Follow it up with spicy grilled Jamaican jerk chicken, nuanced with lime and served with peanut sauce and rum-spiked coconut-banana ketchup; it comes with two side dishes—perhaps roasted garlic/skin-on mashed potatoes and mixed vegetables. Swig down a few of the Grill's excellent made-from-scratch margaritas with your meal, but do leave room for some graham cracker–crusted praline cheesecake smothered with pecans.

INEXPENSIVE

The Rathskellar. 3003 Paradise Rd., between Riviera Blvd. and Convention Center Dr. ☎ **702/734-6888.** Reservations recommended. Burgers and sandwiches $4.25–$7.50, main courses $8.75–$11.95. AE, CB, DC, DISC, MC, V. Sun–Thurs 5–10pm, Fri–Sat 5–11pm. GERMAN/AMERICAN.

The Rathskellar is a rollicking downstairs adjunct to the Alpine Village Inn (see above), a cozy beer hall with red-and-white checkered tablecloths and a floor strewn with peanut shells (there are bowls of peanuts on every table). A pianist and singer entertain nightly, and everyone sings along. Choices here include a sauerbraten sandwich on pumpernickel rye served with German potato salad; a hot, open-faced turkey sandwich served with mashed potatoes, cranberry sauce, and gravy (salad bar included); barbecued pork ribs with baked beans; half-pound burgers; and beer-battered deep-fried buffalo wings with french fries. For dessert, there's apple or peach strudel à la mode. An extensive children's menu makes this a popular choice for family dining.

7 East Las Vegas/Flamingo Road

VERY EXPENSIVE

✪ **The Tillerman.** 2245 E. Flamingo Rd., at Channel 10 Dr. (just west of Eastern Ave.). ☎ **702/731-4036.** Reservations not accepted. Main courses $15.95–$36.95. AE, CB, DC, DISC, MC, V. Nightly 5–11pm, bar/lounge until midnight. STEAK/SEAFOOD.

Ask any local for a list of favorite restaurants, and you can be sure the Tillerman in east Las Vegas will be on it. Its verdant, plant-filled interior is under a lofty, beamed cathedral ceiling with retractable skylights. Candlelit dining areas offer seating amid a grove of ficus trees, and the woodsy ambience is furthered by exquisite oak paneling and tree-trunk pillars. A circular stained-glass window provides a lovely focal point. There's additional seating on the mezzanine level, where diners enjoy treetop views. All the top Strip performers are regular Tillerman customers.

Your meal here begins with a relish tray and a basket of delicious, oven-fresh breads. Also complimentary is a Lazy Susan salad bar served at your table with a choice of homemade dressings, including a memorable chunky blue cheese. Portions are immense, so appetizers are really not necessary, but then again, they're too good to pass up. Especially notable: ultrafresh, plump red medallions of yellowfin tuna blackened and served almost rare in spicy mustard sauce. Meat entrees include prime center-cut New York strip steak, fork-tender filet mignon, and a center-cut veal chop. And there are at least a dozen fresh seafood specials each night; we've had a memorable piece of snowy white halibut, charcoal-broiled and brushed with pecan pesto. Entrees come with a white and wild rice mixture tossed with slivered almonds and chives and fresh vegetables. Homemade desserts, such as Bavarian cream with strawberries and bananas, change nightly. The wine list highlights California selections.

Note: Since the Tillerman doesn't take reservations, arrive early to avoid waiting.

MODERATE

✪ **Fog City Diner.** 325 Hughes Center Dr., off Flamingo Rd. at Howard Hughes Pkwy. (between Koval Lane and Paradise Rd.). ☎ **702/737-0200.** Reservations recommended. Main courses $6.50–$13.95. AE, CB, DC, DISC, MC, V. Sun–Thurs 11:30am–10pm, Fri–Sat 11:30am–11pm. AMERICAN.

San Francisco transplant, the Fog City Diner (it was featured in a Visa commercial for years) is one of the better dining choices in Las Vegas. It's not fancy food, per se—meat loaf, clam chowder, and so forth—but it's all prepared with impeccable taste with new, clever gourmand twists on familiar Blue Plate Specials. In other words, this is not your mother's meat loaf. (No offense to your mother.) Here, it comes blackened and with a tomato chutney gravy that is out of this world. The menu changes seasonally, but with a constant emphasis on extremely fresh fish. They are very proud of said fish, which is trucked in every day from Los Angeles; they claim it is the freshest and most marvelously prepared of anywhere in Las Vegas. Even antifish folk might find their minds changed by the aforementioned clam chowder and the Pacific Northwest oysters. A section on the menu has a variety of small dishes; they call it "American dim sum," a variety of portions for grazing. These might include Mu-Shu pork burritos (which are more Mu-Shu than burrito—that's just the shape) or seared butter soft ahi tuna with tomato chow chow. Making a meal by grazing on a selection of these is worth considering. Entrees are often accompanied by hearty portions of garlic mashed potatoes. They also carry La Brea Bakery bread (the much famed Los Angeles bakery), and though it's not cheap, the garlic/leek/basil bread is hard to pass up. For dessert, they will strongly urge you to try the moist chocolate chile tart in orange rind sauce, topped with a scoop of Häagen-Dazs coffee ice cream. Yes, chile and chocolate. It sounds extremely weird, but our waiter correctly described the spice of the chile as something that simply prickles the back of your throat as you swallow a bite. It's unusual and well worth trying.

The restaurant itself is part diner, part train car, with leather booths and a post-deco/Orient Express interior. It's more casual than anything else. You can also eat at the even more informal onyx oyster bar facing the open kitchen. Don't miss the jokes scattered about (signs saying "no crybabies" or referring to "those silly clove cigarettes").

Ricardo's. 2380 Tropicana Ave., at Eastern Ave. (northwest corner). ☎ **702/ 798-4515.** Reservations recommended. Main courses $7.50–$12.95; lunch buffet $6.95; children's plates $2.95–$3.95, including milk or soft drink with complimentary refills. AE, CB, DC, DISC, MC, V. Mon–Thurs 11am–10pm, Fri–Sat 11am–11pm, Sun 11am–10pm. MEXICAN.

This hacienda-style restaurant is a great favorite with locals. Start off with an appetizer of deep-fried battered chicken wings served with melted cheddar (ask for jalapeños if you like your cheese sauce hotter). Nachos smothered with cheese and guacamole are also very good here. For an entree, you can't go wrong with chicken, beef, or pork fajitas served sizzling on a hot skillet atop sautéed onions, mushrooms, and peppers; they come with rice and beans, tortillas, a selection of salsas, guacamole, and tomato wedges with cilantro.

All the usual taco/enchilada/tamale combinations are also listed. A delicious dessert is *helado* Las Vegas: ice cream rolled in corn flakes and cinnamon, deep fried, and served with honey and whipped cream. Be sure to order a pitcher of Ricardo's great margaritas. The same menu is available all day, but a buffet is offered at lunch. The kids' menu, on a place mat with games and puzzles, features both Mexican and American fare.

INEXPENSIVE

✪ **Mediterranean Café and Market.** 4147 S. Maryland Pkwy., at Flamingo Rd., in the Tiffany Square strip mall. ☎ **702/731-6030.** Main courses $3.99–$8.49 (all sandwiches under $5). AE, MC, DISC, V. Daily 8am–10pm. MEDITERRANEAN.

It is an immeasurable thrill to find this totally authentic, mom-and-pop Middle Eastern restaurant in Las Vegas, where high-quality ethnic eateries are scarce.

Everything here is homemade and delicious. You might order up a gyro (slivers of rotisseried beef and lamb enfolded into a pita with lettuce and tomato). Other good choices are a phyllo pie layered with spinach and feta cheese, served with hummus; skewers of grilled chicken and vegetable kabobs with lavash bread and hummus; and a combination platter of hummus, tabouli, stuffed grape leaves, and falafel. All entrees come with pita bread and salad. Try a side order of *bourrani* (creamy yogurt dip mixed with steamed spinach, sautéed garlic, and slivered almonds). Finish up with baklava and rich Turkish coffee. Wine and beer are available. You can also come by in the morning for Middle Eastern breakfasts. A Mediterranean market adjoins.

8 West Las Vegas

EXPENSIVE

The Garlic Cafe. 3650 S. Decatur Blvd., at Spring Mountain Rd. ☎ **702/221-0266.** Reservations recommended. Main courses $9.25–$27.95. AE, DC, MC, V. Daily 5–10pm. INTERNATIONAL.

If you don't like garlic, there is no reason to read further. If you do like garlic, just start heading toward the Garlic Cafe right now. You can read this on the way. Garlic is the food of the gods, and Warren, the owner/chef/creator of this cafe understands that. Unlike similar ventures (the Stinking Rose in San Francisco, for example), this is a more international menu. Warren found that garlic was a unifying theme around the world, so here are dishes from Thailand, Jamaica, Japan, Hungary, and so on. You can decide on the level of garlic in your dish. Their garlic scale usually runs from 1 to 5 (each level is one entire head of garlic, so "5" equals five whole heads), but they will go as high as you want. The current record holder is up to 60. The waiters will help you decide what level is best for any given dish; certain ones (like the duck) would get overwhelmed by too much of our favorite seasoning.

Everyone gets a roast *skordalia* (partly pureed garlic) and bagel chip appetizer, but you can order still others; the choices differ nightly but will always include a perfectly roasted head of garlic. The entree portions are huge (which makes up for the somewhat high prices), and they are very nicely presented. Not to mention imaginatively—okay, incredibly eccentrically—named. Like the Salmon in Garfunkel Crust (a fillet of salmon in a garlic-basil cracker crust with béarnaise sauce) or Grandpa Murray in a Hurry "Don't Worry!" Chicken Curry. If you are nice, maybe they will let you take the menu home so you don't have to try to remember what you ate. Finish it off with some garlic ice cream. It's not as weird as it sounds, a very good vanilla with just a hint of garlic that somehow works in a sweet and sour kind of way. The real fun comes with the chocolate-covered (roasted) garlic clove.

The food is not that memorable, but it is competently made and the garlic works as well as you would like. Plus, it's all just a lot of fun, as is imagining the poor soul next to you later at the black-jack tables. No, they don't hand out Breath Assure when you leave. Strangely enough, this restaurant has not yet caught on too much with the tourists, despite having a theme.

MODERATE

Cathy House. 5300 W. Spring Mountain Rd. (in Spring Valley). ☎ **702/876-3838.** Reservations recommended. Main Courses $6.75–$13.75. AE, MC, V. Daily 11am–10:30pm. CHINESE.

Las Vegas actually has a Chinatown—a very large strip mall (naturally) on Spring Mountain Road near Wynn. There are several Asian restaurants there, including the average Plum Tree Inn, which serves dim sum. But ask locals who look like they know, and they will send you instead farther up Spring Mountain Road to the Cathy House (on the opposite side of the street). This only looks far from the Strip on a map; it's really about a 7-minute drive from Treasure Island. Ordering dim sum, if you haven't experienced it, is sort of like being at a Chinese sushi bar, in that you order many individual, tasty little dishes. Of course, dim sum itself is nothing like sushi. Rather, it's a range of potstickers, pan-fried dumplings, *baos* (soft, doughy buns filled with meat like barbecued pork), translucent rice noodles wrapped around shrimp, sticky rice in lotus leaves, and so forth.

Some of it's steamed, some is fried—for that extra good grease! You can make your own dipping sauce by combining soy sauce, vinegar, and hot pepper oil. The wait staff pushes steam carts filled with little dishes; point, and they will attempt to tell you what each one is. Each dish ranges from approximately $1 to $3; each server makes a note of what you just received, and the total is tallied at the end. (For some reason, it almost always works out to about $9 a person.) Dim sum is usually available only until midafternoon.

The standout at the Cathy House was a vegetable bao that included Chinese glass noodles. Lightly browned and not overly doughy like many baos, it was slightly sweet and utterly delicious. The shrimp wrapped in rice noodles were big and plump, while anything that was fried was so good we decided to ignore our arteries for awhile. Cathy House (which features quite a good view through the windows on one side) also has a full dinner menu, which includes the strawberry chicken invented by Chin's; it's considerably cheaper here.

Viva Mercados. 6182 W. Flamingo, at Jones. ☎ **702/871-8826.** Main courses $7.95–$16.95. AE, DISC, V, MC. Sun–Thurs 11am–10pm, Fri–Sat 11am–11pm. MEXICAN.

Ask any local about Mexican food in Vegas, and almost certainly he or she will point to Viva Mercados as the best in town. That recommendation, plus the restaurant's health-conscious attitude toward food preparation, makes this worth the roughly 10-minute drive from the Strip.

Given all those warnings lately about Mexican food and its heart attack–inducing properties, Viva Mercados' approach to food is nothing to be sniffed at. No dish is prepared with or cooked in any kind of animal fat. Nope, the lard so dear to Mexican cooking is not found here. The oil used is an artery-friendly canola. Additionally, this makes the place particularly appealing to vegetarians, who will also be pleased by the regular veggie specials. Everything is quite fresh, and they do particularly amazing things with seafood. Try the Maresco Vallarta, which is orange roughy, shrimp, and scallops cooked in a coconut tomato sauce, with capers and olives. They have all sorts of noteworthy shrimp dishes and 11 different salsas, ranked 1 to 10 for degree of spice. (Ask for advice, first.) The staff is friendly (try to chat with owner Bobby Mercado) and the portions hearty.

✪ **Ware's T Bones Texas Style Bar-B-Que.** 2740 N. Green Pkwy., at Sunset (inside Swizzle Stick Lounge). ☎ **702/435-5937.** Sandwiches $3.95–$5.25. Main courses $9.25–$14.95. Cash only. Daily 9am–10pm. BARBECUE.

William Ware hails from Alabama but went to culinary school in New York City. He opened up the Hard Rock Cafe in Los Angeles but has since gone on to operate his own restaurants. Las Vegas was incredibly lucky the day he decided to leave L.A. and come here. His first outlet was so popular he recently opened a second. Neither is near anything that you might call a beaten path, though the Flamingo Road restaurant (the complete address is at the end of this review) is virtually in the lap of **Sam's Town.** Guests staying there (and those with a car) should come here immediately.

Ware uses his own recipe for salad dressings and for the barbecue sauce, which is more sweet than hot (which may be a drawback for those who figure it's not barbecue unless you've seared your mouth). It's a light, tasty sauce that puts the heavy, gloppy stuff they serve in chains (and throughout most Vegas locales) to shame. And what it is covering is superb. The meat is blackened but tender perfection. Pick up a pork or beef rib and watch the meat slide right off. The brisket is buttery soft—you won't need a knife to cut it, as it falls apart under your fork.

Just about everything is good (including the sides of corn muffins and slaw), but be sure to check out the barbecue chicken salad. It's available as an entree, but rather than waste the stomach space (so you can leave room for those pork ribs), sweetly ask if you can have a small serving as an appetizer. Not only is the chicken dynamite, but it's covered with Ware's own honey mustard dressing (an original tart/sweet creation totally unlike anything else you've had with that name) and tossed with apples and walnuts. It will make your mouth sing. Note also the "Feast for Two" special: For $24.95, you get two half chickens, three beef ribs, six pork ribs, half a pound of brisket, a pint of slaw, a pint of beans, and two corn muffins. This meal could easily feed three rather than two. Ware's also serves hearty country breakfasts until 4pm.

Ware's second outlet is at 4734 E. Flamingo Rd., at Mountain Vista and Boulder Highway (in Albertson's Shopping Center) (☎ 702/435-5937).

INEXPENSIVE

✪ **Enigma Cafe.** 918¹/₂ S. Fourth St., at Charleston. ☎ **702-386-0999.** No items over $6. Cash only. Mon 7am–3pm, Tues–Fri 7am–midnight, Sat–Sun 9am–midnight. CALIFORNIA/MEDITERRANEAN.

Finding the Enigma Cafe is almost as good as finding a breeze on a really hot Vegas day. Or maybe it's more like suddenly finding yourself transported out of Vegas and into California. Owners Julie and Len have taken two 1930s-era cottages and turned them into a cafe/coffeehouse/art space that, during the day, is a restful, garden patio setting (orders are taken inside one house; inside the other is the art gallery, with more seating) with folk and classical music playing. At night the space blooms with candles, live music, and poetry readings.

The menu is a huge relief: healthful, interesting sandwiches ("Mossy Melt" is tuna salad "revived up with" horseradish and havarti, toasted open face) and familiar ones (ham and Swiss, but well garnished), salads (again with a range from the ordinary green variety to "Dr. Bombay's" curried chicken breast with veggies) to hummus burritos and the "Tippy Elvis Supreme" (named after a local polka band/art project), which is peanut butter and bananas (what else?). You can get a side platter of hummus, feta cheese, veggies, and pita, or have a thick fruit smoothie. And that doesn't even begin to cover their wide range of coffee drinks. Best of all, it's cheap. Considering the soothing affect it has on your mind, spirit, wallet, and stomach, Enigma is like a vacation from your vacation. This is actually very close to both the Strip and Downtown, particularly the latter, where good, healthful food is hard to find.

9 Downtown

VERY EXPENSIVE

Andre's. 401 S. 6th St., at Lewis Ave., a few blocks south of Fremont St. ☎ **702/385-5016.** Reservations required. Main courses $19.75–$33. AE, CB, DC, MC, V. Nightly from 6pm; closing hours vary. FRENCH.

Owner-chef Andre Rochat has created a rustic country-French setting in a converted 1930s house in Downtown Las Vegas. In addition to a catacomb of cozy interior rooms, there's a lovely, ivy-walled garden patio under the shade of a mulberry tree. This is a major celebrity haunt where you're likely to see Strip headliners. One night, Tom Hanks, Steven Spielberg, and James Spader were all spotted joining some pals for a bachelor party.

The menu changes seasonally. On a recent visit, appetizers included jumbo sea scallops rolled in a crunchy macadamia nut crust with citrus beurre blanc and red beet coulis. And among the entrees, a fan of pink, juicy slices of sautéed duck came with a confit of port wine and onions. A medley of vegetables—perhaps pommes lyonnaise, asparagus, broccoli hollandaise, and baby carrots—accompanies each entree, and sorbets are served between courses. For dessert, there are Andre's classic fruit tarts: flaky butter crusts layered with Grand Marnier custard and topped with fresh,

Dining Downtown

Andre's
Binion's Horshoe
 Coffee Shop
Carson Street Café
Hugo's Cellar
Limerick's

Buffets
Golden Nugget
 Buffet
Lady Luck Banquet
 Buffet
Main Street Station
 Garden Court
Sam Boyd's Fremont
 Paradise Buffet

plump berries. An extensive wine list (more than 900 labels) is international in scope and includes many rare vintages; consult the sommelier.

Hugo's Cellar. Four Queen's, 202 Fremont St., at Casino Center Blvd. ☎ **702/385-4011.** Reservations required. Main courses $24–$35. AE, DC, DISC, MC, V. Nightly 5:30–10:30pm. INTERNATIONAL.

Hugo's Cellar is indeed in a cellar, or at least below street level in the Four Queen's Hotel. No, they aren't ashamed of it—quite the opposite. This is their gourmet restaurant, and it's highly regarded by the locals. You pass through a small, dark (romantic, not creepy) bar with a few tables and a friendly bartender, perfect for a little quiet tête-à-tête between hands at the poker tables. Each female guest is given a red rose when she enters the restaurant—the beginning of a series of nice touches. The restaurant space proper is dimly lit, lined with dark wood and brick. It's fairly intimate, but if you really want to be cozy, ask for one of the curtained booths against the wall.

The meal is full of ceremony, perfectly delivered by a well-trained and cordial wait staff. Salads, included in the price, are prepared at your table, from a cart full of choices. (In Vegas style, though, most of said choices are on the calorie-intensive side.) A tiny cup with palate-cleansing sorbet prepares you for the main course. Unfortunately, despite the high regard, the main courses are not all that novel (various cuts of meat, seafood, chicken prepared different ways) and can be disappointing. Promising choices include the Chicken "Hugo" (with basil and pine nuts prepared in a cream sauce) or the Rack of Lamb Indonesian with Indonesian spices. Vegetables are included, as is a finish of chocolate-dipped fruits with cream.

The service is impeccable (you have little to no wait between courses), and it really makes you feel pampered. That salad, the small dessert, and so forth are included, making a hefty price tag appear a bit more reasonable, especially when compared to Strip establishments that aren't much better, and can cost nearly twice as much. While the main food is not spectacular, the salads and desserts were fine. It is not worth going out of your way for the food, but it perhaps is for the whole package.

EXPENSIVE

Limerick's. Fitzgerald's Casino Holiday Inn, 301 Fremont St., at 3rd St. ☎ **702/388-2400.** Reservations recommended. Main courses $13.95–$21.00. AE, MC, V, D. Nightly 5:30–10:30pm. STEAK/SEAFOOD.

An extensive renovation a year ago turned a down-at-the-heels eatery into a posh steakhouse. Decorated in the classic Olde English gentlemen's club style, Limerick's is meant to be an oasis of gracious dining away from hectic casino life, and the overall effect is comforting and moderately womblike, particularly in the cozy booths at the back. Unfortunately, casino noise still creeps in, but it's not overly bothersome. The menu is classic, upscale steakhouse: beef, chops, some lobster, and chicken. The portions are Vegas-sized (the small prime rib was 14 ounces), so bring an appetite (and a love of red meat), or take your leftovers back to the room to feed the kids for a couple of days. The filet mignon was tender enough to cut with a fork, while the lamb chops came with a pecan mustard glaze. People who don't eat red meat might want to try the apricot chicken. Appetizers are mostly seafood, though there is a fine-sounding baked brie with strawberry preserves. "Chef's choice" desserts change nightly, and the wine list is good and extensive.

INEXPENSIVE

Binion's Horseshoe Coffee Shop. Binion's Horseshoe, 128 E. Fremont St., at Casino Center Blvd. ☎ **702/382-1600.** Main courses $4.25–$14.95 (most under $8). AE, CB, DC, DISC, MC, V. Daily 24 hours. AMERICAN.

Down a flight of steps from the casino floor, this is no humble hotel coffee shop. It's heralded by a gorgeous stained-glass dome and entered via doors embellished with antique beveled-glass panels. The interior is equally impressive, with a magnificent pressed copper ceiling, rich oak paneling, walls hung with original oil paintings you'll wish you owned, and displays of antiques, turn-of-the-century magazine covers, and black-and-white photographs of the Old West. Notice, too, an exhibit of vintage playing cards that depict real kings and queens (Henry VIII and Anne Boleyn, for example).

The menu lists all the traditional Las Vegas coffee shop items: sandwiches, burgers, Southern-fried chicken, steak and seafood entrees, along with breakfast fare. And you can't beat Binion's specials: two eggs with an immense slab of grilled ham, home fries, toast, and tea or coffee ($2.99 from 6am to 2pm); a 10-ounce New York steak dinner with baked potato, salad, and roll and butter ($3.99 from 10pm to 5:45am); a 7-ounce New York steak with eggs, home fries, and toast ($2.99 from 10pm to 5:45am); 10-ounce prime rib dinner, including soup or salad, potato, and vegetables ($5.25 from 5 to 9:45pm)—$6.25 for a 16-ounce T-bone steak instead of prime rib. All bar drinks are available, and there's peanut butter cream pie for dessert.

Carson Street Café. Golden Nugget, 129 E. Fremont St. between 1st St. and Casino Center Blvd. ☎ **702/385-7111.** Main courses mostly $5.95–$14.95. AE, CB, DC, DISC, MC, V. Daily 24 hours. AMERICAN.

Las Vegas has many delightful 24-hour hotel restaurants. The Golden Nugget's is reminiscent of an elegant street cafe on the Champs-Elysées, albeit one overlooking a gorgeous hotel lobby instead of a Paris street. Its jewel-toned interior, under a white-fringed green awning, features murals of park scenes and topiary, white latticing, and seating amid potted orange trees and planters of greenery.

And the food is notably excellent. A wide-ranging menu offers terrific salads (such as Oriental chicken), overstuffed deli sandwiches, burgers, Mexican fare (chicken burritos, fajita sandwiches), numerous breakfast items, and entrees running the gamut from filet mignon to country-fried steak with mashed potatoes and vegetables.

From 4 to 11pm, a 10-ounce prime rib dinner (with baked potato and a vegetable) is $9.95. And from 11pm to 7am an 8-ounce grilled ham steak with eggs, hash browns, and toast costs $3.95. There's a full bar. Dessert options include fresh-baked eclairs, strawberry shortcake, and hot fudge or butterscotch sundaes.

10 Buffets & Sunday Brunches

Lavish low-priced buffets are a Las Vegas tradition, designed to lure you to the gaming tables, feeling like you got such a bargain for your meal you can afford to drop more money. They're a gimmick, and we love them. Something about filling up on too much prime rib and shrimp just says *Vegas* to us. Of course, there is quite a range, from some perfunctory steam table displays and salad bars heavy on iceberg lettuce, to unbelievably opulent spreads with caviar and free flowing champagne. Some of the food is awful, some of it merely works as fuel, some of it is memorable. No trip to Las Vegas is complete without trying one or two. There are dozens of hotel buffets in town; the most noteworthy are described below. Mind you, almost all buffets have some things in common. Unless otherwise noted, every one listed below will have a carving station, a salad bar (quality differs), and hot main courses and side dishes. We will try only to point out when a buffet has something original or notable.

Note: Buffet meals are extremely popular, and reservations are usually not taken. Arrive early (before opening) or late to avoid a long line, especially on weekends.

ON OR NEAR THE STRIP
VERY EXPENSIVE

✪ **Bally's Sterling Sunday Brunch.** 3645 Las Vegas Blvd. S. ☎ **702/ 739-4111.** Reservations recommended. Brunch is $49.95. Sun only 9:30am– 2:30pm.

This brunch is served in the clubby elegant precincts of Bally's Steakhouse. There's a waffle and omelette station, a sushi and sashimi bar, and a brimming dessert table. You might choose smoked fish with bagels and cream cheese or help yourself from a mound of fresh shrimp. Entrees vary weekly. On a recent visit the possibilities included rolled chicken stuffed with pistachios and porcini mushrooms, beef tenderloin, steak Diane, seared salmon with beet butter sauce and fried leeks, roast duckling with black currant and blueberry sauce, and penne Florentine with pine nuts and smoked chicken in vodka sauce. Of course, there are deli and breakfast meats, vegetables and scrumptious salads, cheeses, raw bar offerings, seasonal fruits and berries, and side dishes such as stuffed potatoes with caviar and sour cream. Champagne flows freely.

EXPENSIVE

✪ **Tropicana Sunday Brunch Buffet.** 3801 Las Vegas Blvd. S. ☎ **702/739-2376.** $25.95 for adults, $15.95 for children 10 and under. Sun only 9:30am–2pm.

On one visit, this impressive feast was comprised of sushi, ceviche, raw oysters, cold shrimp, smoked seafood (trout, salmon, whitefish, and sable), caviar; a carving station that can also include rack of lamb, salmon Florentine, and roast pork; a waffle and omelette station, a full complement of breakfast meats and potato dishes, cheeses and cold cuts, an extensive salad bar, steak and tuna tartare, fresh vegetables, pasta dishes, numerous entrees (stuffed Maine lobster, red snapper in dill butter sauce, and roast pork with mustard sauce, among others), unlimited champagne, and dozens of desserts (including bananas Foster).

MODERATE

✪ **Bally's Big Kitchen Buffet.** 3645 Las Vegas Blvd. S. ☎ **702/739-4111.** Breakfast $8.95; brunch $9.95; dinner $12.95. Breakfast daily 7a–11am; brunch daily 11am–2:30pm; dinner daily 4:30–10pm.

Everything is extremely fresh and of the highest quality. There's always a bountiful salad bar, a good choice of fruits and vegetables, entrees (perhaps seafood casserole in a creamy dill sauce, baked red snapper, pork chops sautéed in Cajun spices, barbecued chicken, and broiled steak in peppercorn sauce), pastas, rice and potato dishes, cold cuts, and a vast array of fresh-baked desserts. The brunch buffet includes breakfast fare and all-you-can-eat shrimp, while the dinner buffet adds Chinese selections.

✪ **Caesars Palace Palatium Buffet.** 3570 Las Vegas Blvd. S. ☎ **702/731-7110.** Breakfast $7.95; lunch $9.95; dinner $16.95; Sat brunch $14.95; Sun brunch $16.95 adults, children 4 to 12 half price, under 3 free (includes unlimited champagne). Breakfast Mon–Fri 8–11:30am; lunch Mon–Fri 11:30am–3:30pm; dinner daily 4:30–10pm; brunch Sat–Sun 8:30am–3:30pm.

Selections at lunch and dinner include elaborate salad bars, fresh-baked breads, and much, much more. The evening meal includes a cold seafood station. Especially lavish are weekend brunches with omelette stations (in addition to egg dishes), breakfast meats, fresh-squeezed juices, potatoes prepared in various ways, pastas, rice casseroles, carved meats, cold shrimp, smoked salmon, and a waffle and ice-cream sundae bar in addition to two dessert islands spotlighting cakes and pastries. That's not the half of it.

✪ **Mirage Buffet.** 3400 Las Vegas Blvd. S. ☎ **702/791-7111.** Breakfast $7.50; lunch $8.95; dinner $12.95; Sun brunch $13.95; reduced prices for children ages 4 to 10, children under 4 free. Mon–Sat 7–10:45am, 11am–2:45pm, and 3–9:30pm; Sun 8am–9:30pm.

The Mirage offers lavish spreads in a lovely garden-themed setting with palm trees, a plant-filled stone fountain, and seating under verdigris eaves and domes embellished with flowers. You pay somewhat more here than at other buffets, but you certainly get what you pay for. The salad bars alone are enormous, filled with at least 25 different choices such as Thai beef, seafood, salad niççoise, tabbouleh, Chinese chicken, Creole rice, and tortellini. At brunch champagne flows freely, and a scrumptious array of smoked fish is added to the board, along with such items as fruit-filled crêpes and blintzes. And every meal features a spectacular dessert table (the bread pudding in bourbon sauce is noteworthy). For healthful eating there are many light items to choose from, including sugar- and fat-free puddings. And on Sundays a nonalcoholic sparkling cider is a possible champagne alternative.

INEXPENSIVE

Excalibur's Round Table Buffet. 3850 Las Vegas Blvd. S. ☎ **702/597-7777.** Breakfast $3.99; lunch $4.99; dinner $5.99. Breakfast daily 7–11am; lunch daily 11am–4pm; dinner daily 4–10pm.

This strikes the perfect balance of cheap prices, mandatory tacky decor, and adequate food. This is what you want in a cheap Vegas buffet. But on a recent trip they didn't have mashed potatoes or macaroni salad, which are essential for an archetypal buffet. The plates are large, so you don't have to make as many trips to the buffet tables.

The Flamingo Hilton Paradise Garden Buffet. 3555 Las Vegas Blvd. S. ☎ **702/733-3111.** Breakfast $6.50; lunch $7.50; dinner $9.95 (includes 2 glasses of wine). Breakfast daily 6am–noon; lunch daily noon–2:30pm; dinner daily 4:30–10pm.

At dinner, there is an extensive international food station (which changes monthly) presenting French, Chinese, Mexican, German, or Italian specialties. A large salad bar, fresh fruits, pastas, vegetables, potato dishes, and a vast dessert display round out the offerings. Lunch is similar, featuring a mix of international cuisines as well as a stir-fry station and a soup/salad/pasta bar. At breakfast, you'll find all the expected fare, including a made-to-order omelette station and fresh-baked breads.

✪ **The Luxor Pharaoh's Pheast Buffet.** 3900 Las Vegas Blvd. S. ☎ **702/262-4000.** Breakfast $4.49; lunch $5.49; dinner $7.49. Breakfast daily 7–11am; lunch daily 11am–4pm; dinner daily 4–11pm.

The food is better than most cheap buffets, including a Mexican station with some genuinely spicy food, Chinese stir fry, and different Italian pastas. Desserts were disappointing. A beer and wine cart makes the rounds. Word has probably gotten out, unfortunately, because the lines are always enormous.

✪ **The Rio's Carnival World Buffet.** 3700 W. Flamingo Rd. ☎ **702/ 252-7777.** Breakfast $5.55; lunch $7.77; dinner $9.99; brunch $7.99 (champagne is $1 per glass). Breakfast Mon–Fri 7–10:30am; lunch Mon–Fri 11am– 3pm; dinner daily 3:30–10pm; brunch Sat–Sun 7am–3:30pm.

This is an excellent buffet with cheerfully decorative food booths set up like stations in an upscale food court. A barbecued chicken and ribs station offers side dishes of baked beans and mashed potatoes. Other stations offer stir-fry (chicken, beef, pork, and vegetables), Mexican taco fixings and accompaniments, Chinese fare, a Japanese sushi and teppanyaki grill, a Brazilian mixed grill, Italian pasta and antipasto, and fish-and-chips. There's even a diner setup for hot dogs, burgers, fries, and milk shakes. All this is in addition to the usual offerings of most Las Vegas buffets. Everything is fresh and beautifully prepared and presented.

Tropicana Island Buffet. 3801 Las Vegas Blvd. S. ☎ **702/739-2222.** Brunch $9.95; dinner $10.95. Brunch daily 7am–1pm; dinner daily 5–10pm.

This buffet is served in a large and delightful dining room. Dinners here feature an extensive salad bar and peel-and-eat-shrimp.

CONVENTION CENTER AREA
MODERATE
✪ **Las Vegas Hilton Buffet of Champions.** 3000 Paradise Rd. ☎ **702/ 732-5111.** Breakfast $7.99; lunch $8.99; dinner $12.99; brunch $11.99 (includes unlimited champagne). Children 12 and under half price. Breakfast Mon–Fri 7–10am; lunch Mon–Fri 11am–2:30pm; dinner daily 5–10pm; brunch Sat–Sun 8am–2:30pm.

The fare is fresh and delicious. Dinner additionally features all-you-can-eat crab and shrimp.

DOWNTOWN
MODERATE
✪ **The Golden Nugget Buffet.** 129 E. Fremont St. ☎ **702/385-7111.** Breakfast $5.75; lunch $7.50; dinner $10.25; brunch $10.25. Breakfast Mon– Sat 7–10:30am; lunch Mon–Sat 10:30am–3pm; dinner Mon–Sat 4–10pm; Sun brunch 8am–10pm.

This buffet has often been voted number one in Las Vegas. The buffet tables are laden with an extensive salad bar (about 50 items), fresh fruit, and marvelous desserts including Zelma Wynn's (Steve's mother) famous bread pudding. Every night fresh seafood is featured. Most lavish is the all-day Sunday champagne brunch, which adds such dishes as eggs Benedict, blintzes, pancakes, creamed herring, and smoked fish with bagels and cream cheese. *Note:* This stunning buffet room is also the setting for a $2.99 late-night meal of steak and eggs with home fries and biscuits with gravy; it's served 11pm to 4am.

○ **Main Street Station Garden Court.** 200 N. Main Street. **702/ 787-1896.** Breakfast $4.99; lunch $6.99; dinner $8.99. Friday seafood buffet $12.99. Sun champagne brunch $7.99. Children 3 and under free. Breakfast 7–10:30am; brunch 7am–3pm; lunch 11am–3pm; dinner 4–10pm.

The Main Street Station Garden Court buffet is one of the best in town, much less in Downtown. This buffet features nine live-action stations (meaning you can watch your food being prepared), including wood-fired brick oven pizza (delicious), many fresh salsas at the Mexican station, a barbecue rotisserie, fresh sausage at the carving station, and Chinese, Hawaiian, and Southern specialties (soul food and the like). On Friday nights, they have all this plus countless kinds of seafood all the way up to lobster.

INEXPENSIVE

The Lady Luck Banquet Buffet. 206 N. 3rd St. ☎ **702/477-3000.** Breakfast $4.99; lunch $5.49; dinner $7.77. Breakfast daily 6–10:30am; lunch daily 10:30am–2pm; dinner daily 4–10pm.

Dinner includes all-you-can-eat prime rib and frequently there are Chinese, Polynesian, and Italian specialties as well. Offerings additionally include an extensive salad bar, a make-your-own-sundae bar, an array of fresh-baked pies and cakes, and beverages.

○ **Sam Boyd's Fremont Paradise Buffet.** 200 E. Fremont St. ☎ **702/ 385-3232.** Breakfast $4.95; lunch $5.95; dinner $8.95 ($13.95 for Seafood Fantasy); brunch $7.95. Breakfast Mon–Sat 7–10:30am; lunch Mon–Sat 11am–3pm; dinner Mon, Wed, Thurs 4–10pm (Sat until 11pm); Seafood Fantasy Sun and Tues 4–10pm (Fri until 11pm); Sun brunch 7am–3pm.

Meals here are on the lavish side. Sunday, Tuesday, and Friday nights the buffet is renamed the Seafood Fantasy, and food tables, adorned with beautiful ice sculptures, are laden with lobster claws, crab legs, shrimp, raw oysters, smoked salmon, clams, and entrees such as steamed mussels, shrimp scampi, and scallops Provenççale— all in addition to the usual meat carving stations and a few nonseafood entrees. And finally, the Fremont has a delightful champagne Sunday brunch served by "island girls" in colorful Polynesian garb. It includes not only unlimited champagne, but a full carving station, lox with bagels and cream cheese, an omelette station, and desserts.

6

What to See & Do in Las Vegas

*Y*ou aren't going to lack for things to do in Las Vegas. More than likely, you have come here for the gambling, which should keep you pretty busy (we say with some understatement). But you can't sit at a slot machine forever (or maybe you can). In any event, it shouldn't be too hard to find ways to fill your time between poker hands.

Just walking on the Strip and gazing at the gaudy, garish, absurd wonder of it all can occupy quite a lot of time. This is the number-one activity we recommend in Vegas; at night, it is a mind-boggling sight like no other. But if you need something else to do, or if you are trying to amuse yourself while the rest of your party gambles away, this chapter will guide you. Don't forget to check out the free attractions, such as the Mirage's volcano and white tiger exhibit, Treasure Island's pirate battle, and the new Masquerade Show at the Rio Hotel.

But there's much more to a Las Vegas vacation than gaming action and headliner entertainment. Nearby Hoover Dam is a major sightseeing attraction, and Lake Mead is one of several pristinely beautiful recreation areas. In our opinion, the ideal Las Vegas vacation combines the glitz and glitter of casino hotels with explorations of the area's natural beauty.

Be sure to take a look at attractions listed for children, many of which may also interest adults.

1 Attractions in Las Vegas

✪ **Caesars Magical Empire.** Caesars Palace, 3570 Las Vegas Blvd. S. ☎ **800/445-4544** or 702/731-7333. Admission (including a three-course meal and wine, gratuities extra): $65–$75. Reservations required. Daily 4:30–11:30pm. Children must be at least 10 years of age.

Caesars spent a lot of money constructing this facility, and it shows. It's an impressive place of tunnels, grottos, revolving rooms, theaters, and so forth, with a surprise around every corner. Upon arrival, you are assigned to a group of no more than 24, which is escorted through catacombs by Centurion guards to a private dining room.

There, you are treated to an intimate magic show by your own private magician. Assisted by some very funny wait staff, there is usually a little story played out as you eat your dinner. Up close magic is performed between courses. Afterwards, you are taken through the rest of the Cavern (beware the Forbidden Crypt of Ramses if you have anything even remotely resembling motion sickness—they ask only if you have "balance problems"); you'll end up in a seven-story dome, with massive Egyptian columns and sculptures, where you can see several other magic shows ranging in size. Here, you can experience Lumineria, a 5-minute show combining smoke, dancing fire, and high-tech lighting effects (cover your eyes before the finale—it's nearly blinding). You can also chat with some skeletons (Habeas and Corpus) on the walls and, best of all, request songs from Invisibella, the player piano ghost with a nearly unlimited repertoire and a great sense of humor. All throughout are additional spots with some kind of trick to them; be sure to ask the bartenders for advice. (And look for ghosts in the bathroom mirrors.) The three-course dinner isn't bad (salad and dessert were pretty good, main course average, though it featured a tasty polenta), and the whole experience is playful and genuinely fun. You can stay as long as you want, even after you have seen all the shows (though that could take awhile as they rotate performers in the venues). There are two different bars inside, with video poker in case you are jonesing. You could hang out for hours in the Grotto Bar, as we did, making requests to Invisibella. Allow yourself at least 3 hours to see everything once. Considering how much show, spectacle, food, and just plain entertainment you get, this is one of the best values in the city.

Note: While you're at Caesars, check out the talking statues at the Forum Shops and catch an OMNIMAX movie (the latter described in this chapter below).

Caesars OMNIMAX Theatre. Caesars Palace, 3570 Las Vegas Blvd. S. ☎ 800/634-6698 or 702/731-7901. Admission $7 adults; seniors, children 2–12, hotel guests, and military personnel $5. Show times vary. You must purchase tickets at the box office (open daily 9am–11pm) on the day of the performance.

If you've never seen one of these 3-D-like films, you're in for a treat. The OMNIMAX Theatre here is housed in a geodesic dome: a space-age environment with 368 seats that recline 27°, affording a panoramic view of the curved 57-foot screen. The movies, projected via 70mm film (which is 10 times the frame size of ordinary 35mm film), offer an awesome visual display enhanced by a state-of-the-art

Las Vegas Attractions

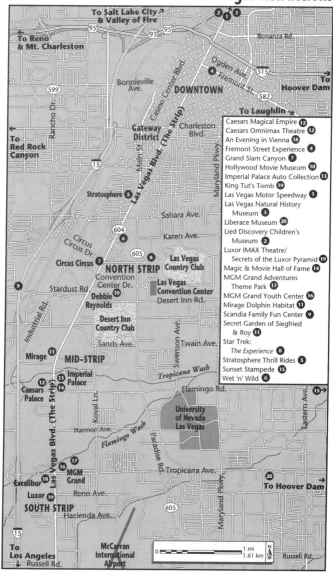

Caesars Magical Empire **12**
Caesars Omnimax Theatre **12**
An Evening in Vienna **18**
Fremont Street Experience **4**
Grand Slam Canyon **7**
Hollywood Movie Museum **10**
Imperial Palace Auto Collection **13**
King Tut's Tomb **19**
Las Vegas Motor Speedway **1**
Las Vegas Natural History
  Museum **3**
Liberace Museum **20**
Lied Discovery Children's
  Museum **2**
Luxor IMAX Theatre/
  Secrets of the Luxor Pyramid **19**
Magic & Movie Hall of Fame **14**
MGM Grand Adventures
  Theme Park **17**
MGM Grand Youth Center **16**
Mirage Dolphin Habitat **11**
Scandia Family Fun Center **9**
Secret Garden of Siegfried
  & Roy **11**
Star Trek:
  The Experience **8**
Stratosphere Thrill Rides **5**
Sunset Stampede **15**
Wet 'n' Wild **6**

sound system (89 speakers engulf the audience in sound). Depending on the film being shown, viewers might soar over the Rocky Mountains, plummet down steep waterfalls, ride the rapids, travel into outer space, or perch at the rim of an erupting volcano. Shows change frequently, but whatever you see will be stupendous.

✪ **An Evening in Vienna.** Excalibur Hotel, 3850 Las Vegas Blvd. S. ☎ **702/ 597-7600.** Admission $7.95 adults, $5.95 for children under 12 and seniors (including tax). Mon–Thurs 2pm, Sat–Sun 2pm. Dark Fri. Seating is on a first-come, first-served basis. Tickets can be purchased up to 3 days in advance at Excalibur ticket booths.

This is not your average, glitzy, high production value Vegas show—quite the opposite. In fact, it's so low key it almost comes as a shock to the system. The magnificent white Lipizzaner stallions hail originally from Spain, but were developed at the Spanish Riding School in Vienna. The horses are trained in the elegant and graceful movements of *dressage* and *haute école*. But the real attraction is the "airs above the ground," gravity-defying, seemingly physically impossible leaps the stallions perform naturally for play. They have been shown for centuries in Vienna (Disney made a movie about them), and a touring company has set up permanent residence at the Excalibur. The company re-creates what the Vienna show would be like, with riders in formal uniforms, and the horses performing to classical music. (Watch as the complicated dressage footwork by the horses is choreographed so well to the music that it appears the horse is dancing.) Obviously, it lacks the grand air the real thing would have, and it really suffers in comparison to the extravaganzas performed everywhere else. These comparisons are unfair; the stuff you see here is performed without tricks of lighting or mirrors, and unlike other white mammals on the Strip, these horses are really doing something. If you have a kid who loves horses, or if you love horses, this is a must-see. Children with short attention spans may be bored. But the price makes this the best bargain show in town, and, frankly, after the constant sensory bombardment that is Las Vegas—particularly Vegas shows—spending an hour here is a great relief.

✪ **Fremont Street Experience.** Fremont St., between Main St. and Las Vegas Blvd. in downtown Las Vegas. Shows nightly. Free.

For some years, downtown Vegas has been losing ground to the Strip. But thanks to a $70 million revitalization project, that is starting to change. Fremont Street, the heart of "Glitter Gulch," has been closed off and turned into a pedestrian mall. The Fremont Street Experience is a 5-block open-air pedestrian mall, a landscaped strip of outdoor cafes, vendor carts, and colorful kiosks purveying food and merchandise. Overhead is a 90-foot-high steel-mesh "celestial vault." At night, it is the *Sky Parade:* a high-tech light and laser show (the canopy is equipped with more than 2.1 million lights) enhanced by a concert hall quality sound system, which takes place four times nightly. But there's music in between shows as well. Not only does the canopy provide shade, it cools the area through a misting system in summer and warms you with radiant heaters in winter. The difference this makes can not be overemphasized; what was once a ghost town of tacky, rapidly aging buildings, in an area with more undesirables than not, is now a bustling (at least at night), friendly, safe place (they have private security guards who hustle said undesirables away). It's a place where you can stroll, eat, or even dance to the music under the lights. The crowd it attracts is more upscale than in years past, and of course, it's a lot less crowded than the hectic Strip. *Note:* A good place to view the light show is from the balcony at Fitzgerald's Hotel.

Hollywood Movie Museum. Debbie Reynolds Hotel, 305 Convention Center Dr. ☎ **702/7-DEBBIE.** Admission $7.95 adults, $5.95 children 3–12. Mon–Fri 10am–10pm, with tours every hour on the hour.

Debbie Reynolds has been buying up Hollywood memorabilia for decades. Her $30 million collection, comprising items from more than a half century of American movies, celebrates Hollywood's Golden Age. Changing exhibits showcase some 3,000 costumes—the famous white dress worn by Marilyn Monroe in *The Seven Year Itch,* Elizabeth Taylor's *Cleopatra* headdress, a pair of Judy Garland's ruby slippers from *The Wizard of Oz,* and the dancing shoes of Fred Astaire and Cyd Charisse, among them. Additionally, there are props, artifacts, and furnishings from classic films (she has a 36,000-square-foot warehouse filled with them).

Imperial Palace Auto Collection. Imperial Palace Hotel, 3535 Las Vegas Blvd. S. ☎ **702/731-3311.** Admission $6.95 adults, $3 seniors and children under 12, free for children under 5 and AAA members. Daily 9:30am–11:30pm.

If you're not a "car person," don't assume you won't be interested in this premier collection of antique, classic, and special-interest vehicles. There's more here than just cars and trucks. Check out the graceful lines and handsome sculpture of one of the 43 Model J Dusenbergs (the largest collection in the world valued at over $50 million). The craftsmanship and attention to detail make these cars, and others here, true works of art. There's also a great deal of history. Take a walk down President's Row where you can see JFK's

1962 "bubbletop" Lincoln Continental, Lyndon Johnson's 1964 Cadillac, Eisenhower's 1952 Chrysler Imperial 20-foot-long parade car, Truman's 1950 Lincoln Cosmopolitan with gold-plated interior, FDR's unrestored 1936 V-16 Cadillac, and Herbert Hoover's 1929 Cadillac.

Las Vegas Motor Speedway. 7000 Las Vegas Blvd. N., directly across from Nellis Air Force base (take I-15 north to Speedway exit 54). ☎ **702/644-4443** for ticket information. Tickets $10–$75 (higher prices for major events).

This 107,000-seat facility, the first new superspeedway to be built in the Southwest in more than two decades, opened with a 500K Indy Racing League event. A $100 million state-of-the-art motor sports entertainment complex, it includes a 1.5-mile superspeedway, a 2.5-mile FIA-approved road course, paved and dirt short-track ovals, and a 4,000-foot drag strip. Also on the property are facilities for Go-Kart, Legends Car, Sand Drag, and Motocross competition. The new speedway is accessible via shuttle buses to and from major casino hotels.

✪ **Liberace Museum.** 1775 E. Tropicana Ave., at Spencer St. ☎ **702/798-5595.** Admission $6.50 adults, $4.50 seniors over 60, $3.50 students, $2 children 6–12, free for children under 6. Mon–Sat 10am–5pm, Sun 1–5pm.

You can keep your Louvres and Vaticans and Smithsonians; *this* is a museum. Housed, like everything else in Vegas, in a strip mall, this is a shrine to the glory and excess that was the art project known as Liberace. You've got your costumes (bejeweled), your many cars (bejeweled), your many many pianos (bejeweled), and many jewels (also bejeweled). It just shows what can be bought with lots of money and no taste. Unless you have a severely underdeveloped appreciation for camp—or take your museum going very seriously—you shouldn't miss it. The museum is 2^1/$_2$ miles east of the Strip on your right.

Luxor IMAX Theater. Luxor Las Vegas, 3900 Las Vegas Blvd. S. ☎ **702/262-4000.** Admission $7 for IMAX 2-D, $8.50 for 3-D. A combined ticket, including both episodes of *Secrets of the Luxor Pyramid* (described below), is $19. Sun–Thurs 10am–11pm, Fri–Sat 10am–11:30pm. Show times vary depending on the length of the film.

This is a state-of-the-art theater that projects the film on a seven-story screen. There are two different films running, one in standard two dimensions, the other 3-D. The glasses for the latter are really cool headsets that include built-in speakers, bringing certain sounds right into your head. The movies change periodically, but always include some extraordinary special effects. If you have a fear of heights, make sure to ask for a seat on one of the lower levels.

Magic and Movie Hall of Fame. O'Shea's Casino, 3555 Las Vegas Blvd. S., between Sands Ave. and Flamingo Rd. ☎ **702/737-1343.** Admission $9.95 adults, $3 children under 12 accompanied by an adult. Tues–Sat 10am–6pm. Magic shows at 11:30am and l:30, 3, and 4:30pm.

The price of entry here is very reasonable, considering you can almost always get a $5 discount coupon out front or in the casino's food court. Admission includes a half-hour show in the Houdini Theatre (note performance hours above) featuring magician/ventriloquist Valentine Vox.

After the performance, visitors tour a vast museum that houses props and artifacts of famous magicians such as Houdini.

The Secret Garden of Siegfried and Roy and the ✪ Mirage Dolphin Habitat. Mirage Hotel, 3400 Las Vegas Blvd. S. ☎ **702/791-7111.** Admission $10, free for children under 11. Mon–Sun 10am–5:30pm. Closed Wed. (Dolphin exhibit only $5 Wed.) Hours subject to change.

Siegfried and Roy's famous white tigers have long had a free exhibit in the Mirage. They still do, but now they have an additional space, a gorgeous area behind the dolphin exhibit. Here, the white tigers are joined by white lions, Bengal tigers, an Asian elephant, a panther, and a snow leopard. (Many of these are bred by Siegfried and Roy and are also in their nightly show.) It's really just a glorified zoo, featuring only the big-ticket animals; however, it is a very pretty place, with plenty of foliage and some bits of Indian- and Asian-themed architecture. Visitors are given little portable phone-like objects on which they can play a series of programs, listening to Roy and Mirage owner Steve Wynn discuss conservation or deliver anecdotes.

The Dolphin habitat is more satisfying. It was designed to provide a healthy and nurturing environment and to educate the public about marine mammals and their role in the ecosystem. The Mirage displays only dolphins already in captivity—no dolphins will be taken from the wild. You can watch the dolphins frolic both above and below ground through viewing windows, in three different pools. (There is nothing quite like the kick you get from seeing a baby dolphin play.) The knowledgeable staff members, who surely have the best job in Vegas, will answer questions. The staff also plays ball with the dolphins; they toss large beach balls into the pools, and the dolphins hit them out with their noses, leaping out of the water cackling with dolphin glee. You catch the ball, getting nicely wet, and toss it back to them. If you have never played ball with a dolphin, shove that happy child next to you out of the way and go for it.

STAR TREK: The Experience. Las Vegas Hilton, 3000 Paradise Rd. ☎ **702/ 732-5111.** Admission will be about $10. Hours not yet available.

Trekkers take note: Opening by the end of 1997, STAR TREK: The Experience promises to "boldly go where no entertainment experience has gone before." Visitors will become Starfleet crew members on an intergalactic journey that utilizes simulator rides, interactive videos, morphing, and virtual-reality stations, holograms, and state-of-the-art computer games. Your voyage will begin in a "history-of-the-future" museum filled with authentic *Star Trek* costumes, weaponry, and props. From the Starfleet Gallery Room, you'll be "beamed up" to the Bridge of the Starship Enterprise and board a shuttlecraft for a simulated journey through the universe.

Upon successful completion of your mission, you'll disembark at Deep Space Nine to play (there's a state-of-the-art video-game room), dine, shop, and encounter aliens in the 24th century. A Cardassian-style restaurant will serve futuristically named foods, such as Glop-on-a-Stick, and, in the lounge, you'll order food and drinks from machines equipped with voice-recognition capabilities.

Stratosphere Thrill Rides. Stratosphere, 2000 Las Vegas Blvd. S. ☎ **702/ 380-7777.** Admission for either ride is $5, plus $5 to ascend the tower (if you dine in the buffet room or Top of the World, there's no charge to go up to the tower). Sun–Thurs 10am–midnight, Fri–Sat 10am–2am. Minimum height requirement for both rides is 48 inches.

Atop the 1,149-foot Stratosphere Tower are two marvelous thrill rides. The **Let It Ride High Roller** (the world's highest roller coaster) was recently revamped to go at even faster speeds as it zooms around a hilly track that is seemingly suspended in midair. Even more fun is the **Big Shot,** a breathtaking free-fall ride that thrusts you 160 feet in the air along a 228-foot spire at the top of the tower, then plummets back down again. Sitting in an open car, you seem to be dangling in space over Las Vegas. We have one relative, a thrill ride enthusiast, who said he never felt more scared than when he rode the Big Shot. After he survived, he promptly put his kids on it, who loved it.

2 Getting Married

This is one of the most popular things to do in Las Vegas. Why? It's very easy to get married here. Too easy. See that total stranger standing next to you? Grab him or her and head down to the **Clark Country Marriage License Bureau** to get your license (200 S. 3rd at Briger Avenue, ☎ 702/455-3156). It's open Monday to Sunday from 8am to midnight, 24 hours legal holidays). Then find a wedding chapel—not hard since they line the north end of the Strip (Las Vegas Boulevard South) in droves—and tie the knot. Just like that. No blood test, no waiting period—heck, not even an awkward dating period.

You can pick a chapel just by driving down the Strip past the Stratosphere, but we've listed four of our favorites. Or you can also call **Las Vegas Weddings and Rooms** (☎ **800/488-MATE**), a one-stop shop for wedding services. They'll find a chapel or outdoor garden that suits your taste (not to mention such only-in-Vegas venues as the former mansions of Elvis Presley and Liberace), book you into a hotel for the honeymoon, arrange the ceremony, and provide every accessory you need. Theme weddings are a specialty. They even have a New Age minister on call who can perform a Native American ceremony. And yes, you can get married by an Elvis impersonator.

✪ **Cupid's Wedding Chapel.** 827 Las Vegas Blvd. S. ☎ **800/543-2933** or 702/598-4444. Sun–Thurs 10am–10pm, Fri–Sat 10am–1am.

"The little chapel with the big heart." Well, they just might be. The manager explains that, unlike other chapels on the Strip, they schedule weddings an hour apart. This gives them time for the full production number; they pride themselves on offering "a traditional church wedding at chapel prices." "I am a diehard romantic," said the manager. "I want huggin', kissin', and I don't care if they faint—a wedding is a place for romance." You just know she cries at each and every service they perform.

The Little White Chapel. 1301 Las Vegas Blvd. S. **800/545-8111** or 702/382-5943. Open 24 hours.

This is arguably the most famous of the chapels on the strip; maybe because they have the big sign saying Michael Jordan and Joan Collins were married there (not to each other); maybe because they were the first to do the drive-up window. It is indeed little and white. However, they feel like a factory line, processing wedding after wedding after wedding, 24 hours a day; move 'em in and move 'em out. (No wonder they put in that drive-up window!) If you want something special, there are probably better choices, but for a true Vegas wedding experience, this is Kitsch Wedding Central.

✪ **A Special Memory Wedding Chapel.** 800 S. Fourth St., at Gass. ☎ **800/9-MARRYU** or 702/384-2211. Sun–Thurs 8am–10pm, Fri–Sat 8am–midnight.

This is a terrific new wedding chapel, particularly when compared to the rather tired facades of the classics on the Strip. This is absolutely the place to go if you want a traditional, big production wedding; you won't feel in the least bit tacky or in any other way like you got married in Vegas. It's a New England–style church building, complete with steeple. The interior looks like a proper church (well, a plain one—don't think ornate gothic cathedral). Should all this just be too darn nice and proper for you, they also offer a drive-up window (where they do about 300 weddings a month!).

San Francisco Sally's Victorian Chapel. 1304 Las Vegas Blvd. S. ☎ **800/658-8677** or 702/385-7777. Sun–Thurs 10am–4pm, Fri–Sat 10am–8pm.

An extremely tiny wedding chapel bursting at the seams with Victorian frills (fringed lamps, swags of lace curtains). They basically offer "an Olde Tyme Parlor Wedding." This is perfect if you want a very intimate wedding—like you, your intended, and someone to officiate. It literally can't hold more than six people. But if you love Victoriana, or you want to play dress up (they rent out costumes) at your wedding, this is the place. The women who run it refer to themselves as "a bunch of mother hens" and are delightful and will pamper you to within an inch of your life. (One couple drops in every year just to say hi.)

3 Especially for Kids

Like much of the rest of the world, you may be under the impression that Las Vegas has evolved from an adults-only fantasyland into a vacation destination suitable for the entire family. This is a myth. The gargantuan hotels that spent small fortunes on redecorating in an attempt to lure families with vast quantities of junk food and a lot of hype now vehemently deny that any such notion ever crossed their collective minds, and, no, they don't know how that roller coaster got into the parking lot.

To put things simply, Las Vegas makes money—lots and lots of money—by promoting gambling, drinking, and sex. These are all fine pursuits if you happen to be an adult, but if you haven't reached the magical age of 21, you really don't count in this town. In any case, the casinos and even the Strip itself are simply too stimulating, noisy, and smoky for young kids. Older progeny may have a tolerance for crowds and the incessant pinging of the slot machines, but they will be thoroughly annoyed with you when casino security chastises them if they so much as stop to tie their shoelaces anywhere near the gaming tables.

Nevertheless, you may have a perfectly legitimate reason for bringing your children to Las Vegas (like Grandma was busy, or you were just stopping through on your way from somewhere else), so here are some places to take the children both on and off the Strip.

Circus Circus (see p. 115) has ongoing circus acts throughout the day, a vast video game and pinball arcade, and dozens of carnival games on its mezzanine level. Behind the hotel is Grand Slam Canyon, detailed below. **Excalibur** (see p. 108) also offers video and carnival games, plus thrill cinemas and free shows (jugglers, puppets, and so on). At **Caesars Palace,** both the Magical Empire (for kids 12 and older only, see p. 105) and OMNIMAX movies (see p. 106) are a thrill for everyone in the family. The ship battle in front of **Treasure Island** (see box on p. 70) is sure to please, as will the erupting volcano (see p. 35) and the Secret Garden of Siegfried and Roy and dolphin habitat at the **Mirage** (see p. 111). Ditto the various attractions at the **Luxor Las Vegas,** such as the Imax Theater (see p.110).

Kids will enjoy **The Magic and Movie Hall of Fame** (see p. 111), but they'll want to leave before you do.

Appropriate shows for kids include *King Arthur's Tournament* at Excalibur (see p. 27), *An Evening in Vienna* (this is the name for the show starring the extraordinary Lippizaner stallions—see p. 108), *Siegfried and Roy* at the Mirage (see p. 159), *Lance Burton* at the Monte Carlo (see p. 157), *Starlight Express* at the Hilton (see p. 161), *EFX* at the MGM Grand (see p. 153), and Cirque du Soleil's *Mystère* at Treasure Island (see p. 151). As a general rule, early shows are less racy than late-night shows.

Grand Slam Canyon Theme Park. 2889 Las Vegas Blvd. S., behind Circus Circus Hotel. ☎ **702/734-3939.** Admission free; pay per ride. Park hours vary; call ahead.

This isn't a half-bad place to spend a hot afternoon, especially now that Circus Circus, the casino/hotel that built this indoor amusement park, has undergone a face-lift. The glass dome that towers overhead lets in natural light, a solace to those of us who look peaked under the glow of the artificial kind. A double-loop roller coaster careens around the simulated Grand Canyon, and there's the requisite water flume, a laser tag area, and a modest number of other rides for kids of all ages. A dinosaur-bone excavation area will provide a good time for preschoolers and a place to rest for the supervising adults. Video games and an arcade are separate from the attractions, cutting down just a tad on the noise level. Jugglers and magicians provide impromptu entertainment. Our only caveat is don't leave kids here alone. They could easily get lost.

Las Vegas Natural History Museum. 900 Las Vegas Blvd. N., at Washington. ☎ **702/384-3466.** Admission $5 adults, $2.50 children 4–12. Mon–Sun 9am–4pm

Conveniently located across the street from the Lied Children's Museum (described below), this humble temple of taxidermy harkens back to elementary school field trips circa 1965, when stuffed elk and brown bears forever protecting their kill were as close as most of us got to exotic animals. Worn around the edges but very sweet and relaxed, the museum is enlivened by a hands-on activity room and two life-sized dinosaurs that roar at one another intermittently. A small boy was observed leaping toward his dad upon watching this display, so you might want to warn any sensitive little ones that the big tyrannosaurs aren't going anywhere. Surprisingly, the gift shop here is particularly well stocked with neat items you won't mind too terribly buying for the kids.

Lied Discovery Children's Museum. 833 Las Vegas Blvd. N., across from Cashman Field ☎ **702/382-5437.** Admission $5 for adults, $4 for kids 12–17, $3 for kids 3–11. Wed–Sat 10am–5pm, Sun 12pm–5.

A hands-on science museum designed for curious kids, the bright, airy, two-story Lied makes an ideal outing for toddlers and young children. With lots of interactive exhibits to examine, including a miniature grocery store, a bubble tube for encasing oneself inside a soap bubble, a radio station, and music and drawing areas, you'll soon forget your video poker losses. Clever, thought-inducing exhibits are everywhere. Learn how it feels to be handicapped by playing basketball from a wheelchair. Feed a wooden "sandwich" to a cutout of a snake and to a human cutout, and see how much nutrition each receives. See how much sunscreen their giant stuffed mascot needs to keep from burning. On weekend afternoons from 1pm until 3pm, free drop-in art classes are offered, giving you a bit of time to ramble around the gift store or read the fine print on the exhibit placards. The Lied also shares space with a city library branch, so after the kids run around, you can calm them back down with a story or two.

MGM Grand Adventures. Behind the MGM Grand Hotel, 3799 Las Vegas Blvd. S. ☎ **702/891-7777.** Admission only (no rides): $2. Admission with unlimited rides: hotel guests $9, everyone else $11. Sky Screamer: one person $22.20, two people $17.50 each, three people $12.50 each. Open daily (hours vary seasonally).

This theme park, slapped together without a great deal of thought on a former parking lot, looks as if some Hollywood set designers dropped off a variety of hokey movie facades and then, unburdened, cheerfully rode off into the sunset. The attractions, such as a clothes-soaking log flume and kiddie bumper cars, are sparsely scattered among a great many food and T-shirt emporiums. It leaves one with the impression that fun has a lot to do with the contents of one's pocketbook and/or stomach. For some peculiar reason, the park sports three tiny boxing arenas where you and a friend can suit up like samurai and duke it out. This is also home of the Sky Screamer, a combination bungee jump/swing that will thrill kids old enough (and daring enough) to give it a try. There is a separate charge for this ride on top of park admission, although you can pay $2 for park entrance alone—a better deal if you only wish to fly through the air. It's also fun just to sit on a bench and watch people on this contraption.

Scandia Family Fun Center. 2900 Sirius Ave., at Rancho Dr. between Sahara Ave. and Spring Mountain Rd. off-ramps. ☎ **702/364-0070.** Admission free, but there's a fee for each game or activity. Super Saver Pass $10.95 (includes 1 round of miniature golf, two rides, and 5 game tokens); Unlimited Wristband Package $14.95 (includes unlimited bumper boat and car rides, unlimited miniature golf, and 10 tokens for batting cages or arcade games). Sept to early June: Sun–Thurs 10am–11pm, Fri–Sat until midnight; mid-June to Aug: Sun–Thurs 10am–midnight, Fri–Sat until 1am.

This family amusement center just a few blocks off the Strip offers three 18-hole miniature golf courses ($5.50 per game, children under 6 free), a state-of-the-art video arcade with 225 machines, miniature car racing, bumper boats ($3.95 per ride, small children ride free with an adult), and automated softball- and baseball-pitching machines for batting practice ($1.25 for 25 pitches). A snack bar is on the premises.

Wet 'n' Wild. 2601 Las Vegas Blvd. S., just south of Sahara Ave. ☎ **702/878-7811.** Admission $21.95 adults, half-price seniors over 55, $15.95 children under 10, free for children under 3. Daily early May to Sept 30, 10am–6 or 8pm (sometimes later). Season and hours vary somewhat from year to year, so call ahead.

When temperatures soar, head for this 26-acre water park right in the heart of the Strip and cool off while jumping waves, careening down steep flumes, and running rapids. Among the highlights: Royal Flush, a thrill ride that washes you down a precipitous chute into a saucer-like bowl at 45 miles per hour, then flushes you into a bottomless pool; Surf Lagoon, a 500,000-gallon wave pool; Banzai

Banzai, a roller-coasterlike water ride (aboard a plastic sled, you race down a 45°-angled 150-foot chute and skip porpoiselike across a 120-foot pool); Der Stuka, the world's fastest and highest water chute; Raging Rapids, a simulated white-water rafting adventure on a 500-foot-long river; Lazy River, a leisurely float trip; Blue Niagara, a dizzying descent inside intertwined looping tubes from a height of six stories; Willy Willy (a hydra-hurricane that propels riders on inner tubes around a 90-foot-diameter pool at 10 miles per hour); Bomb Bay (enter a bomblike casing 76 feet in the air for a speedy vertical flight straight down to a pool target); and the Black Hole (an exhilaratingly rapid space-themed flume descent in the dark enhanced by a bombardment of colorful fiber-optic star fields and spinning galaxy patterns en route to splashdown). There are additional flumes, a challenging children's water playground, and a sunbathing area with a cascading waterfall, as well as video and arcade games. Food concessions are located throughout the park, and you can purchase swimwear and accessories at the Beach Trends Shop. Also, be on the lookout for discount coupons. Many Las Vegas packages include a free admission (sometimes partial day).

4 Playing Golf & Tennis

GOLF   There are dozens of local golf courses, including very challenging ones—the Sheraton Desert Inn Country has hosted many PGA tournaments. Beginner and intermediate golfers might prefer the other courses listed.

Angel Park Golf Club. 100 S. Rampart Blvd., between Charleston Blvd. and Westcliff St. ☎ **888/446/5358** or 702/254-4653.

This 36-hole par-70/71 public course, was designed by Arnold Palmer. In addition to the 18-hole Palm and Mountain Courses, Angel Park offers a night-it Cloud 9 course (12 holes for daylight play, 9 at night), where each hole is patterned after a famous par-3. **Yardage:** Palm Course 6,438 championship, 5,721 regular, 4,565 ladies; Mountain Course 6,783 championship, 6,272 regular, 5,143 ladies. **Facilities:** pro shop, nightlit driving range, 18-hole putting course, restaurant, snack bar, cocktail bar, beverage cart.

Black Mountain Golf and Country Club. 500 Greenway Rd., in nearby Henderson. ☎ **702/565-7933.**

Two new greens have recently been added to this 18-hole, par-72 semi-private course, which requires reservations 4 days in advance. **Yardage:** 6,541 championship, 6,223 regular, 5,478 ladies.

Facilities: pro shop, putting green, driving range, restaurant, snack bar, and cocktail lounge.

Craig Ranch Golf Club. 628 W. Craig Rd., Losee Rd. and Martin Luther King Blvd. ☎ **702/642-9700.**

This is an 18-hole, par-70 public course. **Yardage:** 6,001 regular, 5,221 ladies. **Facilities:** driving range, pro shop, PGA teaching pro, putting green, and snack bar.

Desert Inn Golf Club. 3145 Las Vegas Blvd. S. ☎ **702/733-4290.**

The Desert Inn course gets the nod from champions. It's an 18-hole, par-72 resort course. **Yardage:** 7,150 championship, 6,715 regular, 5,800 ladies. **Facilities:** driving range, putting green, pro shop, and restaurant. You can reserve 90 days in advance for Sunday through Thursday, 2 days in advance for Friday and Saturday. This is the most famous and demanding course in Las Vegas. *Golf Digest* calls it one of America's top resort courses. The driving range is open to Desert Inn and Caesars guests only; anyone can play the course, but nonguests pay a higher fee.

Desert Rose Golf Club. 5483 Clubhouse Dr., 3 blocks west of Nellis Blvd., off Sahara Ave. ☎ **702/431-4653.**

This is an 18-hole, par-71 public course. **Yardage:** 6,511 championship, 6,135 regular, 5,458 ladies. **Facilities:** driving range, putting and chipping greens, PGA teaching pro, pro shop, restaurant, and cocktail lounge.

Las Vegas Hilton Country Club. 1911 Desert Inn Rd., between Maryland Pkwy. and Eastern Ave. ☎ **702/796-0016.**

This is an 18-hole, par-72 public course. **Yardage:** 6,815 championship, 6,418 regular, 5,741 ladies. **Facilities:** pro shop, golf school, driving range, restaurant, and cocktail lounge. Hilton guests enjoy preferred tee times and rates.

TENNIS   Tennis buffs should choose one of the many hotels in town that have tennis courts.

Bally's (☎ 702/739-4598) has eight night-lit hard courts. Fees per hour range from $10 to $15 for guests, $15 to $20 for nonguests. Facilities include a pro shop. Hours vary seasonally. Reservations are advised.

The **Flamingo Hilton** (☎ 702/733-3444) has four outdoor hard courts (all lit for night play) and a pro shop. They are open to the public Monday to Friday from 7am to 8pm, Saturday and Sunday from 7am to 6pm. Rates are $20 per hour for nonguests, $12 for guests. Lessons are available. Reservations are required.

The **Riviera** (☎ 702/734-5110) has two outdoor hard courts (both lit for night play) that are open to the public, subject to availability; hotel guests have priority. They are open 24 hours. There is no charge for guests; nonguests pay $10 per hour. Reservations are required.

The **Desert Inn** (☎ 702/733-4557) has five outdoor hard courts (all lit for night play) and a pro shop. They are open to the public. Hours are daybreak to 10pm. Rates are $10 per person for a daily pass (you book for an hour but can stay longer if no one is waiting); they are free for guests. Reservations are necessary.

In addition to hotels, the **University of Nevada, Las Vegas (UNLV),** Harmon Avenue just east of Swenson Street (☎ 702/895-0844), has a dozen courts (all lit for night play) that are open weekdays from 6am to 9:45pm, on weekends from 8am to 9pm. Rates are $5 per person, per day on weekdays; $10 weekends. You should call before going to find out if a court is available.

5 An Excursion to Hoover Dam & Lake Mead

30 miles SE of Las Vegas

This is one of the most popular excursions from Las Vegas, visited by 2,000 to 3,000 people daily. Wear comfortable shoes; the dam tour involves quite a bit of walking. The best plan would be to tour the dam in the morning and enjoy some of the area's scenic beauty and recreation facilities in the afternoon.

ESSENTIALS

GETTING THERE   By Car   Take U.S. 93 south from Las Vegas (it's a continuation of Fremont Street Downtown). As you near the dam, you'll see a five-story parking structure tucked into the canyon wall on your left. Park here and take the elevators or stairs to the walkway leading to the new Visitor Center.

If you would rather go on an **organized tour, Gray Line** (☎ 702/384-1234) offers several Hoover Dam packages, all of them including admission and a tour of the dam. The 5¹/₂-hour **Hoover Dam Express** excursion, departing daily at 8am and noon, also includes a stop at Cranberry World; the price is $22.95 for adults, $20.45 for children 10 to 16 and seniors over 62, $17.95 for children under 10. More elaborate is the **Grand Hoover Dam Tour,** also departing daily at 10am and returning at 6pm, which includes the World of Clowns and a 1¹/₂-hour paddlewheeler cruise on Lake Mead; adults $36.50, children 10 to 16 and seniors $34.10,

Lake Mead & Vicinity

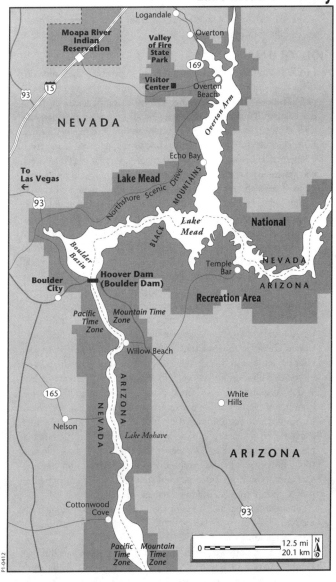

under 10 $31.60. You can inquire at your hotel sightseeing desk about other bus tours.

HOOVER DAM

In 1928, prodded by the seven states through which the Colorado River runs during the course of its 1,400-mile journey to the Gulf of California, Congress authorized construction of a dam at Boulder Canyon (later moved to Black Canyon). The Senate's declaration of intention was that "A mighty river, now a source of destruction, is to be curbed and put to work in the interests of society." Construction began in 1931. An army of more than 5,200 laborers was assembled, and work proceeded 24 hours a day. Completed in 1936, 2 years ahead of schedule, the dam stopped the river's annual floods and conserved water for irrigation, industrial, and domestic use. Equally important, it became one of the world's major electrical generating plants, providing low-cost, pollution-free hydroelectric power to a score of surrounding communities. Hoover Dam's $175 million cost has been repaid with interest by the sale of inexpensive power to a number of California cities and the states of Arizona and Nevada. The dam is a government project that paid for itself—a feat almost as awe-inspiring as its engineering.

The dam itself is a massive curved wall, 660 feet thick at the bottom and tapering to 45 feet where the road crosses it at the top. It towers 726.4 feet above bedrock (about the height of a 60-story skyscraper) and acts as a plug between the canyon walls to hold back up to 9.2 trillion gallons of water in Lake Mead—the reservoir created by its construction. All the architecture is on a grand scale, with beautiful art deco elements unusual in an engineering project. Note, for instance, the monumental 30-foot bronze sculpture, *Winged Figures of the Republic,* flanking a 142-foot flagpole at the Nevada entrance. According to its creator, Oskar Hansen, the sculpture symbolizes "the immutable calm of intellectual resolution, and the enormous power of trained physical strength, equally enthroned in placid triumph of scientific achievement."

The dam has become a major sightseeing attraction along with Lake Mead—America's largest artificial reservoir and a major Nevada recreation area.

Seven miles northwest of the dam on U.S. 93, you'll pass through **Boulder City,** which was built to house managerial and construction workers. Sweltering summer heat (many days it is 125°F) ruled out a campsite by the dam, whereas the higher elevation of Boulder City offered lower temperatures. The city emerged within a single year, turning a desert waste into a community of 6,000 with tree-shaded lawns, homes, churches, parks, restaurants, hotels, and schools.

TOURING THE DAM

The **Hoover Dam Visitor Center,** a vast three-level circular concrete structure with a rooftop overlook, opened in 1995. You'll enter the Reception Lobby, where you can buy tickets, peruse informational exhibits, photographs, and memorabilia, and view three 12-minute video presentations in a rotating theater. Additional exhibition galleries are in the works at this writing. The Overlook Level provides an unobstructed view of Lake Mead, the dam, the power plant, the Colorado River, and Black Canyon. You can visit an exhibit center across the street where a 10-minute presentation in a small theater focuses on a topographical map of the 1,400-mile Colorado River and the 14 dams and diversions along it. This building also houses a turbine and generator model, an information desk, and serves as a ticket purchase point for Lake Mead cruises. A gift shop and food concession are under construction in the parking structure.

Thirty-minute tours of the dam depart from the Reception Lobby every few minutes daily, except Christmas and Thanksgiving. The Visitor Center opens at 8:30am, and the first tour departs soon after. The last tour leaves at 5:40pm, and the center closes at 6:30pm. Admission is $5 for adults, $2.50 for senior citizens and children 10 to 16, free for children under 10. More extensive hard-hat tours can be arranged by calling in advance (☎ 702/294-3522).

The tour begins with a 530-foot elevator descent deep into the dam's interior to one of the many galleries used for maintenance and inspection. There are more than 2 miles of galleries inside the dam at various levels. From the gallery, you'll proceed into the power plant, downstream through the thickness of the dam. Note, en route, the terrazzo floors that are inlaid with basketry and pottery designs of southwestern Native American tribes. From the visitor's balcony of the Nevada wing, you'll see eight huge hydroelectric generators (nine from the Arizona wing). These generators are driven by individual turbines located 40 feet below the floor. Water is delivered from the reservoir to the turbines (through canyon walls) via massive 30-foot-diameter pipes called penstocks. You'll learn about the manufacture of these generating units, each of which produces sufficient electrical energy to supply the domestic needs of a city of 95,000 people. After visiting the generating room below, you'll go outside to see a tunnel through the 600-foot canyon wall that provides access to vehicles entering the power plant area. However, heavy equipment is lowered by a cableway that has a capacity of 150 tons! Looking up, you can see the control room for the cable operation. Moving on to the Arizona wing, your guide (with the aid of a diagram) will explain construction procedures of the four tunnels that were drilled and blasted through solid rock and used to divert the river around the dam site. These diversion tunnels averaged 4,000 feet in length and 56 feet in diameter. When construction work advanced beyond the point where it was no longer necessary to divert water around the dam site, the tunnels were permanently sealed off. You'll also learn about the four intake towers which control the supply of water drawn from Lake Mead for the power plant turbines and the spillways which, one on each side of the lake, control its maximum depth and ensure that no flood will ever overflow the dam. Finally, visitors stand in one of the diversion tunnels and view one of the largest steel water pipes ever made (its interior could accommodate two lanes of automobile traffic).

LAKE MEAD NATIONAL RECREATION AREA

Under the auspices of the National Park Service, the 1.5-million-acre Lake Mead National Recreation Area was created in 1936 around Lake Mead (the reservoir lake resulted from the construction of Hoover Dam) and later Lake Mohave to the south (formed with the construction of Davis Dam). Before the lakes emerged, this desert region was brutally hot, dry, and rugged—unfit for human habitation. Today it is one of the nation's most popular playgrounds, attracting about nine million visitors annually. The two lakes comprise 290.7 square miles. At an elevation of 1,221.4 feet, Lake Mead itself extends some 110 miles upstream toward the Grand Canyon. Its 550-mile shoreline, backed by spectacular cliff and canyon scenery, forms a perfect setting for a wide variety of water sports and desert hiking.

INFORMATION   The **Alan Bible Visitor Center,** 4 miles northeast of Boulder City on U.S. 93 at Nev. 166 (☎ **702/293-8990**), can provide information on all area activities and services. You can pick up trail maps and brochures here, view informative films, and find out about scenic drives, accommodations, ranger-guided hikes, naturalist programs and lectures, bird-watching, canoeing, camping, lakeside RV parks, and picnic facilities. The center also sells books and videotapes about the area. It's open daily 8:30am to 4:30pm.

For information on accommodations, boat rentals, and fishing, call **Seven Crown Resorts** (☎ 800/752-9669).

ACTIVITIES   Hiking   The best season for hiking is November through March (too hot the rest of the year). Some ranger-guided hikes are offered via the Alan Bible Visitor Center, which also stocks detailed trail maps. Three trails—ranging in length from ³/₄ mile to 6 miles—originate at the Visitor Center.

Boating & Fishing   A store at **Lake Mead Resort and Marina** under the auspices of Seven Crown Resorts (☎ **800/752-9669** or 702/293-3484), rents fishing boats, ski boats, personal watercraft, and patio boats. It also carries groceries, clothing, marine supplies, sporting goods, waterskiing gear, scuba and fishing equipment, and bait and tackle. You can get a fishing license here ($45.50 a year, $30.50 for 10 days, $17.50 for 3 days, $8.50 for children 12 to 15, under 12 free). The staff is knowledgeable and can apprise you of good fishing spots. Largemouth bass, striped bass, channel catfish, crappie, and bluegill are all found in Lake Mead.

Other convenient Lake Mead marinas offering similar rentals and equipment are **Las Vegas Bay** (☎ **702/565-9111**), which is even closer to Las Vegas, and **Callville Bay** (☎ **702/565-8958**), which is the least crowded of the five on the Nevada Shore.

Lake Cruises   A delightful way to enjoy Lake Mead is on a cruise aboard the ***Desert Princess*** (☎ **702/293-6180**), a Mississippi-style paddle wheeler. Cruises depart year-round from the Hoover Dam Ferry Terminal, which is near Lake Mead Lodge. At some time in the near future (possibly already as you read this), they will also depart from a dock right at the Hoover Dam Visitor Center; a ticket booth will be on the premises. It's a relaxing, scenic trip (enjoyed from an open promenade deck or one of two fully enclosed, climate-controlled decks) through Black Canyon and past colorful rock formations known as the "Arizona Paint Pots" en route to Hoover Dam, which is lit at night. Prices begin at $14.50 for adults for a luncheon cruise. Call for departure times.

7

About Casino Gambling

What? You didn't come to Las Vegas for the Liberace Museum? We are shocked. *Shocked.*

Yes, there are gambling opportunities in Vegas. We've noticed this. You will, too. The tip-off will be the slot machines in the airport as soon as you step off the plane. Or the slot machines in the convenience stores as soon as you drive across the state line. Let's not kid ourselves, gambling is what Vegas is about. The bright lights, the shows, the showgirls, the food—it's all there just to lure you in and make you open your wallet. (The free drinks certainly help ease the latter as well.)

You can disappoint them if you want, but what would be the point? *This is Las Vegas.* You don't have to be a high roller. You would not believe how much fun you can have with a nickel slot machine. You won't get rich, but neither will most of those guys playing the $5 dollar slots, either. Of course, that's not going to stop anyone from trying. Almost everyone plays in Vegas with the hopes of winning The Big One. That only a few ever do doesn't stop them from trying again and again and again. That's how the casinos make their money, by the way.

Remember that there is no system that is sure to help you win. We all have our own systems, and our own ideas. Reading books and listening to others at the tables will help you pick up some tips, but if there were a surefire way to win, the casinos would have taken care of it (and we will leave you to imagine just what that might entail). Try to have the courage to walk away when your bankroll is up, not down. Remember, your children's college fund is just that, and not a gambling budget supplement.

The first part of this chapter tells you the basics of betting. Knowing how to play the games not only improves your odds but makes playing more enjoyable. In addition to the instructions below, you'll find dozens of books on how to gamble at all casino hotel gift shops, and many casinos offer free gaming lessons on the premises. The second part of this chapter describes all the major casinos in town. Remember that gambling is supposed to be entertainment; picking a gaming table where the other players are laughing, slapping each other on the back, and generally enjoying themselves tends to make for considerable more fun than a table where everyone is sitting around in stony silence, morosely staring at their cards. Unless you really need to concentrate, pick a table where everyone seems to be enjoying themselves, and you will too, even if you don't win. Maybe.

1 The Games

BACCARAT

The ancient game of baccarat, or *chemin de fer,* is played with eight decks of cards. Firm rules apply, and there is no skill involved other than deciding whether to bet on the bank or the player. Any beginner can play, but check the betting minimum before you sit down as this tends to be a high-stakes game. The cards are shuffled by the croupier and then placed in a box that is called the "shoe."

Players may wager on "bank" or "player" at any time. Two cards are dealt from the shoe and given to the player who has the largest

BACCARAT RULES
PLAYER'S HAND

Having

0-1-2-3-4-5	Must draw a third card.
6-7	*Must stand.*
8-9	Natural. Banker cannot draw.

BANKER'S HAND

Having	**Draws**	**Does Not Draw**
	When giving Player 3rd card of:	When giving Player 3rd card of:
3	1-2-3-4-5-6-7-9-10	8
4	2-3-4-5-6-7	1-8-9-10
5	4-5-6-7	1-2-3-8-9-10
6	6-7	1-2-3-4-5-8-9-10
7	*Must stand.*	
8-9	Natural. Player cannot draw.	

If the player takes no third card, the banker must stand on 6. No one draws against a natural 8 or 9.

wager against the bank, and two cards are dealt to the croupier acting as banker. If the rule calls for a third card (see rules on chart shown on the previous page), the player or banker, or both, must take the third card. In the event of a tie, the hand is dealt over.

The object of the game is to come as close as possible to the number 9. To score the hands, the cards of each hand are totaled and the *last digit* is used. All cards have face value. For example: 10 plus 5 equals 15 (score is 5); 10 plus 4 plus 9 equals 23 (score is 3); 4 plus 3 plus 3 equals 10 (score is 0); and 4 plus 3 plus 2 equals 9 (score is 9). The closest hand to 9 wins.

Each player has a chance to deal the cards. The shoe passes to the player on the right each time the bank loses. If the player wishes, he or she may pass the shoe at any time.

Note: When you bet on the bank and the bank wins, you are charged a 5% commission. This must be paid at the start of a new game or when you leave the table.

BIG SIX

Big Six provides pleasant recreation and involves no study or effort. The wheel has 56 positions on it, 54 of them marked by bills from $1 to $20 denominations. The other two spots are jokers, and each pays 40 to 1 if the wheel stops in that position.

All other stops pay at face value. Those marked with $20 bills pay 20 to 1, the $5 bills pay 5 to 1, and so forth.

BLACKJACK

The dealer starts the game by dealing each player two cards. In some casinos they're dealt to the player faceup, in others facedown, but the dealer always gets one card up and one card down. Everybody plays against the dealer. The object is to get a total that is higher than that of the dealer without exceeding 21. All face cards count as 10; all other number cards except aces count as their number value. An ace may be counted as 1 or 11, whichever you choose it to be.

Starting at his or her left, the dealer gives additional cards to the players who wish to draw (be "hit") or none to a player who wishes to "stand" or "hold." If your count is nearer to 21 than the dealer's, you win. If it's under the dealer's, you lose. Ties are a push and nobody wins. After all the players are satisfied with their counts, the dealer exposes his or her facedown card. If his two cards total 16 or less, the dealer must "hit" (draw an additional card) until reaching 17 or over. If the dealer's total goes over 21, he or she must pay all the players whose hands have not gone "bust." It is important to note here that the blackjack dealer has no choice as to whether he or she should stay or draw. A dealer's decisions are predetermined and known to all the players at the table.

HOW TO PLAY

Here are eight "rules" for blackjack.

1. Place the amount of chips that you want to bet on the betting space on your table.

2. Look at the first two cards the dealer starts you with. If your hand adds up to the total you prefer, place your cards *under your bet money,* indicating that you don't wish any additional cards. If you elect to draw an additional card, you tell the dealer to "hit" you by making a sweeping motion with your cards or point to your open hand (watch your fellow players).

3. If your count goes over 21, you go "bust" and lose—even if the dealer also goes "bust" afterward. Unless hands are dealt faceup; *you then turn your hand faceup on the table.*

4. If you make 21 in your first two cards (any picture card or 10 with an ace), you've got blackjack. *You expose your winning hand immediately,* and you collect $1^{1}/_{2}$ times your bet—unless the dealer has blackjack, too, in which case it's a push and nobody wins.

5. If you find a "pair" in your first two cards (say, two 8s or two aces) you may "split" the pair into two hands and treat each card as the first card dealt in two separate hands. *Turn the pair faceup, on the table,* place the original bet on one of these cards, then place an equal amount on the other card. *Split aces are limited to a one-card draw on each.*

6. You may double your original bet and make a one-card draw after receiving your initial two cards. *Turn your hand faceup,* and you'll receive one more card facedown.

7. Anytime the dealer deals himself or herself an ace for the "up" card, you may insure your hand against the possibility that the hole card is a 10 or face card, which would give him or her an automatic blackjack. To insure, you place an amount up to one-half of your bet on the "insurance" line. If the dealer does have a blackjack, you do not lose, even though he or she has your hand beat, and you keep your bet and your insurance money. If the dealer does not have a blackjack, he or she takes your insurance money and play continues in the normal fashion.

8. *Remember:* The dealer *must* stand on 17 or more and *must* hit a hand of 16 or less.

PROFESSIONAL TIPS

Advice of the experts in playing blackjack is as follows.

1. *Do not* ask for an extra card if you have a count of 17, 18, 19, 20, or 21 in your cards, no matter what the dealer has showing in his or her "up" card.

2. *Do not* ask for an extra card when you have 12, 13, 14, 15, 16, or more if the dealer has a 2, 3, 4, 5, or 6 showing in his or her "up" card.

3. *Do* ask for an extra card or more when you have a count of 12 through 16 in your hand if the dealer's "up" card is a 7, 8, 9, 10, or ace.

There's a lot more to blackjack-playing strategy than the above, of course. So consider this merely as the bare bones of the game.

A final tip: Avoid insurance bets; they're sucker bait!

CRAPS

The most exciting casino action is always at the craps tables. Betting is frenetic, play fast-paced, and groups quickly bond yelling and screaming in response to the action.

The Table   The craps table is divided into marked areas (Pass, Come, Field, Big 6, Big 8, and so on), where you place your chips to bet. The following are a few simple directions.

Pass Line   A "Pass Line" bet pays even money. If the first roll of the dice adds up to 7 or 11, you win your bet; if the first roll adds up to 2, 3, or 12, you lose your bet. If any other number comes up, it's your "point." If you roll your point again, you win; but if a 7 comes up again before your point is rolled, you lose.

Don't Pass Line   Betting on the "Don't Pass" is the opposite of betting on the Pass Line. This time, you lose if a 7 or an 11 is thrown on the first roll, and you win if a 2 or a 3 is thrown on the first roll.

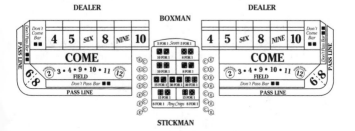

If the first roll is 12, however, it's a push (standoff), and nobody wins. If none of these numbers is thrown and you have a point instead, in order to win, a 7 will have to be thrown before the point comes up again. A "Don't Pass" bet also pays even money.

Come Betting on "Come" is the same as betting on the Pass Line, but you must bet *after* the first roll or on any following roll. Again, you'll win on 7 or 11 and lose on 2, 3, or 12. Any other number is your point, and you win if your point comes up again before a 7.

Don't Come This is the opposite of a "Come" bet. Again, you wait until after the first roll to bet. A 7 or an 11 means you lose; a 2 or a 3 means you win; 12 is a push, and nobody wins. You win if 7 comes up before the point. (The point, you'll recall, was the first number rolled if it was none of the above.)

Field This is a bet for one roll only. The "Field" consists of seven numbers: 2, 3, 4, 9, 10, 11, and 12. If any of these numbers is thrown on the next roll, you win even money, except on 2 and 12, which pay to 2 to 1 (at some casinos 3 to 1).

Big 6 & 8 A "Big 6 and 8" bet pays even money. You win if either a 6 or an 8 is rolled before a 7.

Any 7 An "Any 7" bet pays the winner five for one. If a 7 is thrown on the first roll after you bet, you win.

"Hard Way" Bets In the middle of a craps table are pictures of several possible dice combinations together with the odds the casino will pay you if you bet and win on any of those combinations being thrown. For example, if 8 is thrown by having a 4 appear on each die, and you bet on it, the bank will pay 10 for 1; if 4 is thrown by having a 2 appear on each die, and you bet on it, the bank will pay 8 for 1; if 3 is thrown, the bank pays 15 for 1. You win at the odds quoted if the *exact* combination of numbers you bet on comes up. But you lose either if a 7 is rolled or if the number you bet on was rolled any way other than the "Hard Way" shown on the table. In-the-know gamblers tend to avoid "Hard Way" bets as an easy way to lose their money. And note that the odds quoted are *not* 3 to 1, 4 to 1, or 8 to 1; here the key word is *for*—that is, 3 for 1 or 8 for 1.

Any Craps Here you're lucky if the dice "crap out"—if they show 2, 3, or 12 on the first roll after you bet. If this happens, the bank pays for 8 for 1. Any other number is a loser.

Place Bets You can make a "Place Bet" on any of the following numbers: 4, 5, 6, 8, 9, and 10. You're betting that the number you choose will be thrown before a 7 is thrown. If you win, the payoff is as follows: 4 or 10 pays at the rate of 9 to 5; 5 or 9 pays at the rate of 7 to 5; 6 or 8 pays at the rate of 7 to 6. "Place Bets" can be removed at any time before a roll.

Some Probabilities   Because each die has six sides numbered from 1 to 6—and craps is played with a pair of dice—the probability of throwing certain numbers has been studied carefully. Professionals have employed complex mathematical formulas in searching for the answers. And computers have data-processed curves of probability.

Suffice it to say that 7 (a crucial number in craps) will be thrown more frequently than any other number over the long run, for there are six possible combinations that make 7 when you break down the 1 to 6 possibilities on each separate die. As to the total possible number of combinations on the dice, there are 36.

Comparing the 36 possible combinations, numbers, or point combinations, run as follows:

> *2 and 12* may be thrown in *1 way only.*
> *3 and 11* may be thrown in *2 ways.*
> *4 and 10* may be thrown in *3 ways.*
> *5 and 9* may be thrown in *4 ways.*
> *6 and 8* may be thrown in *5 ways.*
> *7* may be thrown in *6 ways.*

So 7 has an advantage over all other combinations, which, over the long run, is in favor of the casino. You can't beat the law of averages. Players, however, often have winning streaks—a proven fact in ESP studies—and that's when the experts advise that it's wise to increase the size of bets. But when a losing streak sets in, stop playing!

KENO

This is one of the oldest games of chance. Originating in China, the game can be traced back to a time before Christ, when it operated as a national lottery. Legend has it that funds acquired from the game were used to finance construction of the Great Wall of China.

Keno was first introduced into the United States in the 1800s by Chinese railroad construction workers. Easy to play, and offering a chance to sit down and converse between bets, it is one of the most popular games in town—despite the fact that *the house percentage is greater than that of any other casino game!*

To play, you must first obtain a keno form, available at the counter in the keno lounge and in most Las Vegas coffee shops.

		PRICE PER WAY	PRICE PER GAME
$50,000.00 LIMIT TO AGGREGATE PLAYERS EACH GAME			
MARK NUMBER OF SPOTS OR WAYS PLAYED		**NO. OF GAMES**	**TOTAL PRICE**

WINNING TICKETS MUST BE COLLECTED IMMEDIATELY AFTER EACH KENO GAME IS CALLED.

1	2	3	4	5	6	7	8	9	10
11	12	13	14	15	16	17	18	19	20
21	22	23	24	25	26	27	28	29	30
31	32	33	34	35	36	37	38	39	40

WE PAY ON MACHINE ISSUED TICKETS - TICKETS WITH ERRORS NOT CORRECTED BEFORE START OF GAME WILL BE ACCEPTED AS ISSUED.

41	42	43	44	45	46	47	48	49	50
51	52	53	54	55	56	57	58	59	60
61	62	63	64	65	66	67	68	69	70
71	72	73	74	75	76	77	78	79	80

WE ARE NOT RESPONSIBLE FOR KENO RUNNERS TICKETS NOT VALIDATED BEFORE START OF NEXT GAME.

In the latter, you'll usually find blank keno forms and thick black crayons on your table. Fill yours out, and a miniskirted keno runner will come and collect it. After the game is over, she'll return with your winning or losing ticket. If you've won, it's customary to offer a tip, depending on your winnings.

Looking at your keno ticket and the keno board, you'll see that it is divided horizontally into two rectangles. The upper half (in China the yin area) contains the numbers 1 through 40, the lower (yang) half contains the numbers 41 through 80. You can win a maximum of $50,000—even more on progressive games—though it's highly unlikely (the probability is less than a hundredth of a percent). Mark up to 15 out of the 80 numbers; bets range from about 70¢ on up. A one-number mark is known as a one-spot, a two-number selection is a two-spot, and so on. After you have selected the number of spots you wish to play, write the price of the ticket in the right-hand corner where indicated. The more you bet, the more you can win if your numbers come up. Before the game starts, you have to give the completed form to a keno runner—or hand it in at the keno lounge desk—and pay for your bet. You'll get back a duplicate form with the number of the game you're playing on it. Then the game begins. As numbers appear on the keno board, compare them to the numbers you've marked on your ticket. After 20 numbers have appeared on the board, if you've won, turn in your ticket immediately for a payoff—before the next game begins. Otherwise, you will forfeit your winnings, a frustrating experience to say the least.

On a straight ticket that is marked with one or two spots, all of your numbers must appear on the board for you to win anything. With a few exceptions, if you mark from 3 to 7 spots, 3 numbers must appear on the board for you to win anything. Similarly, if you mark 8 to 12 spots, usually at least 5 numbers must come up for you to win the minimum amount. And if you mark 13 to 15 spots, usually at least 6 numbers must come up for a winning ticket. To win the maximum amount ($50,000), which requires that all of your numbers come up, you must select at least 8 spots. The more numbers on the board matching the numbers on your ticket, the more you win. If you want to keep playing the same numbers over and over, you can replay a ticket by handing in your duplicate to the keno runner; you don't have to keep rewriting it.

In addition to the straight bets described above, you can split your ticket, betting various amounts on two or more groups of numbers. To do so, circle the groups. The amount you bet is then divided by the number of groups. You could, if you so desired, play as many as 40 two-spots on a single ticket. Another possibility is to play three groups of four numbers each as eight spots (any two of the three groups of four numbers can be considered an eight spot). It does get a little complex, since combination betting options are almost infinite. Helpful casino personnel in the keno lounge can help you with combination betting.

POKER

Poker is *the* game of the Old West. There's at least one sequence in every Western where the hero faces off against the villain over a poker hand. In Las Vegas poker is a tradition, although it isn't played at every casino.

There are lots of variations on the basic game, but one of the most popular is Hold 'Em. Five cards are dealt faceup in the center of the table, and two are dealt to each player. The player uses the best five of seven, and the best hand wins. The house dealer takes care of the shuffling and the dealing and moves a marker around the table to alternate the start of the deal. The house rakes 1% to 10% (it depends on the casino) from each pot. Most casinos include the usual seven-card stud and a few have hi-lo split.

If you don't know how to play poker, don't attempt to learn at a table. Find a casino that teaches it in free gaming lessons.

Pai gow poker (a variation on poker) has become increasingly popular. The game is played with a traditional deck plus one joker. The joker is a wild card that can be used as an ace or to complete a straight, a flush, a straight flush, or a royal flush. Each player is dealt seven cards to arrange into two hands—a two-card hand and a five-card hand. As in standard poker, the highest two-card hand is two aces, and the highest five-card hand is a royal flush. The five-card hand *must* be higher than the two-card hand (if the two-card hand is a pair of sixes, for example, the five-card hand must be a pair of sevens or better). Any player's hand that is set incorrectly is an automatic loss. The object of the game is for both of the player's hands to rank higher than both of the banker's hands. Should one hand rank exactly the same as the banker's hand, this is a tie (called a "copy"), *and the banker wins all tie hands.* If the player wins one hand but loses the other, this is a "push," and no money changes hands. The house dealer or any player may be the banker. The bank is offered to each player, and each player may accept or pass. Winning hands are paid even money, less a 5% commission.

ROULETTE

Roulette is an extremely easy game to play, and it's really quite colorful and exciting to watch. The wheel spins, and the little ball bounces around, finally dropping into one of the slots, numbered 1 to 36, plus 0 and 00. You can bet on a single number, a

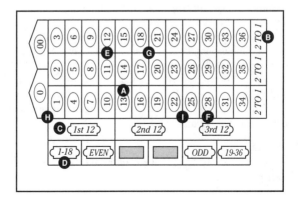

ROULETTE BETS AND ODDS

ROULETTE CHART KEY	ODDS	TYPE OF BET
		Straight Bets
A	35 to 1	*Straight-up:* All numbers, plus 0 and 00.
B	2 to 1	*Column Bet:* Pays off on any number in that horizontal column.
C	2 to 1	*First Dozen:* Pays off on any number 1 through 12. Same for second and third dozen.
D	Even Money	
		Combination Bets
E	17 to 1	*Split:* Pays off on 11 or 12.
F	11 to 1	Pays off on 28, 29, or 30.
G	8 to 1	*Corner:* Pays off on 17, 18, 20, or 21.
H	6 to 1	Pays off on 0, 00, 1, 2, or 3.
I	5 to 1	Pays off on 22, 23, 24, 25, 26, or 27.

combination of numbers, or red or black, odd or even. If you're lucky, you can win as much as 35 to 1 (see the table above). The method of placing single-number bets, column bets, and others is fairly obvious. The dealer will be happy to show you how to "straddle" two or more numbers and make many other interesting betting combinations. Each player is given different-colored chips so that it's easy to follow the numbers you're on.

A number of typical bets are indicated by means of letters on the roulette layout depicted here. The winning odds for each of these sample bets are listed. These bets can be made on any corresponding combinations of numbers.

SLOTS

You put the coin in the slot and pull the handle. What, you thought there was a trick to this?

Actually, there is a bit more to it. But first, some background. Old-timers will tell you that slots were invented to give wives something to do while their husbands gambled. Slots used to be stuck at the edges of the casino and could be counted on one hand, maybe two. But now they *are* the casino. The casinos make more from slots than from craps, blackjack, and roulette combined. There are 115,00 slot machines (not including video poker) in the county alone. Some of these are at the airport, steps from you as you deplane. It's a just a matter of time before the planes flying into Vegas feature slots that pop up as soon as you cross the state line.

But in order to keep up with the increasing competition, the plain old machine, where reels just spun, has become nearly obsolete. Now, they are all computerized and have added buttons to push, so you can avoid carpel tunnel syndrome yanking the handle all night. (The handles are still there on many of them.) The idea is still simple: Get three (sometimes four) cherries (clowns, sevens, dinosaurs, whatever) in a row, and you win something. Each machine has its own combination; some will pay you something with just one symbol showing; on most the more combinations there are, the more opportunities for loot. Some will even pay if you get three blanks. Study each machine to learn what it does.

The **payback** goes up considerably if you bet the limit (from two to as many as 45 coins). But while the payoff can be much bigger, the odds *against* winning also go up when you put in the limit. (So if you hit something on a machine and realize your $25 win would have been $500 had you only put in more money, take a deep breath, stop kicking yourself, and remember you might not actually have hit that winning combination so easily had you bet the limit.)

Progressive slots are groups of machines where the jackpot gets bigger every few moments (just as lottery jackpots build up). Bigger and better games keep showing up; for example, there's Anchor Gaming's much-imitated **Wheel of Gold,** wherein if you get the right symbol, you get to spin a roulette wheel, which guarantees you a win of a serious number of coins. **Totem Pole** is the Godzilla of slot machines, a behemoth that allows you to spin up to three reels at once (provided you put in the limit). And of course, there's our personal favorite, **Piggy Bankin'.** This has a LED display on which a silly tune plays and a pig cavorts (at erratic times, he trots across the screen, oinks, giggles when you lose, and imitates Elvis, among other playful actions). It's so much fun to watch you start putting in the coins just to get the pig to move, forget about the money. But meanwhile, money is building up in the piggy bank, an extra bonus you win if you hit the right symbol.

Other gimmick machines include **Clear Winner,** where you can satisfy your curiosity about the inner workings of a slot machine, and **Rockin' Reels,** which looks like a jukebox. And of course, there are always those **Big Giant Slot** machines, gimmicky devices found in almost every casino. They may not win as often as regular slots (though there is no definite word on it one way or the other), but not only are they just plain fun to spin, they often turn into audience participation gambling, as watchers gather to cheer you on to victory.

Are there surefire ways to win on a slot machine? No. But you can lose more slowly. The slots are on computer timers, and there are times when they are hitting and times when they are not. A bank of empty slots probably (but not certainly) means they aren't hitting. Go find a line where lots of people are sitting around with trays full of money. (Of course, yours will be the one that doesn't hit.) A good rule of thumb is that if your slot doesn't hit something in four or five pulls, leave it and go find another. It's not as though you won't have some choice in the matter. Also, each casino has some bank of slots that they advertise as more loose or with a bigger payback. Try these. It's what they want you to do, but what the heck.

SLOT CLUBS

If you play slots or video poker, it definitely pays to join a slot club. These so-called clubs are designed to attract and keep customers in a given casino by providing incentives—meals, shows, discounts on rooms, gifts, tournament invitations, discounts at hotel shops, VIP treatment, and (more and more) cash rebates. Of course, your rewards are greater if you play just in one casino, but your mobility is limited.

When you join a slot club (inquire at the casino desk), you're given something that looks like a credit card, which you must insert into an ATM-like device whenever you play. (Don't forget to retrieve your card when you leave the machine, as we sometimes do—though that may work in your favor if someone comes along and plays the machine without removing it.) The device tracks your play and computes bonus points.

Which slot club should you join? Actually, you should join one at any casino where you play, since even the act of joining usually entitles you to some benefits. It's convenient to concentrate play where you're staying; if you play a great deal, a casino hotel's slot-club benefits may be a factor in your accommodations choice. Consider, though, particularly if you aren't a high roller, the Slot Clubs Downtown. You get more bang for your buck because you don't have to spend as much to start raking in the goodies.

One way to judge a slot club is by the quality of service when you enroll. Personnel should politely answer all your questions (for instance, is nickel play included? or is there a time limit for earning required points?) and be able to tell you exactly how many points you need for various bonuses.

To maximize your slot-club profits and choose the club that's best for you is a complex business. If you want to get into it in depth, order a copy of Jeffrey Compton's *The Las Vegas Advisor Guide to Slot Clubs* ($9.95 plus shipping), which examines just about every facet of the situation (☎ **800/244-2224**). Compton gives high ratings to the clubs at Caesars Palace, the Desert Inn, the Mirage, Treasure Island, the Flamingo Hilton, the Rio, the Sahara, Sam's Town, the Four Queens, the Golden Nugget, and Lady Luck.

SPORTS BOOKS

Most of the larger hotels in Las Vegas have sports book operations— they look a lot like commodities-futures trading boards. In some, almost as large as theaters, you can sit comfortably and watch ball games, fights, and, at some casinos, horse races on huge TV screens. To add to your enjoyment, there's usually a deli/bar nearby that serves sandwiches, hot dogs, soft drinks, and beer. As a matter of fact, some of the best sandwiches in Las Vegas are served next to the sports books. Sports books take bets on virtually every sport.

VIDEO POKER

Rapidly coming up on slots in popularity, video poker works the same way as regular poker, except you play against the machine. You are dealt a hand, you pick which cards to keep and which to discard, and then get your new hand. And hopefully, collect your winnings. They are somewhat more of a challenge and more active than slots because you have some control (or at least illusion of control) over your fate, and they are easier than playing actual poker with a table full of folks who probably take it very seriously.

There are a number of varieties of this machine, with **Jacks are Better, Deuces Wild,** and so forth. Be sure to study your machine before you sit down. (The best returns are offered on the **Jacks Are Wild** machines, when the payback for a pair of Jacks or better is 2 times your bet, and 3 times for three of a kind.) Some machines offer Double Down: After you have won, you get a chance to draw cards against the machine, with the higher card the winner. If you win, your money is doubled and you are offered a chance to go again. Your money can increase nicely during this time, and you can also lose it all very fast, which is most annoying. Technology is catching up with Video Poker, too. Now they even have touch screens, which offer a variety of different poker games, blackjack, and video slots—just touch your screen and choose your poison.

2 The Casinos

Casino choice is a personal thing. Some like to find their lucky place and stick with it, while others love to take advantage of the nearly endless choices Vegas offers. Everyone should casino-hop at least once to marvel (or get dizzy) at the decor/spectacle and the sheer excess of it all. But beyond decoration, there isn't too much difference. You've got your slot machines, gaming tables, big chandeliers.

Virtually all casinos make sure they have no clocks or windows—they do not want you to interrupt your losing streak by realizing how much time has passed. Of course, we've all heard the legend that Vegas casinos pump in fresh oxygen to keep the players from getting tired and wanting to pack it in. The veracity of this is hard to confirm, but we can only hope it's true, especially when we think of that time we looked up after a long stretch of gambling and discovered it was Thursday.

Don't be a snob, and don't be overly dazzled by the fancy casinos. Sometimes you can have a better time at one of the older places Downtown, where stakes are lower, pretensions are nonexistent, and the clientele often friendlier.

What follows are brief descriptions of most of the major casinos in Vegas, including a claustrophobia rating, whether or not they have a Big Giant Slot Machine (it's a sucker bet, but we love them), and a completely arbitrary assessment based on whether or not we won there.

Bally's Las Vegas   Bally's casino is one of the most clean and well lit and definitely has that high-rent appeal. It's large (the size of a football field) with lots of colorful signage. The big ceiling makes for a low claustrophobia level. There's a Most Valuable Player Slot Club, offering members cash rebates, room discounts, free meals and show tickets, and invitations to special events, among other perks. The casino hosts frequent slot tournaments, and free gaming lessons are offered. There is not, however, a Big Giant Slot machine. For shame.

Barbary Coast The Barbary Coast has a cheerful 1890s-style casino ornately decorated with $2 million worth of gorgeous stained-glass skylights and signs, as well as immense crystal-dangling globe chandeliers over the gaming tables. It's worth stopping in just to take a look around when you're in the central "four corners" area of the Strip. The casino has a free Fun Club for slot players; participants earn points toward cash and prizes.

Binion's Horseshoe Professionals who know say that "for the serious player, the Binions *are* this town." Benny Binion could neither read nor write, but boy, did he know how to run a casino. His venerable establishment has gotten eclipsed over the years, but it claims the highest betting limits in Las Vegas on all games (probably in the entire world, according to a spokesperson). It offers single-deck blackjack and $2 minimums, 10-times odds on craps, and high progressive jackpots. We especially like the older part of the casino here, which—with its flocked wallpaper, gorgeous lighting fixtures, and gold-tasseled burgundy velvet drapes—looks like a turn-of-the-century Old West bordello. Unfortunately, all this adds up to a very high claustrophobia level. They have two Big Giant Slot machines, at least one of which has been very very good to us. Binion's is located Downtown at 128 E. Fremont St. between Casino Center Boulevard and First Street.

While you're visiting Binion's casino, be sure to see the display of $1 million (comprised of 100 $10,000 bills) encased in a gold horseshoe-shaped vault. If you'd like a photograph of yourself with all that moolah, you can get one taken free from 4pm to midnight daily.

Caesars Palace Caesars casino is simultaneously the ultimate in gambling luxury and the ultimate in Vegas kitsch. Cocktail waitresses in togas parade about, as you gamble under the watchful gaze of faux marble Roman statues. The very high ceiling makes for a very low claustrophobia level, especially thanks to the recent face-lift, which has lightened up the paint and made the whole casino much brighter. A notable facility is the state-of-the-art Race and Sports Book, with huge electronic display boards and giant video screens. (Caesars pioneered computer-generated wagering data that can be communicated in less than half a second and sophisticated satellite equipment that can pick up virtually any broadcast sporting event in the world.) It's a gorgeous and elegant place to gamble, but we've never won there, so we hate it.

California Hotel/Casino The California is a festive place filled with Hawaiian shirts and balloons. This friendly facility actually provides sofas and armchairs in the casino area—an unheard-of luxury in this town. This is the first place we found our favorite Piggy Bankin' machines.

Circus Circus   This vast property has three full-size casinos that, combined, comprise one of the largest gaming operations in Nevada (more than 100,000 square feet). More important, they have an entire circus midway set up throughout, so you are literally gambling with trapeze stunts going on over your head. The other great gimmick is the slot machine carousel—yep, it turns while you spin the reels. Unfortunately, the casino is crowded, noisy, and there are lots of children passing through. That, plus some low ceilings (not in the Big Top, obviously), make for a very high claustrophobia rating. Although the recent upgrades and remodeling aim to improve matters.

Desert Inn   Possibly the most genuinely elegant casino in Vegas, it's also one of the smallest for a major hotel. They don't care—they are looking for one good James Bond figure, rather than the masses. Crystal chandeliers here replace the usual neon glitz, and gaming tables are comfortably spaced. The ambience is reminiscent of intimate European gaming houses and is downright quiet. Some might find this almost creepy. Others may find it a huge relief. Since there are fewer slot machines here than at most major casinos, there's less noise in ringing bells and clinking coins. Most table games have a $5 minimum. The very high ceiling gives it a nonexistent claustrophobia rating.

Excalibur   As you might expect, the Excalibur casino is replete with suits of armor, stained-glass panels, knights, dragons, and velvet and satin heraldic banners, with gaming action taking place beneath vast iron and gold chandeliers fit for a medieval castle fortress. This all makes it fine for kitsch-seekers, but anyone hating crowds or with a low noise-pain threshold will hate it. The overall effect is less like a castle and more like a dungeon. A popular feature here is Circus Bucks, a progressive slot machine that builds from a jackpot base of $500,000; players can win on a $3 pull. One of us won a lot of money here and refused to share it with the other, so our final judgment about the casino is, well, mixed.

Fitzgeralds   They recently redid their casino in greens and golds, and the overall effect is not quite as tacky as you might expect. In fact, it's rather friendly, and with a medium to low claustrophobia level. The casino is actually two levels—from the upstairs part you can access a balcony from which you get an up-close view of the Fremont St. Experience. Their mascot, Mr. O'Lucky (a costumed leprechaun), roams the casino. You don't have to be nice to him. They have dollar Piggy Bankin' machines.

Flamingo Hilton If you've seen the movie *Bugsey,* you won't recognize this as Mr. Seigel's baby. The Flamingo is in the middle of redoing their casino area, which is just as well, because right now, it is overly crowded in feel, thanks to overall tight confines. It sprawls across a large space, meandering around corners, so it's very difficult to get out of. Actual daylight does stream in from windows and glass doorways on the Strip, however. There are slots here offering Cadillacs and Continentals as jackpots. One of our favorite slot machines is here, but we won't tell you which one to save it for ourselves. Sorry.

Four Queens New Orleans's themed, with turn-of-the-century-style globe chandeliers, which make for good lighting and a low claustrophobia level. It's small, but the dealers are helpful, which is one of the pluses of gambling in the more manageable-sized casinos. The facility boasts the world's largest slot machine—more than 9 feet high and almost 20 feet long; six people can play it at one time! It's the Mother of all Big Giant Slot machines, and frankly, it intimidates even us. Here is also the world's largest blackjack table (it seats 12 players).

Gold Coast Adjacent to the Rio, this casino is not only well lit, but totally unique in Vegas: *It has windows!* It's a little thing, but it really excited us. The Gold Coast is located at 4000 W. Flamingo.

Golden Gate This is one of the oldest casinos in Downtown, and though its age is showing, it's still fun to go there. As you might expect from the name, old San Francisco (think earthquake time) artifacts and decor abound. At one end of the narrow casino is the bar, where a piano player performs ragtime jazz, which is better than the homogenized pap offered in most casino lounges. Unfortunately, the low ceiling, dark period wallpaper, and small dimensions give this a high claustrophobia level. Golden Gate is at 1 Fremont St.

Golden Nugget Frankly, this is not the standout that other Steve Wynn–owned casino properties are. It goes for luxury, of course, but so much is crammed into so little space that the only feeling that emerges is one of overcrowding. That's not to say we didn't like it because we won a lot of money there. And compared to most other Downtown properties, this is the most Strip-like. It is much cleaner and fresher feeling, in an area filled with dingy, time-forgotten spaces.

Gold Spike   Yes, we just criticized dingy, time-forgotten spaces (see above) in Downtown, and the Gold Spike certainly lands in that category. So what? Here, everyone is equal, and everyone is having a good time, or at least they can sincerely join you in your misery. Best of all, they have penny slots! (Not very many, to be sure, and getting a seat at one can require patience.) Hey tightwads, take a buck, and spend a few hours. The Gold Spike is at 400 Ogden at Las Vegas Boulevard., Downtown.

Hard Rock Hotel & Casino   Where Gen X goes to gamble. The Hard Rock has certainly taken casino decor to a whole new level. The attention to detail and the resulting playfulness is admirable, if not incredible. Gaming tables have piano keyboards at one end; some slots have Fender guitar fretboards as arms; gaming chips have band names and/or pictures on them; slot machines are similarly rock themed (check out the Jimi Hendrix machine!); and so it goes. The whole thing is set in the middle of a circular room, around the outskirts of which is various rock memorabilia in glass cases. Rock blares over the sound system, allowing Boomers to boogie while they gamble. All this is genuinely amazing, but the noise level is above even that of a normal casino and we just hated it. It's worth looking at anyway.

Harrah's   Confetti carpeting and fiber-optic fireworks overhead combine with murals and an overall Mardi Gras theme to make a festive environment. Does it help you win more? Who knows. But the different, better energy that has resulted from this recent, costly face-lift certainly couldn't hurt. Don't miss the "party pits," gaming table areas where dealers are encouraged to wear funny hats, celebrate wins, and otherwise break the usual stern dealer facade. Singing, dancing, and the handing out of party favors have all been known to break out. Gambling is supposed to be fun, so enjoy it.

Imperial Palace   The 75,000-square-foot casino here reflects the hotel's pagoda-roofed Asian exterior with a dragon-motif ceiling and giant wind-chime chandeliers. There is a nonsmoking slot machine area separate from the main casino (as opposed to just another part of the room, at best, in other casinos) and a Breathalyzer for voluntary alcohol limit checks on your way to the parking lot. (Useful since there are nine bars on the casino premises.) One Big Giant Slot machine is red, white, and blue; try singing the National Anthem to it, and see if you win more money.

Lady Luck   Even though it's an older casino with the anticipated drop in glamour, it's surprisingly cheerful and with a low to medium claustrophobia level. Decorations give it a festive quality, and cocktail waitresses push drink carts, to mix you up something right on the spot.

Las Vegas Hilton   Austrian crystal chandeliers add a strong touch of class to the Hilton's 67,000-square-foot casino. It's actually on the medium size, but it does have an enormous sports book—at 30,500 square feet, the world's largest race and sports book facility.

Luxor Las Vegas   More accessible than ever thanks to the addition of the air-conditioned people mover from Excalibur, Luxor has been completed remodeled and, in our opinion, improved immeasurably. The additional space gives the casino a much more airy feel, which gives it a low claustrophobia level—in parts you can see all the way up the inside of the pyramid. There's a nonsmoking slot area. We already felt inclined to like this casino thanks to a good run at blackjack, but the redesign has made it even more inviting.

Main Street Station   Part of a long-closed old hotel that has been recently renovated and reopened to great success, this is the best of the Downtown casinos, at least in terms of comfort and pleasant environment. Even the Golden Nugget, nice as it is, has more noise and distractions. The decor here is, again, classic Vegas/old-timey (Victorian-era) San Francisco, but with extra touches (check out the old-fashioned fans above the truly beautiful bar) that make it work much better than other attempts at the same. Strangely, it seems just about smoke-free, perhaps thanks in part to a very high ceiling. The claustrophobia level is zero.

MGM Grand   The world's largest casino—171,500 square feet—is divided into four themed areas, in a futile attempt to make it seem smaller. Much of the Wizard of Oz decorations have been removed, but spend an hour in here and you might well feel like Dorothy after she got hit by the twister.

The Mirage   Gamble in a Polynesian village in one of the prettiest casinos in town. It has a meandering layout, and the low ceiling makes for a medium claustrophobia level, but neither of these things is overwhelming. This remains one of our favorite places to gamble. It's one of the most pleasant, and popular casinos in town so it's crowded more often than not.

Monte Carlo   All huge ceilings and white-light interiors: Obviously, they are trying to evoke gambling in Monaco. While the decor shows lots of attention, it perhaps had too much attention. Bulbs line the ceiling, and everywhere you look is some detail or other. It's busy on both your eyes and ears. So despite the effort put in, it's not a pleasant place to gamble.

New York New York   Another them-run-wild place: tuxes on the backs of gaming chairs, change carts that look like yellow cabs, and so forth, all set in a miniature New York City. It's all fabulous fun, but despite a low claustrophobia level (thanks to an unusually high ceiling), it is a major case of sensory overload akin to the reaction elicited by a first-time look at the Strip. This may prove distracting. On the other hand, we won there, so we love it. And it is, if one can say this about anything in Vegas with a straight face, in spots quite beautiful. Serious gamblers understandably may sniff at it all and prefer to take their business to a more seemly casino, but everyone else should have about the most Vegasey time they can.

Orleans   This is not a particularly special gambling space, though it has a low claustrophobia level. Cajun and Zydeco music is played over the sound system, so you can two-step while you gamble, which can make losing somewhat less painful. It has a Wheel of Fortune machine that works like those other roulette wheel slots, but in this case, actually plays the theme song from the TV show. It will even applaud for you if you win.

The Rio   This Brazilian-themed resort's 85,000-square-foot casino is, despite the presence of plenty of glitter and neon, very dark. It has about the highest claustrophobia rating of the major casinos. Its sports book feels a little grimy. The waitresses wear scanty costumes (particularly in the back), probably in an effort to distract you and throw your game off. Do not let them. The part of the casino in the new Masquerade Village is considerably more pleasant (the very high ceilings help) though still crowded, plus the loud live show adds still more noise.

The Riviera   The Riviera's 100,000-square-foot casino, one of the largest in the world, means that there are plenty of opportunities to get lost and cranky. A wall of windows lets daylight stream in (most unusual), and the gaming tables are situated beneath gleaming brass arches lit by recessed, pink neon tubing. This is one of the few places in town where you can play the ancient Chinese game of *sic bo* (a fast-paced dice game resembling craps).

The Sahara   The Sahara is in the process of changing its casino's look, and adding a large new area, so it might be worth checking out. This is one place where there seem to be more tables than slots and video poker machines, but that might change with the new addition. When we were last there, they had a whole row of Piggy Bankin' machines that were all paying off, so we were happy.

The Stardust   Always mobbed, this popular casino features 90,000 square feet of lively gaming action, including a 250-seat race and sports book with a sophisticated satellite system and more than 50 TV monitors airing sporting events and horse racing results around the clock. We usually do well there, so even though it's a little loud we like it. Check out those one dollar slots just inside the front door—they've been very good to us.

The Stratosphere   Originally set up as to evoke a World's Fair, but ending up more like a circus, the Stratosphere redid the whole area in order to make it more appealing for the many adults who were staying away in droves. The newly redone facility aims for class, but doesn't necessarily achieve that—it's not that it fails, it just no longer has any identity at all. They heavily advertise their high payback on certain slots and video poker: 98% payback on dollar slots and 100% payback on quarter video poker (if you bet the maximum on each). We can't say we noticed a difference, but other people around us were winning like crazy.

Treasure Island   Treasure Island's huge casino is highly themed. If you have ever gone to Disneyland's Pirates of the Caribbean and thought, "Gee, if only this were a casino," this is the place for you. Kids seem to be everywhere because they are dazzled by the pirate stuff. Many people complain they don't like the atmosphere here, possibly because that very theme backfires. Throughout the casino there is something called Slot 2000. Hit a button, and a video screen pops up showing a (female) casino worker, to whom you can talk. She will answer questions, send someone over with drinks, make reservations, and otherwise help make your time there better. If you win a jackpot, she will come on and congratulate you. No, she can't see you, so don't try to flirt.

Tropicana   The Trop casino is quite good-looking, and, yes, highly tropical, with gaming tables situated beneath a massive, stained-glass archway and art nouveau lighting fixtures. In summer it offers something totally unique: swim-up blackjack tables located in the hotel's stunning 5-acre tropical garden and pool area.

8

Las Vegas After Dark

*Y*ou will not lack for things to do at night in Vegas. It is a town that truly comes alive only at night. Don't believe us? Just look at the difference between the Strip during the day, when it's kind of dingy and nothing special, and at night when the lights hit and the place glows in all its glory. Night is when it's happening in this 24-hour town. In fact, most bars and clubs don't even get going until close to midnight. That's because it's only around then that all the many restaurant workers and people connected with the shows get off the clock and can go out and play themselves. It's extraordinary. Just sit down in a bar at 11pm; it's empty. You might well conclude it's dead. Return in 2 hours and find it completely full and jumping.

But you also won't lack for things to do before 11pm. There are shows all over town, ranging from traditional magic to cutting-edge acts like *Mystère*. The showgirls remain, topless and otherwise; Las Vegas revues are what happened to vaudeville, by the way, as chorus girls do their thing in between jugglers, comics, magicians, singers, and specialty acts of dubious category. Even the topless ones are tame; all that changes is the that already scantily clad showgirls are even more so.

Every hotel has at least one lounge, usually offering live music. The days of fabulous Vegas lounge entertainment, where sometimes the acts were of better quality than the headliners (and headliners like Sinatra would join the lounge acts onstage between their own sets), are gone. Most of what remains are homogenous and bland, and serve best as a brief respite or background noise. On the other hand, finding the most awful lounge act in town can be rewarding on its own. (To this end, seek out Cook E. Jarr and the Crumbs, a rapidly aging and tasteless crew universally revered as the worst lounge act in Vegas. They were last spotted at the Continental Hotel.)

Vegas still does attract the best in headliner entertainment in its showrooms and arenas. Bette Midler did an HBO special from the MGM Grand in early 1997, and U2 started its PopArt tour at UNLV's stadium. Liza Minnelli, Harry Belafonte, Penn and Teller,

Melissa Manchester, Wayne Newton, Chaka Khan, Johnny Mathis, Barbara Mandrell, Englebert Humperdick, and Wynnona have all played Vegas recently. (And up until just a few years ago, the legendary Sinatra still did regular stints there.) It is still a badge of honor for comedians to play Vegas, and there is almost always someone of marquee value playing one showroom or the other.

Of course, if you prefer alternative or real rock music, check out the listings below for bars, several of which offer live alternative or blues music. Free alternative papers are the *Scope* (biweekly, with great club and bar descriptions in their listings) and *City Life* (weekly, with no descriptions but comprehensive listings of what's playing where all over town). Both can be picked up at restaurants, bars, record and music stores, and hep retail stores.

Admission to shows runs a wide gamut, from about $18.95 for *An Evening at La Cage* (a female impersonator show at the Riviera) to $80 and more for top headliners or *Siegfried and Roy.* Prices usually include two drinks or, in rare instances, dinner.

To find out who will be performing during your stay, and for up to date listings of shows (prices change, shows close), you can call the various hotels featuring headliner entertainment, using toll-free numbers. Or call the **Las Vegas Convention and Visitors Authority** (☎ **702/892-0711**) and ask them to send you a free copy of *Showguide* or *What's On in Las Vegas* (one or both of which will probably be in your hotel room.)

1 What's Playing Where

Below is a list of the major production shows playing at our press time in Las Vegas. In the following section, we've reviewed some of the major ones.

- Aladdin Hotel, *Country Tonite* (country music review)
- Bally's, ✪ *Jubilee!* (Las Vegas–style review)
- Debbie Reynolds Hotel, ✪ *Kenny Kerr Show* (female impersonators) and the ✪ *Debbie Reynolds Show* (Las Vegas–style review featuring Debbie)
- Excalibur, *An Evening in Vienna* (afternoon show featuring the Lippizaner Stallions, described in chapter 7) and *King Arthur's Tournament* (medieval-themed review)
- Flamingo Hilton, *Forever Plaid* (off-Broadway review featuring '60s music) and *The Great Radio City Spectacular* (Las Vegas–style review featuring the Radio City Music Hall Rockettes)
- Golden Nugget, ✪ *Country Fever* (country music review)

- Harrah's, *Spellbound* (magic review)
- Imperial Palace, *Legends in Concert* (musical impersonators)
- Jackie Gaughan's Plaza, *The Xtreme Scene* (sexy Las Vegas–style review)
- Las Vegas Hilton, *Starlight Express* (Andrew Lloyd Webber's Broadway show)
- MGM Grand, ✪ *EFX* (special-effects review featuring David Cassidy)
- The Mirage, ✪ *Siegfried and Roy* (magical extravaganza)
- Monte Carlo, ✪ *Lance Burton: Master Magician* (magic show and review)
- Rio Suite Hotel, Danny Gans (impressions)
- Riviera Hotel, *An Evening at La Cage* (female impersonators), *Crazy Girls* (sexy Las Vegas–style review), and *Splash* (aquatic review)
- Stardust, *Enter the Night* (Las Vegas–style review)
- Stratosphere Tower, ✪ *American Superstars* (an impression-filled production show), *Viva Las Vegas* (Las Vegas–style review)
- Treasure Island, ✪ Cirque du Soleil's *Mystère* (unique circus performance)
- Tropicana, *Folies Bergère* (Las Vegas–style review)

2 The Major Production Shows

Since this portable guide is more limited in scope than our regular *Frommer's Las Vegas* guide, we've only included reviews of the better or more important shows.

American Superstars. Stratosphere, 2000 Las Vegas Blvd. S. ☎ **800/ 99-TOWER** or 702/380-7777.

One of the increasing number of celebrity impersonator shows (cheaper than getting the real headliners), "American Superstars" is one of the few where said impersonators actually sing live. Five performers do their thing; celebs impersonated vary depending on the evening. A typical Friday night featured Gloria Estefan, Charlie Daniels, Madonna, Michael Jackson, and Diana Ross and the Supremes. The performers won't be putting the originals out of work any time soon, but they aren't bad. Actually, they are closer in voice than in looks to the celeb in question (half the black performers were played by white actors), which is an unusual switch for Vegas impersonators. The "Charlie Daniels" actually proved to be a fine fiddler in his own right and was the hands-down crowd favorite. The live band actually had a look alike of their own,

Kato Kaelin on drums (it's good that he's getting work). The youngish crowd (by Vegas standards) included a healthy smattering of children and seemed to find no faults with the production. The action is also shown on two large, and completely unnecessary, video screens flanking the stage, so you don't have to miss a moment.

- **Showroom Policies:** Smoking not permitted; maitre d' seating.
- **Price:** Admission $25.25 includes tax.
- **Show Times:** Fri–Wed at 8 and 10pm. Dark Thurs.
- **Reservations:** Up to 3 days in advance.

✪ **Cirque du Soleil's Mystère.** Treasure Island, 3300 Las Vegas Blvd. S. ☎ **800/392-1999** or 702/894-7723.

The in-house ads for *Mystère* (say "miss-TAIR") say "Words don't do it justice," and for once, that's not just hype. The show is so visual that trying to describe it is a losing proposition. And simply calling it a circus is like calling the Hope Diamond a gem or the Taj Mahal a building. It's accurate, but something seems a little left out of the description.

Cirque de Soleil began in Montréal as a unique circus experience, not only shunning the traditional animal acts in favor of gorgeous feats of human strength and agility, but also adding elements of the surreal and the absurd. The result seems like a collaboration between Salvador Dali and Luis Buñel, with a few touches by Magritte and choreography by Twyla Tharp. Mirage Resorts has built them their own theater, an incredible space with an enormous dome and super hydraulics that allow for the Cirque performers to fly in space. Or so it seems.

While part of the fun of the early Cirque was seeing what amazing stuff they could do on a shoestring, seeing what they can do with virtually unlimited funds is spectacular. Unlike, arguably, other artistic ventures, Cirque took full advantage of their new largess, and their art only rose with their budget. The show features one simply unbelievable act after another (seemingly boneless contortionists and acrobats, breathtakingly beautiful aerial maneuvers), interspersed with Dada-ist, commedia dell'arte clowns, and everyone clad in costumes like nothing you've ever seen before. All this and a giant snail. The show is dreamlike, suspenseful, funny, erotic, mesmerizing, and just lovely. At times, you might even find yourself moved to tears. However, for some children, it might be a bit too sophisticated and arty. Even if you've seen Cirque before, it's worth coming to check out, thanks to the large production values. It's a world-class show, no matter where it's playing. That this is playing in Vegas is astonishing.

- **Showroom Policies:** Nonsmoking with preassigned seating.
- **Price:** $64.90 adults, $32.40 for children under 11 (drinks and tax extra).
- **Show Times:** Wed–Sun at 7:30 and 10:30pm. Dark Mon–Tues.
- **Reservations:** You can reserve by phone via credit card up to 7 days in advance (do reserve early since it often sells out).

✪ **Country Fever.** Golden Nugget, 129 E. Fremont St. ☎ **800/777-4658** or 702/386-8100.

A few years back, the Golden Nugget redecorated its showroom walls with a display of Western paraphernalia, neon cacti, steer heads, and cowboy boots. It's the setting for *Country Fever*—the best foot-stompin', hand-clappin' country music show in town—featuring a cast of tremendously talented singers and dancers, including bare-buttocked showgirls in fringed country thongs and cowboy boots (this *is* Las Vegas!). They're backed up by an outstanding nine-piece band called The Posse. The cast also includes a gospel choir and a first-rate stand-up comic, Kirby St. Romaine. Special kudos to the exuberant star of the show, T. J. Weaver. Since light fare is served, arrive at least an hour early, so you're through with it when the show begins.

- **Showroom Policies:** Nonsmoking with maître d' seating.
- **Price:** $25 (including a drink and a basket of taco chips with two dipping sauces and chicken tenders; gratuity extra).
- **Show Times:** Sat–Thurs at 7:00 and 9:45pm. Dark Fri.
- **Reservations:** You can reserve up to 4 days in advance.

✪ **Danny Gans: The Man of Many Voices.** Rio Suites, 3700 W. Flamingo Rd. ☎ **800/PLAY-RIO** or 702/252-7777.

Danny Gans has taken over the newly refurbished Copacobana Showroom for an indefinite run. If he's still on when you visit, don't miss him. Gans, who has starred on Broadway, is an impressionist extraordinaire. Natalie Cole, who heard him perform her father's famous song, "Unforgettable," exclaimed, "No one has ever done a better impression of my dad." His show is also unforgettable. In addition to startlingly realistic impressions of dozens of singers (everyone from Sinatra to Springsteen), he does movie scenes (such as Fonda and Hepburn in *On Golden Pond),* Bill Clinton, weird duets (Michael Bolton and Dr. Ruth, or Stevie Wonder singing to Shirley MacLaine—"I Just Called to Say I Was You"), and, of course, a first-rate Elvis. A mind-boggling highlight is Gans's rendition of "The Twelve Days of Christmas" in 12 different voices, which necessitates rapidly switching back and forth from such diverse impressions as Paul Lynde, Clint Eastwood, Peter Falk, and Woody Allen, among others. This show gets a standing ovation every night.

- **Showroom Policies:** Nonsmoking with maître d' seating.
- **Price:** $44.95 (including two drinks, tax and gratuities).
- **Show Times:** Wed–Sun at 8pm. Dark Mon–Tues.
- **Reservations:** Tickets can be ordered up to 30 days in advance.

✪ **EFX.** MGM Grand, 3799 Las Vegas Blvd. S. ☎ **800/929-1111** or 702/891-7777.

Essentially the first major show of the post–Cirque de Soliel era, *EFX*'s $40 million makeover (thanks to new star David Cassidy) has used its money wisely, updating the classic Vegas revue into essentially a live action version of the modern over-the-top Strip hotels. It's not so much cheese anymore, as expensive and occasionally jaw-dropping cheese. Which is not to say it's bad—quite the opposite. The nominal story line, about a man who has lost his imagination, allows the very likable Cassidy, playing on his regular guy image, to assume the personas of King Arthur, P. T. Barnum, Houdini, and H. G. Wells, in order to deliver set pieces of better-than-usual dancing, magic, singing, acrobatics, and illusion. And, of course, special effects (*EFX* is the movie industry term for same). The sets are lavish beyond belief, the costumes and some of the acting show the Cirque influence (faintly Grand Guignol), and the choreography is considerably more imaginative and fresh than any other such show in town. The songs are somewhat bland, but sung almost totally live, and some prove surprisingly hummable. And the effects (flying saucers and cast members, fire-breathing dragons, 3-D time travel, lots of explosions) show where the money is. Cranks may occasionally spot wires, and sometimes said effects are a little painful on the eyes and ears (and they overdo it on the fog machine). The ticket price isn't cheap, so it might be worth taking the less expensive seats in the mezzanine, as the view is just as good from there.

- **Showroom Policies:** Nonsmoking with preassigned seating.
- **Price:** $51.50–$72.
- **Show Times:** Tues–Sat at 7:30 and 10:30pm. Dark Sun–Mon.
- **Reservations:** You can reserve by phone any time in advance.

Enter the Night. The Stardust, 3000 Las Vegas Blvd. S. ☎ **800/824-6033** or 702/732-6111.

It's kind of cute how the Stardust has tried to stage a full-size top-less revue on a small- to medium-size stage. Okay, maybe not *cute*, but the production does seem to be busting at its seams, and it never quite reconciles its aspirations with its reality. There is no plot or point to this; the theme is "enter the night" (of course) and about the passion and mystery that will then ensue, but the songs and actions are vague as to how this is supposed to come about. Instead, what you get is one of those "why is that girl parading around in her underwear?" sort of shows. It's a question that can be quite relevant, depending on your seats, since a circular catwalk extends into the audience; some seats are perched right on the rail edge of this, virtually squashing the occupant's face into a showgirl midriff. In fact, some of those topless breasts could put out an eye. (Besides, it spoils the illusion when you are close enough to see all that pancake makeup.) Your seat placement is worth noting for this reason, if you don't want to be that up close and personal with a virtually naked total stranger. Others might pay extra.

Anyway, it's a revue, featuring songs about listening to your heart, dancing (the Space Age Viking dance number was a camp highlight), and one blonde (presumably Aki, "Showgirl for the 21st Century") in a flesh-colored G-string performing nearly nude *en pointe* ballet. All this is delivered with a Mickey Mouse Club enthusiasm, which is a bit disconcerting when half the performers are partially naked. There is also nearly naked ice-skating, which was actually better than you might think; the skaters are very good and make use of the world's tiniest patch of ice in dramatic and resourceful ways. They were also a huge crowd pleaser, as was the delightful Argentinean gaucho act.

- **Showroom Policies:** Nonsmoking with preassigned seating.
- **Price:** Most seats $29.85, booths $35 to $55 (includes two drinks, tax, and gratuity).
- **Show Times:** Tues, Wed, Thurs, Sat at 7:30 and 10:30pm, Sun–Mon at 8pm only. Dark Fri.
- **Reservations:** You can reserve up to a month in advance by phone.

An Evening at La Cage. Riviera Hotel and Casino, 2901 Las Vegas Blvd. S. ☎ **800/634-6753** or 702/734-9301.

No, not inspired by the French movie nor the recent American remake, nor even the Broadway musical. Actually, it's more the stage show from *Priscilla, Queen of the Desert*. Female impersonators dress up as various entertainers (with varying degrees of success) to lip-synch to said performers greatest hits (with varying degrees of success). Celebs lampooned can include Cher, Bette Midler, Judy Garland, Whitney Houston, Dionne Warwick and, intriguingly, Michael Jackson. A Joan Rivers impersonator, looking not unlike the original but sounding (even with the aid of, oddly, a constant echo) not at all like her is the hostess, delivers scatological phrases and stale jokes. They do make the most of a tiny stage with some pretty stunning lighting, though the choreography is bland. Still, it's a crowd pleaser—one couple was back for their fourth (all comped) visit.

- **Showroom Policies:** Nonsmoking with maître d' seating.
- **Price:** $26.66–$32.16 (includes two drinks; gratuity extra).
- **Show Times:** Wed–Mon at 7:30 and 9:30pm, with an extra show at 11:15pm Wed. Dark Tues.
- **Reservations:** Tickets can be purchased at the box office only, in advance if you wish.

The Great Radio City Spectacular. Flamingo Hilton, 3555 Las Vegas Blvd. S. ☎ 702/733-3333.

This is the wholesome showgirls show. If you aren't familiar with the venerable Rockettes tradition, the short black-and-white film on their history that opens the production will get you up-to-date. It also sets the stage for the big entrance by the ladies, arguably the world's best known chorus line. There is a headliner who accompanies them—this star changes frequently. As of this writing, it was Paige O'Hara, the voice of Belle from Disney's *Beauty and the Beast.* Regardless of who it is, the star's musical numbers are interspersed with a variety of dance productions by the Rockettes that serve as a veritable history of dance, ranging from tap to forties swing, waltzes, March of the Wooden Soldiers, and the like. Of course, the signature Rockettes' high-kicking line is worked into at least half the numbers. That's their greatest hit—if Ms. O'Hara remains with the show, you can count on seeing her do hers, from the aforementioned "Beast." The variety acts are standard Vegas: A juggler who keeps up a disturbing, David Helfgott–like banter under his breath and a magician who tries too hard. The standout here was the trained dogs act, which reduced even cynical viewers to goo. These are all pound-rescued mutts with plenty of star quality, and they work the crowd like pros.

- **Showroom Policies:** Nonsmoking with maître d' seating.
- **Price:** Dinner show based on main-course price ($53.95–$64.28 includes tax, and gratuity). Cocktail show $46.12 (includes two drinks, tax, and gratuity).

- **Show Times:** Nightly dinner show at 7:45pm, cocktail show at 10:30pm.
- **Reservations:** You can reserve by phone 2 weeks in advance.

✪ **Jubilee!** Bally's, 3645 Las Vegas Blvd. S. ☎ **800/237-7469** or 702/739-4567.

A classic Vegas spectacular, crammed with singing, dancing, magic, acrobats, elaborate costumes and sets, and of course, bare breasts. It's a basic review, with production numbers featuring homogenized versions of standards (Gershwin, Cole Porter, some Fred Astaire numbers) sometimes sung live, sometimes lip-synched, and always accompanied by lavishly costumed and frequently topless showgirls. Humorous set pieces about Samson and Delilah and the sinking of the *Titanic* show off some pretty awesome sets, while the finale features aerodynamically impossible feathered and bejeweled costumes and headpieces designed by Bob Mackie. So what if the dancers are occasionally out of step and the action sometimes veers into the dubious (a Vegas-style revue about a disaster that took over 1,000

---

12 Inaccuracies in the Movie *Showgirls*
by the Showgirls in Jubilee!

1. Nomi Malone wouldn't be in a Las Vegas production because she can't sing (or act).
2. Showgirls do not live in trailers.
3. Showgirls aren't discovered in strip bars.
4. Showgirls do not pimp themselves at conventions or trade shows.
5. Hotel owners do not throw lavish cast parties.
6. A lead dancer does not become a celebrity.
7. No one learns a show in a day.
8. Pushing someone down the stairs doesn't get you a lead role; it gets you fired.
9. Ice is used backstage to treat injuries, not to erect nipples.
10. Leaving rehearsal to go to Spago to drink champagne is generally frowned upon.
11. Showgirls are not coke-sniffing, champagne-drinking lesbians.
12. Anyway, Showgirls do not drink champagne backstage—we prefer Jack Daniels!

lives?) or even the inexplicable (a finale praising "beautiful," and bare-breasted, girls suddenly stops for three lines of "Somewhere Over the Rainbow")? With plenty of rhinestones and nipples on display, this is archetypal Vegas entertainment and the best of that presently offered.

- **Showroom Policies:** Nonsmoking with preassigned seating.
- **Price:** $49.50 (tax included, drinks extra).
- **Show Times:** Sun–Mon at 8pm, Tues–Thurs and Sat at 8 and 11pm. Dark Fri.
- **Reservations:** You can reserve up to 6 weeks in advance.

✪ **Kenny Kerr Show.** Debbie Reynolds Hotel, 305 Convention Center Dr. ☎ **800/633-1777** or 702/7-DEBBIE.

A sophisticated female-impersonator revue starring "hostess" Kenny Kerr, *Boylesque* has been playing somewhere in Las Vegas since 1970. This now eponymously titled version is his best show yet: He's looking great, his repartee is sparkling, and his vast array of costumes is simply stunning. An evening with Kenny is marvelously outrageous and over-the-top, with lots of double-entendre jokes and even a bit of beefcake. A talented cast, backed up by a dance troupe, does take-offs (mostly lip-synching, but Kenny really sings) on Marilyn Monroe, Dolly Parton, Janet Jackson, Diana Ross, Barbra Streisand, Liza Minnelli, and others—even Pocahontas. But most impressive is the lively improvisational patter of Kerr himself, who fields questions, some of them very personal, with humor and panache and creates an intimate rapport with his audience.

- **Showroom Policies:** Nonsmoking with maître d' seating.
- **Price:** $21.95 (includes tax).
- **Show Times:** Mon–Sat 10:30pm.
- **Reservations:** You can reserve by phone up to 3 days in advance.

✪ **Lance Burton: Master Magician.** Monte Carlo, 3770 Las Vegas Blvd. S. ☎ **800/311-8999** or 702/730-7000.

Magic acts are a dime a dozen in Vegas of late—along with impersonator acts, they seem to have largely replaced the topless showgirls of lore. Most seem more than a little influenced by the immeasurable success of Siegfried and Roy. So when someone pops up who is original—not to mention charming and, yes, actually good at his job—it comes as a relief.

Monte Carlo dumped a lot of money into building the lush Victorian music hall–style Lance Burton Theater for the star, and it was worth it. Handsome and folksy (he hails from Lexington, Kentucky), Burton is talented and engaging, for the most part shunning the big-ticket special effects that seem to have swamped most other shows in town. Instead, he offers an extremely appealing production that starts small, with "close up" magic. These rather lovely tricks, he tells us, are what won him a number of prestigious magic competitions. They are truly extraordinary (we swear that he tossed a bird up in the air, and the darn thing turned into confetti in front of our eyes. Really.) Burton doesn't have patter, per se, but his dry, laconic, low-key delivery is plenty amusing and in contrast to other performers in town who seem as if they have been spending way too much time at Starbucks. He does eventually move to bigger illusions, but his manner follows him—he knows the stuff is good, but he also knows the whole thing is a bit silly, so why not have fun with it? Accompanying him are some perky showgirls, who border on the wholesome, and talented comic juggler Michael Goudeau. The latter is a likable goofball who instantly wins you over (or should) when he juggles three beanbag chairs. All this and extremely comfortable movie theater–style plush seats with cupholders. And for a most reasonable price.

- **Showroom Policies:** Nonsmoking with preassigned seating.
- **Price:** $34.95 (includes tax, drinks extra).
- **Show Times:** Tues–Sat at 7:30 and 10:30pm. Dark Sun–Mon.
- **Reservations:** Tickets can be purchased 60 days in advance.

Legends in Concert. Imperial Palace, 3535 Las Vegas Blvd. S. ☎ **702/ 794-3261.**

A crowd pleaser, which is probably why it's been running since May 1983. Arguably the best of the Vegas impersonator shows (though it's hard to quantify such things), "Legends" does feature performers live, rather than lip-synching. Acts vary from night to night (in a showroom that could use a face-lift) on a nice large stage with modern hydraulics but twinkle lighting that is stuck in a *Flip Wilson Show* time warp. The personal touches here include scantily clad (but well choreographed) male and female dancers and an utterly useless green laser. When we went, the performers included Neil Diamond (whose "America" was accompanied by red-, white-, and blue-clad showgirls covered in flags of all nations. Go figure), an actual piano-playing Elton John, the Blues Brothers (a reasonable John Belushi, but a not even close Dan Ackroyd), and the inevitable Diana Ross, Four Tops, and the young thin Elvis (who performs hits from the fat old Elvis years). The latter, by the way, was preceded by a reverent multimedia presentation (the stage also has video screens that show not only the live action but clips by the real celebs). Best of all, Wayne Newton was there. Yes, the *real* one. During the Blues Brothers bit, the band showed a rare display of spontaneity. When one audience member called out a request for "country," they actually broke into the theme from *Rawhide*. Maybe it was a planned moment, but we were impressed that it didn't seem that way.

- **Showroom Policies:** Nonsmoking, with maître d' seating.
- **Price:** $29.50 (includes two drinks or one Polynesian cocktail such as a mai tai or zombie; tax and gratuity extra).
- **Show Times:** Mon–Sat at 7:30 and 10:30pm. Dark Sun.
- **Reservations:** You can make reservations by phone up to 2 weeks in advance.

✪ **Siegfried and Roy.** The Mirage, 3400 Las Vegas Blvd. S. ☎ **800/ 627-6667** or 702/792-7777.

A Vegas institution for more than two decades, illusionists Siegfried and Roy started as an opening act, became headliners at the Frontier, and finally were given their own $30 million show and $25 million theater in the Mirage. They (and their extensive exotic animal menagerie) have amply repaid this enormous investment by selling out every show since. No wonder the Mirage has them booked "until the end of time."

But while the spectacle is undeniable (and the money right on the stage), the result is overproduced. From the get go, there is so much light, sound, smoke, and fire; so many dancing girls, fire-breathing dragons, robots, and other often completely superfluous effects; not to mention an original (and forgettable) Michael Jackson song, that it overwhelms the point of the whole thing. Or maybe it's *become* the point of the whole thing. The magic, which was the Austrian duo's original act, after all, seems to have gotten lost. Sometimes literally. The tricks are at a minimum, allowing the flash pots, lasers, and whatnot to fill out the nearly 2-hour show. More often than not, when a trick is actually being performed, our attention was elsewhere, gawking at an effect, a showgirl, or something. Only the gasps from the audience members who actually happened to be looking in the right place let us know we missed something really neat.

Tellingly, the best part of the show is when all that stuff is switched off, and Siegfried and Roy take the stage to perform smaller magic and chat with the audience. The charm that helped get them so far shines through, and spontaneity is allowed to sneak in. The

Wayne Newton's Top 10 Favorite Lounge Songs

Wayne Newton is the consummate entertainer. He has performed more than 25,000 concerts in Las Vegas alone, and in front of more than 25 million people worldwide. Wayne has received more standing ovations than any other entertainer in history. Along with his singing credits, his acting credits are soaring—one of his more recent credits is Vegas Vacation. *Make sure you catch him playing at the MGM Grand.*

No trip to Vegas is complete without seeing the King of Las Vegas . . .WAYNE NEWTON!

1. "You're Nobody, 'Til Somebody Loves You" (*You don't have a body unless somebody loves you!)*
2. "Up A Lazy River" (or *"Up Your Lazy River!")*
3. "Don't Go Changin' (Just The Way You Are)" (*The clothes will last another week!)*
4. "Having My Baby" *(Oh God!!)*
5. "The Windmills Of My Mind" *(A mind is a terrible thing to waste!)*
6. "The Wind Beneath My Wings" *(Soft and Dry usually helps!)*
7. "Copacabana"
8. "When the Saints Go Marching In"
9. "I Am, I Said" *(HUH?!)*
10. "The Theme From the Love Boat" (or *"Would A Dingy Do?")*

white tigers are certainly magnificent, but they don't do much other than get cuddled (charmingly) by Roy and badly lip-synch to pretaped roars. The duo are clearly doing something right, judging from the heartfelt standing ovations they receive night after night. But more than one couple was heard to say it was not the best show they had seen, and also to express a feeling that it was overpriced. At these ticket costs (essentially $90 *per person*!) almost anything is. Go if you can't live without seeing a true, modern Vegas legend, but one can find better entertainment values in town.

- **Showroom Policies:** Nonsmoking with preassigned seating.
- **Price:** $89.35 (includes two drinks, souvenir brochure, tax, and gratuity).
- **Show Times:** Performances are Fri–Tues at 7:30 and 11pm, except during occasional dark periods.
- **Reservations:** Tickets can be purchased 3 days in advance.

Starlight Express. Las Vegas Hilton, 3000 Paradise Rd. ☎ **800/222-5361** or 702/732-5755.

Starlight Express does seem perfectly appropriate for Vegas: It's both flashy and fast paced. In 1993, the Hilton transformed its famed showroom into a gorgeous 1,500-seat oval theater to house it. The plot involves a little boy's train set as the individual cars race for some championship title. The gimmick is that the trains are played by actors on roller skates. As opposed to evoking actual trains, the actors never seem like more than actors on roller skates, wearing (admittedly extremely heavy) costumes that look like they were assembled at a junk yard. The songs are forgettable, the main plot hard to follow, the love story inexplicable. On the other hand, the actors work very hard as they whiz about a set that goes into and through the audience; they hit impressive speeds, and some perform breakneck flips. It also seems to inspire repeat visits; a good portion of the audience cheers when key figures make their entrances. It also seems like a good show for kids, with clean content and a solid moral.

- **Showroom Policies:** Nonsmoking with preassigned seating.
- **Price:** $19.50–$45 (tax and drinks extra); $19.50 for children 4 to 12.
- **Show Times:** Tues, Thurs, Sat, Sun at 7:30 and 10:30pm; Mon and Wed at 7:30pm. Dark Fri.
- **Reservations:** You can reserve by phone up to 3 months in advance.

3 Piano Bars

In addition to the below listed, consider the ultraelegant **Palace Court Terrace Lounge,** adjoining the Palace Court restaurant at Caesars or **Gatsby's** at the MGM Grand (see chapter 6), which also has a sophisticated and stunning adjoining piano bar. And **Cafe Niccole** (see chapter 6) has a small, but agreeable genuine piano bar.

Alexis Park Resort: Pisces Bistro. 375 E. Harmon Ave. ☎ **702/796-3300.** No cover or minimum.

The very upscale Alexis Park offers live entertainment in a beautiful room under a 30-foot domed ceiling; planters of greenery cascade from tiered balconies. When the weather permits, it's lovely to sit at umbrella tables on a terra-cotta patio overlooking the pool. Live music is featured Tuesday through Saturday nights from 8pm till about midnight; a versatile pianist and vocalist perform everything from show tunes to oldies to Top 40. Light fare is available.

The Carriage House: Kiefer's. 105 E. Harmon Ave. ☎ **702/739-8000.** No cover or minimum.

This rooftop restaurant has a plushly furnished adjoining piano bar/ lounge. Windowed walls offer great views of the Las Vegas neon sky-line, making this a romantic setting for cocktails and hors d'oeuvres. There's piano music Thursday through Saturday from 7 to 11pm.

Nicky Blair's. 3925 Paradise Rd., between Flamingo and Twain. ☎ **702/ 792-9900.** No cover or minimum.

A Los Angeles legend, Nicky Blair closed the doors of his venerable L.A. establishment to open a new version here. Pity the Rat Pack is gone; this would be their hangout in the '90s. A U-shaped bar domi-nates an elegantly dark space, with hardwood floors and banquettes up against one wall. There are plenty of bartenders and waitresses on hand to serve the middle-aged, upscale (and largely local) clien-tele. The tables seem well spaced, so a romantic tête-á-tête should be possible. You can order the full menu from the restaurant. The piano goes from 7pm until close, which is midnight Monday through Thursday, 2am Friday and Saturday.

4 Other Bars

In addition to the below listed, consider hanging out at **Country Star,** the **Hard Rock Cafe,** and **Planet Hollywood,** all described in chapter 6. You might also check out the incredible nighttime view at the bar atop the **Stratosphere Hotel**—nothing beats it. There's also the **Viva Las Vegas Lounge** at the Hard Rock Hotel, where eventually every rock-connected person in Vegas (band member, industry weasel) will eventually pass through.

Holy Cow. 2432 Las Vegas Blvd. S., at Sahara Ave. ☎ **702/732-COWS.**

Maybe you go to serious bars for serious drinking, but anyplace with a giant bovine on the roof and an extensive cow theme on the inside can't be all bad. Cows are everywhere—cow paintings, cow-motif lighting fixtures, a "sidewalk of fame" of cow hoof prints out-side, even slot machines called (irresistibly) "Moolah"—so if you are heifer-a-phobe, stay away. The microbrew pub upstairs offers a free tour, or you can taste its four hand-crafted microbrews (pale ale, wheat beer, brown ale, and a monthly changing brewmaster's spe-cial, which sometimes contains the word *blueberry* in it). Pub grub is also offered, which they assure us requires only one stomach to consume.

Main Street Station: Triple 7 Brew Pub. 100 Main St. ☎ **702/382-1896.**

Yet another of the many things the newish Main Street Station hotel has done right. Stepping into their microbrew pub feels like stepping out of Vegas. Well, maybe except for the dueling piano entertainment. Part modern warehouse look (exposed pipes, microbrew fixtures visible through exposed glass at back, very high ceiling), but with a hammered tin ceiling that continues the hotel's Victorian decor, this is a look more appropriate to North Beach in San Francisco. Dare we say it? The result produces an environment that is a bit on the yuppified side, but escapes being pretentious. And frankly, it's a much needed modern touch for the Downtown area. They have their own brewmaster, a number of microbrews ready to try, and if you are feeling like a quick bite, there is also an oyster and sushi bar, plus fancy burgers and pizzas. It can get noisy during the aforementioned piano duel act, but otherwise casino noise stays out. And Downtown being all too heavy on the old Las Vegas side (which is fine for a time but not *all* the time), this is good for a suitable breather.

Peppermill's Fireside Lounge. 2985 Las Vegas Blvd. South. ☎ **702/ 735-7635.**

Walk through the classic Peppermill's coffee shop (not a bad place to eat, by the way) on the Strip, and you land in their dark, plush, cozy lounge. A fabulously dated view of hip, it has low, circular banquette seats, fake floral foliage, low neon, and electric candles. But best of all is the water and fire pit as the centerpiece—a piece of kitsch thought long vanished from the earth, which attracts nostalgia buffs like moths to flames. It all adds up to a cozy, womblike place. Perfect for crashing down a bit after some time spent on the hectic Strip. The enormous, exotic froufrou tropical drinks (including the signature basketball-sized margaritas) will ensure that you sink into that level of comfortable stupor.

Pink E's. 4170 S. Valley View. ☎ **702/252-4666.**

Sick of the attitude at Club Rio (and well you should be?) Escape directly across the street to Pink E's, where the theme is pink. You were expecting maybe seafoam? Anyway, at least one regular described this as "the only place to go if you are over 25 and have a brain." And like pink. Because everything here is: the many pool tables, the Ping-Pong tables, the booths, the lighting, the lava lamp on the bar, and even the people. In its own way, it's as gimmick-ridden as the Beach dance club, but surely no one would put out a pink pool table in all seriousness? Yeah, they're a ludicrous heresy, but don't you want to play on one? It's a froufrou drink kind of place—sort of like Farrell's Ice Cream Parlor for grown-ups. Go, but wear all black just to be ornery.

Sand Dollar Blues Lounge. 3355 Spring Mountain. ☎ **702/871-6651.**

The kind of funky, no decor (think posters and beer signs), atmosphere-intensive, slightly grimy, friendly bar you either wish your town had or wish it had something other than. Just up the road from Treasure Island, this is a great antidote to artificial Vegas. The Sand Dollar features live blues (both electric and acoustic, with a little Cajun and Zydeco thrown in) every night.

The Sky Lounge (at the Polo Towers). 3745 Las Vegas Blvd. S. ☎ **702/ 261-1000.**

It may not be quite the view offered by the Stratosphere Hotel's bar, but it's pretty darn good and easier to get to. You see too much of the Holiday Inn Boardwalk directly across the street and not quite enough of the MGM Grand to the left, but otherwise there are no complaints. The decor is too modern—well, heavy on the black and purple '80s modern—but overall the place is quiet (especially during the day) and civil. A jazz vocal/piano performs at night (when the views are naturally best). Worth a trip for an escape from the mob, though you won't be the only tourist fighting for window seats.

5 Dance Clubs

✪ **The Beach.** 365 S. Convention Center Dr., at Paradise Rd. ☎ **702/ 731-9298.** $10 cover most nights (higher on some nights and for special events, lower and nonexistent on others).

If you are a fan of loud, crowded party bars filled with tons of good looking fun seekers, then bow in this direction for you have found Mecca. This huge, tropical-themed club is, according to just about anyone you ask, the "hottest" in the city. It's a two-story affair with five separate bars downstairs and another three up. Just in case walking the 20 feet to the closest one is too much of an effort, they also have bikini-clad women serving beer out of steel tubs full of ice (they also roam the floor with shot belts). The drinks are on the pricey side ($3.75 for an 8-ounce domestic beer). Also downstairs is the large two-story dance floor, which dominates the center of the room and is built around a full-service bar at one end. The crowd is aggressively young and pretty, more men than women (70/30 split), and about 60% tourist, which is probably why the place can get away with charging a $10 cover. Party people look no further. Open 24 hours.

Cleopatra's Barge Nightclub. Caesars Palace, 3570 Las Vegas Blvd. S. ☎ **702/731-7110.** No cover; there's a 2-drink minimum Friday and Saturday only.

Live bands play Top 40 dance tunes aboard Cleopatra's Barge, a replica of the majestic ships that sailed the Nile in ancient Egypt. This waterborne dance club is also afloat on "the Nile," complete with oars, ostrich-feather fans, statues of ancient pharaohs, and furled sails. Open Tuesday to Sunday 10pm to 4am.

Club Rio. Rio Suite Hotel, 3700 W. Flamingo Rd. ☎ **702/252-7777.** As advertised: $10 cover for men, local women free, out of state women $5—but frequently when we went by on a weekend night, the cover was $20 for everyone.

This is the hottest night spot in Vegas (along with Beach) as of this writing, but apparently made so by people who don't mind long lines, restrictive dress codes, attitudinal door people, hefty cover charges, and bland dance music. Waits can be interminable and admittance denied thanks to the wrong foot or shirt wear. Once inside, you find a large, circular room with the spacious dance floor taking up much of the space. Giant video screens line the upper parts of the walls, showing anything from shots of the action down below to catwalk footage. Comfy circular booths fill out the next couple of concentric circles; these seem mostly reserved and, when empty, they leave the impression that the place isn't very full—so why the wait? A recent trip heard music that included a Madonna medley and perennial "Celebration," not the most au courant of tunes. The total effect is of a grown-up, not terribly drunken frat and sorority mixer.

✪ **Drink.** 200 E. Harmon Ave., at Koval Lane ☎ **702/796-5519.** Cover $5–$10 ($15–$25 when major artists are performing); women are admitted free Tues nights. There's no minimum.

Where Gen X Vegas hangs out. Hip decor, which in this case means an odd mix of industrial warehouse, peeling plaster, and brick country cottage exterior; somehow, it works. Soundproofing is impressive; you can literally pass from the hard rock room to the dance room with only a second's worth of the two bleeding into each other. A recent saunter in the hard rock room heard a mix of retro and more current rock. (A song by The Cult segued into "Magic Carpet Ride," which went into "Spill the Wine," which went into some anonymous nineties faux metal/hard rock band.) The different sounds mean different appeals for different rooms, thus something for everyone. Despite a young, fashion-conscious crowd, it's friendlier than you would imagine, with virtually no attitude, surprisingly enough. (If you go there after Club Rio, the difference in attitude is almost palpable.) Of the nightly dance clubs, this is the one to go to, unless a hip quotient frightens you. Open Monday to Thursday 'till 3am, Friday and Saturday till 5am. Closed Sunday. Self parking is free, valet parking $3.

Monte Carlo Pub and Brewery. Monte Carlo Resort, 3770 Las Vegas Blvd. S. ☎ **702/730-7777.** No cover or minimum.

After 9pm nightly, this immense warehouselike pub and working microbrewery (see details in chapter 6) turns from a casual restaurant into a rollicking, high-energy dance club that is very popular with Gen-X-to-thirtysomething locals. Open until 1am Sunday to Thursday, until 3am Friday and Saturday.

6 Strip Clubs

No, not entertainment establishments on Las Vegas Boulevard South. This would be the *other* kind of "strip." Yes, people come to town for the gambling and the wedding chapels, but the lure of Vegas doesn't stop there.

Cheetah's. 2112 Western Ave. ☎ **702/384-0074.** MC, V (but cash preferred—they have an ATM machine). Cover $5. TOPLESS.

This is the strip club used in the movie *Showgirls,* but thanks to the magic of Hollywood and later renovations by the club, only the main stage will look vaguely familiar to those few looking for Nomi Malone. The management believes, "If you treat people right they will keep coming back," so the atmosphere is friendlier than at other clubs. They "encourage couples—people who want to party come here. We get a 21- to 40-aged party kind of crowd," the manager told us. And indeed there is a sporty, frat bar feel to the place. $10 table dance, $20 couch dance. Open 24 hours.

Club Paradise. 4416 Paradise Rd. ☎ **702/734-7990.** $10 cover, 2 drink minimum (drinks $4.50 and up). MC, V. Unescorted women allowed. TOPLESS.

Possibly the nicest of the strip clubs (the outside looks a lot like the Golden Nugget), the interior and atmosphere are rather like that of a hot nightclub where most of the women happen to be topless. The glitzy stage looks like something from a miniature showroom, and the place is relatively bright by strip club standards. Not too surprisingly, they get a very white collar crowd here. The result is not terribly sleazy, which may please some and turn off others. The club says it is "women friendly," and indeed there were a few couples, including one woman who was receiving a lap dance herself—and didn't seem too uncomfortable. Lap dances $20. Open Monday to Sunday from 6pm to 6am.

Glitter Gulch. 20 Fremont St. ☎ **702/385-4774.** No cover, two-drink minimum (drinks $5.75). TOPLESS.

Right there in the middle of the Fremont St. Experience, Glitter Gulch is either an eyesore or the last bastion of Old Las Vegas, depending on your point of view. The women are not exceptionally thin—fully fleshed, but not fat. As you enter, you are assigned your own (overly clothed) waitress who escorts you to your table. They also offer limo service to the hotels. There is even a line of souvenir clothing. Given such services and its convenient location, this is the perfect place for the merely curious—you can easily pop in, check things out, goggle and ogle, and then hit the road, personal dignity intact. Table dances $20. Open Sunday to Thursday from noon to 4am, Friday and Saturday noon to 6am.

Olympic Gardens. 1531 Las Vegas S. Blvd. ☎ **702/385-8987.** Cover $15 (includes two drinks). AE, DISC, MC, V (they have an ATM machine). Unescorted women allowed. TOPLESS.

Possibly the largest of the strip clubs, this almost feels like a family operation, thanks to the middle-aged women handling the door. They also have a boutique selling lingerie and naughty outfits. Table dances $20, more in VIP room. Open Monday to Sunday from 2pm to 6am.

9

Las Vegas Shopping

*U*nless you're looking for souvenir decks of cards, Styrofoam dice, and miniature slot machines, Las Vegas is not exactly a shopping mecca. It does, however, have several noteworthy malls that can amply supply the basics. And many hotels also offer comprehensive, and sometimes highly themed, shopping arcades, most notably Caesars Palace (details below). You might consider driving Maryland Parkway, which runs parallel to the Strip on the west, and has just about one of everything: Target, Toys 'Я' Us, several major department stores, Tower Records, major drug stores (in case you forgot your shampoo and don't want to spend $8 on a new one in your hotel sundry shop), some alternative culture stores (tattoo parlors and hip clothing stores), and so forth. It goes on for blocks.

1 The Malls

Boulevard Mall. 3528 S. Maryland Pkwy., between Twain Ave. and Desert Inn Rd. ☎ **702/732-8949.** Mon–Fri 10am–9pm, Sat 10am–8pm, Sun 11am–6pm.

The Boulevard is the largest mall in Las Vegas. Its 144-plus stores and restaurants are arranged in arcade fashion on a single floor occupying 1.2 million square feet. Geared to the average consumer (not the carriage trade), it has anchors like Sears, JCPenney, Woolworth, Macy's, Dillard's, and Marshalls. Other notables include The Disney Store, The Nature Company, a 23,000-square-foot Good Guys (electronics), The Gap, Gap Kids, The Limited, Victoria's Secret, Colorado (for outdoor clothing and gear), Howard and Phil's Western Wear, and African and World Imports. There's a wide variety of shops offering moderately priced shoes and clothing for the entire family, books and gifts, jewelry, and home furnishings, plus more than a dozen fast-food eateries. In short, you can find just about anything you need here. There's free valet parking.

Fashion Show Mall. 3200 Las Vegas Blvd. S., at the corner of Spring Mountain Rd. ☎ **702/369-8382.** Mon–Fri 10am–9pm, Sat 10am–7pm, Sun noon–6pm.

This luxurious and centrally located mall, one of the city's largest, opened in 1981 to great hoopla. Designers Adolfo, Geoffrey Beene,

Impressions

Tip Number 3: Win a bunch of money. I can't recommend this too highly. If it hasn't occurred to you, win $1,200 and see for yourself. It's very energizing and really adds to your Vegas fun.
—Merrill Markoe, *Viva Las Wine Goddesses!*

Bill Blass, Bob Mackie, and Pauline Trigere were all on hand to display their fashion interpretations of the "Las Vegas look."

The mall comprises more than 130 shops, restaurants, and services. It is anchored by Neiman-Marcus, Saks Fifth Avenue, Macy's, Robinsons-May, and Dillard's. Other notable tenants: Abercrombie and Fitch, The Disney Store, The Walt Disney Gallery, The Discovery Channel Store, Lillie Rubin (upscale women's clothing), The Gap, Benetton, Uomo, Banana Republic, Victoria's Secret, Caché, Williams-Sonoma Grand Cuisine, The Body Shop, Mondi (upscale women's clothing), Waldenbooks, Louis Vuitton, and Sharper Image. There are several card and book shops, a wide selection of apparel stores for the whole family (including large sizes and petites), nine jewelers, 21 shoe stores, and gift and specialty shops. There are dozens of eating places (see chapter 6 for specifics). Valet parking is available, and you can even arrange to have your car hand washed while you shop.

Galleria at Sunset. 1300 W. Sunset Rd., at Stephanie St. just off I-515 in nearby Henderson. ☎ **702/434-0202.** Mon–Sat 10am–9pm, Sun 11am–6pm.

This upscale 1 million-square-foot shopping center, 9 miles southeast of downtown Las Vegas, opened in 1996, with performing Disney characters on hand to welcome shoppers and a nighttime display of fireworks. The mall has a southwestern motif, evidenced in the use of terra-cotta stone, interior landscaping, cascading fountains, and skylights; eight 20-foot hand-carved pillars flank the main entrance. Anchored by four department stores—Dillard's, JC-Penney, Mervyn's California, and Robinsons-May—the Galleria's 110 emporia include branches of The Disney Store, The Gap/Gap Kids/Baby Gap, The Limited and The Limited Too, Eddie Bauer, Miller's Outpost, Ann Taylor, bebe, Caché, Compagnie International, Lane Bryant, Lerner New York, Victoria's Secret, The Body Shop, B. Dalton, and Sam Goody. In addition to shoes and clothing for the entire family, you'll find electronics, eyewear, gifts, books, home furnishings, jewelry, and luggage here. Dining facilities include an extensive food court and two restaurants.

The Meadows. 4300 Meadows Lane, at the intersection of Valley View and U.S. 95. ☎ **702/878-4849.** Mon–Fri 10am–9pm, Sat–Sun 10am–6pm.

Another immense mall, the Meadows comprises 144 shops, services, and eateries, anchored by four department stores: Macy's, Dillard's, Sears, and JCPenney. In addition, there are 15 shoe stores, a full array of apparel for the entire family (including maternity wear, petites, and large sizes), an extensive food court, and shops purveying toys, books, CDs and tapes, luggage, gifts, jewelry, home furnishings (The Bombay Company, among others), accessories, and so on. Fountains and trees enhance the Meadows' ultramodern, high-ceilinged interior, and a 1995 renovation added comfortable conversation/seating areas and made the mall lighter and brighter. It is divided into five courts, one centered on a turn-of-the-century carousel (a plus for kids). A natural history–themed court has a "desert fossil" floor, and an entertainment court is the setting for occasional live musical and dramatic performances. You can rent strollers at the Customer Service Center.

2 Factory Outlets

Las Vegas has two big factory outlets just a few miles past the southern end of the Strip. If you don't have a car, you can take a no. 301 CAT bus from anywhere on the Strip and change at Vacation Village to a no. 303.

Belz Factory Outlet World. 7400 Las Vegas Blvd. S., at Warm Springs Rd. ☎ **702/896-5599.** Mon–Sat 10am–9pm, Sun 10am–6pm.

Belz houses 145 air-conditioned outlets, including a few dozen clothing stores and shoe stores. It offers an immense range of merchandise at savings up to 75% off retail prices. Among other emporia, you'll find Adolfo II, Casual Corner, Levi's, Nike, Dress Barn, Oshkosh B'Gosh, Leggs/Hanes/Bali, Esprit, Aileen, Bugle Boy, Carters, Reebok, Spiegel, Guess Classics, Oneida, Springmaid, We're Entertainment (Disney and Warner Bros.), Bose (electronics), Danskin, Van Heusen, Burlington, Royal Doulton, Lennox (china), Waterford (crystal), and Geoffrey Beene here. There is also a carousel.

Factory Stores of America. 9155 Las Vegas Blvd., at Serene St. ☎ **702/ 897-9090.** Mon–Sat 10am–8pm, Sun 10am–6pm.

A 30-acre open-air mall with Spanish-style architecture, this is the only outlet center in the country with a casino/bar/lounge on its premises. Its 41 stores include Corning/Revere, Izod, Mikasa, American Tourister, Van Heusen, B.U.M. Equipment, Spiegel, London

Fog, VF (sportswear), Book Warehouse, Geoffrey Beene, and Adolfo II. Come here for clothing, housewares, shoes, china, and much, much more.

3 Hotel Shopping Arcades

Just about every Las Vegas hotel offers some shopping opportunities. The following have the most extensive arcades. *Note:* The Forum Shops at Caesars—as much a sightseeing attraction as a shopping arcade—are in the must-see category.

Bally's   Bally's Avenue Shoppes number around 20 emporia offering pro-team sports apparel, toys, clothing (men's, women's, and children's), logo items, gourmet chocolates, liquor, jewelry, nuts and dried fruit, flowers, handbags, and T-shirts. In addition, there are several gift shops, three restaurants, art galleries, and a pool-wear shop. There are blackjack tables and slot and video poker machines right in the mall, as well as a race and sports book. You can dispatch the kids to a video arcade here while you shop.

Caesars Palace   Since 1978, Caesars has had an impressive arcade of shops called the Appian Way. Highlighted by an immense white Carrara-marble replica of Michelangelo's *David* standing more than 18 feet high, its shops include the aptly named Galerie Michelangelo (original and limited-edition artworks), jewelers (including branches of Ciro and Cartier), a logo merchandise shop, and several shops for upscale men's and women's clothing. All in all, a respectable grouping of hotel shops, and an expansion is in the works.

But in the hotel's tradition of constantly surpassing itself, in 1992 Caesars inaugurated the fabulous Forum Shops, an independently operated 250,000-square-foot Rodeo-Drive-meets-the-Roman-Empire affair complete with a 48-foot triumphal arch entranceway, a painted Mediterranean sky that changes as the day progresses from rosy-tinted dawn to twinkling evening stars, acres of marble, lofty scagliola Corinthian columns with gold capitals, and a welcoming goddess of fortune under a central dome. Its architecture and sculpture span a period from 300 B.C. to A.D. 1700. Storefront facades, some topped with statues of Roman senators, resemble a classical Italian streetscape, with archways, piazzas, ornate fountains, and a barrel-vaulted ceiling. The "center of town" is the magnificent domed Fountain of the Gods, where Jupiter rules from his mountaintop surrounded by Pegasus, Mars, Venus, Neptune, and Diana. And at the Festival Fountain, seemingly immovable "marble" animatronic statues of Bacchus (slightly in his cups), a lyre-playing

Apollo, Plutus, and Venus come to life for a 7-minute revel with dancing waters and high-tech laser-light effects. The shows take place every hour on the hour. The whole thing is pretty incredible, but also very Vegas, particularly the Bacchus show, which is truly frightening and bizarre. Even if you don't like shopping, it's worth the stroll just to giggle.

More than 70 prestigious emporia here include Louis Vuitton, Plaza Escada, Bernini, Christian Dior, A/X Armani Exchange, bebe, Caché, Gucci, Ann Taylor, and Gianni Versace, along with many other clothing, shoe, and accessory shops. Other notables include: a Warner Brothers Studio Store (a sign at the exit reads thatius finitus folkus), The Disney Store, Kids Kastle (beautiful children's clothing and toys), Rose of Sharon (classy styles for large-size women), Sports Logo (buy a basketball signed by Michael Jordan for $695!), Field of Dreams (more autographed sports memorabilia), Museum Company (reproductions ranging from 16th-century hand-painted Turkish boxes to ancient Egyptian scarab necklaces), West of Santa Fe (Western wear and Native American jewelry and crafts), Antiquities (neon Shell gas signs, 1950s malt machines, Americana; sometimes "Elvis" is on hand), Endangered Species Store (ecology-themed merchandise), Brookstone (one-of-a-kind items from garden tools to sports paraphernalia), and Victoria's Secret. There's much more, including jewelry shops and art galleries.

A new 283,000-square-foot expansion, including 37 stores and 2 new restaurants, has just been completed. New residents include FAO Schwartz, Fendi, Polo, NikeTown, a Virgin Records megastore, and Wolfgang Puck's Asian Cafe. The centerpiece of the new area will be a Roman Great Hall of heroic proportions, featuring a dramatic high-tech interactive attraction called "Atlantis."

While you shop, send the kids downstairs for spine-tingling Motion-Simulator Cinema Rides in 3-D. Four 5-minute shows simulate a flight into outer space to destroy a runaway nuclear missile, a submarine race through the ancient ruins of Atlantis, a bicycle ride through a haunted graveyard, and a roller-coaster adventure. (Price is $6 for one film, $8 for a double feature. Children must be at least 42 inches high.)

Dining choices range from a pastrami on rye at the Stage Deli, to a thick, juicy steak at The Palm, to Wolfgang Puck's sublime Spago creations. Several Forum Shops restaurants are described in chapter 6.

The shops are open Sunday to Thursday from 10am to 11pm, Friday and Saturday 10am to midnight. An automated walkway transports people from the Strip to the shopping complex. Heralded by a marble temple housing four golden horses and a charioteer, it is flanked by flaming torchiers and fronted by a waterfall cascading over a bas-relief of the god Neptune—you can't miss it! Often a gladiator with sword and shield is there to greet you at the other end. Valet parking is available.

Circus Circus   About 15 shops between the casino and Grand Slam Canyon which offer a wide selection of gifts and sundries, logo items, toys and games, jewelry, liquor, resort apparel for the entire family, T-shirts, homemade fudge/candy/soft ice cream, and, fittingly, clown dolls and puppets. At Amazing Pictures you can have your photo taken as a pinup girl, muscle man, or whatever else your fantasy dictates. Adjacent to Grand Slam Canyon, there is a new shopping arcade themed along a European village, with cobblestone walkways and fake woods and so forth, decorated with replicas of vintage circus posters. It's much nicer than the tacky one Circus Circus had before. Among the stores are Marshall Russo, Headliners, The Sweet Tooth, and Carousel Classics.

Excalibur   The shops of "The Realm," for the most part reflect the hotel's medieval theme. Dragon's Lair, for example, features items ranging from pewter swords and shields to full suits of armor, and Merlin's Mystic Shop carries crystals, luck charms, and gargoyles. Other shops carry more conventional wares—gifts, candy, jewelry, women's clothing, and Excalibur logo items. A child pleaser is Kids of the Kingdom, which displays licensed character merchandise from Disney, Looney Tunes, Garfield, and Snoopy. Wild Bill's carries Western wear and Native American jewelry and crafts. And at Fantasy Faire you can have your photo taken in Renaissance attire.

Flamingo Hilton   The Crystal Court shopping promenade here accommodates men's and women's clothing/accessories stores, gift shops, and a variety of other emporia selling jewelry, beachwear, Southwestern crafts, fresh-baked goods, logo items, children's gifts, toys, and games.

Harrah's   Harrah's is finishing up a massive new renovation which includes a new shopping center to be called Carnivale Court that will include party stores, Ghirardelli Chocolate, and a magic store. It will all be outdoors, and live entertainment will be strolling around and playing on a bandshell.

Luxor Hotel/Casino   Its new 20,000-square-foot shopping arcade will be finished by 1998. Previously, it had The Source, on the lower level, where you'll find museum-quality Egyptian antiquities such as an alabaster portrait of Ptolemy V (205 B.C.) for $3,000 or a bronze Isis statue (664–25 B.C.) for $10,000. More affordable are beautiful Egyptian jewelry (both straight reproductions and Egypt-inspired designs), gift items (mother-of-pearl inlay boxes and tables, paintings, pottery, scarabs, and amulets), and books about ancient Egypt.

The MGM Grand   The hotel's Star Lane Shops include more than a dozen upscale emporia lining the corridors en route from the monorail entrance. The Knot Shop carries designer ties by Calvin Klein, Gianni Versace, and others. El Portal features luggage and handbags—Coach, Dior, Fendi, Polo Ralph Lauren, and other exclusive lines. Grand 50's carries *Route 66* jackets, Elvis T-shirts, photos of James Dean, and other mementos of the 1950s. MGM Grand Sports sells signed athletic uniforms, baseballs autographed by Michael Jordan, and the like; it is the scene of occasional appearances by sports stars such as Floyd Patterson and Stan Musial. You can choose an oyster and have its pearl set in jewelry at The Pearl Factory. Other Star Lane Shops specialize in movie memorabilia, Betty Boop merchandise, *EFX* wares, children's clothing, decorative magnets, MGM Grand logo items and Las Vegas souvenirs, seashells and coral, candy, and sunglasses. Refreshments are available at a Häagen-Dazs ice-cream counter and Yummy's Coffees and Desserts. In other parts of the hotel, retail shops include a *Wizard of Oz* gift shop, Front Page (for newspapers, books, magazines, and sundries), a spa shop selling everything from beachwear to top-of-the-line European skin care products, a liquor store, a candy store, Kenneth J. Lane jewelry, and Marshall Rousso (men's and women's clothing). In addition, theme park emporia sell Hollywood memorabilia, cameras and photographic supplies, MGM Grand and theme park logo products, toys, fine china and crystal, animation cels, collectibles (limited-edition dolls, plates, figurines), Hollywood-themed clothing and accessories, and Western wear. At Arts and Crafts you can watch artisans working in leather, glass, wood, pottery, and other materials; and at Photoplay Gallery, you can have your picture taken as *Time* magazine's man or woman of the year.

Monte Carlo   An arcade of retail shops here includes Bon Vivant (resort wear for the whole family, dress wear for men), Crown Jewels (jewelry, leather bags, crystal, Fabergé eggs, gift items), a florist, logo shop, jeweler, food market, dessert store, and Lance Burton magic paraphernalia shop.

Rio   The new 60,000-square-foot Masquerade Village is a nicely done addition to the Rio. It's done as a European village and is two stories, featuring a wide variety of shops including the nation's largest Nicole Miller, Speedo, and the N'awlins store, which includes "authentic" voodoo items, Mardi Gras masks, and so forth. It's attached to a cafe that sells beignets (from Cafe Du Monde mix) and chicory coffee.

The Riviera   The Riviera has a fairly extensive shopping arcade comprising art galleries, jewelers, a creative photographer, and shops specializing in women's shoes and handbags, clothing for the entire family, furs, gifts, logo items, toys, phones and electronic gadgets, and chocolates.

Sam's Town   Though Sam's Town does not contain a notably significant shopping arcade, it does house the huge Western Emporium (almost department-store size) selling Western clothing for men and women, boots (an enormous selection), jeans, belts, silver and turquoise jewelry, Stetson hats, Native American crafts, gift items, and old-fashioned candy. You can have your picture taken here in period Western costume. Open daily at 9am; closing hours vary.

Stratosphere   Shopping is no afterthought here. The internationally themed second floor Tower Shops promenade, which will soon house 40 stores, is entered off an escalator from the casino. Some shops are in "Paris," along the Rue Lafayette and Avenue de l'Opéra (there are replicas of the Eiffel Tower and Arc de Triomphe in this section). Others occupy Hong Kong and New York City streetscapes. Already extant emporia include: The Money Company (money-motif items from T-shirts to golf balls), a T-shirt store, a magic shop, Key West (body lotions and more), Victoria's Secret, a magnet shop, Norma Kaplan (for glitzy/sexy women's footwear), an electronics boutique, a logo shop, and several gift shops. There are branches of Jitters (a coffeehouse) and Häagen-Dazs, and stores are supplemented by cart vendors.

Treasure Island   Treasure Island's shopping promenade—doubling as a portrait gallery of famed buccaneers (Blackbeard, Jean Lafitte, Calico Jack, Barbarosa)—has wooden ship figureheads and battling pirates suspended from its ceiling. Emporia here include the Treasure Island Store (your basic hotel gift/sundry shop, also offering much pirate-themed merchandise, plus a section devoted to Calvin Klein clothing), Loot 'n' Booty, Candy Reef, Captain Kid's (children's clothing), and Damsels in Dis'Dress (women's sportswear and accessories). The Mutiny Bay Shop, in the video-game arcade, carries logo items and stuffed animals. In the casino are the Buccaneer Bay Shoppe (logo merchandise) and the Treasure Chest (a jewelry store; spend those winnings right on the spot). And the Crow's Nest, en route to the Mirage monorail, carries Cirque du Soleil logo items. Cirque du Soleil and Mystère logo wares are also sold in a shop near the ticket office.

4   Vintage Clothing

The Attic. 1018 S. Main St. ☎ **702/388-4088.** Daily 9am–6pm. MC, V.

Sharing a large space with **Cafe Neon,** a coffeehouse that also serves Greek-influence cafe food (so you can raise your blood sugar again after a long stretch of shopping), and a comedy club stage, and upstairs from an attempt at a weekly club (as of this writing, the Saturday night Underworld), The Attic has plenty of clothing choices on many racks. During a recent visit, a man came in asking for a poodle skirt for his 8-year-old. They had one.

Buffalo Exchange. 4110 S. Maryland Pkwy., at Flamingo, near Tower Records. ☎ **702/791-3960.** Mon–Sat 11am–8pm, Sun 12pm–6pm. MC, V.

This is actually part of a chain of such stores spread out across the western United States. If the chain part worries you, don't let it— this merchandise doesn't feel processed. Staffed by plenty of incredibly hip alt-culture kids (ask them for what's happening in town during your visit), it is stuffed with dresses, shirts, pants, and so forth. Like any vintage shop, the contents are hit and miss; you can easily go in one day and come out with 12 fabulous new outfits, but you can just as easily go in and come up dry. It is probably the most reliable of the local vintage shops.

The Haight. 1647 E. Charleston. ☎ **702/387-7818.** Mon–Sat 11am–6pm, Sun 12pm–5pm. Cash and checks only.

Impressions

As for Vegas—it couldn't be much weirder if this town were on the moon. The place just seems to pulse with whatever it is that makes the weirdness weird. The place feeds on it. Likes it. And the weirdest thing is—it always has.

—Michael Ventura, *Las Vegas: The Odds on Anything*

Upstairs from an antique store, this is in a small old house, and so not only is the stock in various rooms, they've turned the retro-tiled bathroom into the dressing room. They have a large selection of used Levi's and otherwise specialize in '60s and '70s vintage clothing.

Our House. 1639 E. Charleston. Sun–Fri 11am–6pm, Sat 10am–6pm.

A tiny store filled with the most happening in new and vintage clothing (think club kid wear) and some new jewelry designs. Not a huge selection, but very kinda now, kinda wow. No phone at this time (you can always check Information), but they are right next door to the Haight and the start of the Charleston antique row.

5 Reading Material: Used Books, Comics & a Notable Newsstand

USED BOOKS

Dead Poet Books. 3858 W. Sahara (corner of Valley View, near Albertson's). ☎ **702/227-4070.** Mon–Sat 10am–6pm, Sun 12pm–5pm. AE, DISC, MC, V.

Eliot? Byron? Tennyson? None of the above. Actually, the dead poet in question was a man from whose estate the owners bought their start-up stock. He had such good taste in books, they "fell in love with him" and wanted to name the store in his memory. Just one problem—they never did get his name. So they just called him "the dead poet." He wasn't a poet, but surely anyone with such fine taste in books must have been one in his soul. His legacy continues is this book-lover's haven.

Parkland Books. 3661 Maryland Pkwy. (corner of Twain, in the Maryland Sq.). ☎ **702/732-4474.** Mon–Sat 10am–6pm. DISC, MC, V.

Heavy on the hardbacks and the nonfiction, this nicely musty store offers used and out-of-print stock.

A LAS VEGAS SPECIALTY STORE

Gambler's Book Shop. 630 S. 11th St., just off Charleston Blvd. ☎ **800/522-1777** or 702/382-7555. Mon–Sat 9am–5pm.

Here you can buy a book on any system ever devised to beat casino odds. Owner Edna Luckman carries more than 4,000 gambling-related titles, including many out-of-print books, computer software, and videotapes. She describes her store as a place where "gamblers, writers, researchers, statisticians, and computer specialists can meet and exchange information." On request, knowledgeable clerks provide on-the-spot expert advice on handicapping the ponies and other aspects of sports betting. The store's motto is "knowledge is protection."

COMIC BOOKS

Alternative Reality Comics. 4800 S. Maryland Pkwy. ☎ **702/736-3673.**
Mon–Sat. 11am–7pm, Sun 12pm–6pm.

The place in Vegas for all your comic book needs. They have a nearly
comprehensive selection, with a heavy emphasis on the underground
comics. But don't worry, the superheroes are here, too.

A NOTABLE NEWSSTAND

International Newsstand. 3900 Paradise (in Citibank Plaza). ☎ **702/
796-9901.** Daily 8:30am–9pm. AE, MC, V.

Homesick for local news? No matter where you are from, come here.
It's crammed full of seemingly every city newspaper in the land, plus
a large selection of foreign cities. They surely don't have everything,
but it seems like they do. Okay, the actual count is every major U.S.
city, plus 10 other countries. One impressed shopper said this would
put many a formerly worthy newsstand in any cosmopolitan city to
shame. There is also a wide array of magazines, both foreign and
domestic, though they get less space than at other newsstands thanks
to the newspapers.

6 Antiques

Antiques in Vegas? You mean really old slot machines, or the people
playing the really old slot machines?

Actually, Vegas has quite a few antique stores—nearly two dozen,
of consistent quality and price, nearly all located within a few blocks
of each other. We have one friend, someone who takes interior design *very* seriously, who comes straight to Vegas for most of her best
finds (you should see her antique chandelier collection!).

To get there, start in the middle of the 1600 block of E. Charleston and keep driving east. The little stores, nearly all in old houses
dating from the '30s, line each side of the street. Or you can stop
in at **Silver Horse Antiques** (1651 E. Charleston) and pick up a
map to almost all the locations, with phone numbers and hours of
operation.

See also separate Restaurants and Buffets indexes, below.

Restaurants

BUFFETS